D1389926

"SPECIAL OPERATIONS" SERIES

Project Editor Éric MICHELETTI

"Special Operations" Series

Project Editor Eric MICHELETTI

© Histoire & Collections, 2000
5, avenue de la République - 75541 Paris Cedex 11 - France
ISBN : 2 908 182 734

Eric LEFEVRE

BRANDENBURG DIVISION

COMMANDOS OF THE REICH

Translated by Julia FINEL

HISTOIRE & COLLECTIONS

A reviewed and corrected edition of the book by the same author published in 1983 by 'Presses de la Cité' in the collection 'Troupes de Choc' and under the title *La Division Brandebourg 1939-1945*.

The author, Eric Lefevre, has already written :

- *Les Panzers (Normandie 1944)*. Heimdal, 1978.

- *La Wehrmacht (Uniformes et insignes de l'armée de terre allemande)*. Argout Edition, 1978 and 1979; J. Grancher, 1986.

- *Dunkerque, 26 mai-4 juin 1940 (la Bataille des Dunes)*. Lavauzelle, 1981.

- *Opération Epaulard I (Beyrouth, 21 août-13 septembre 1982)*. Lavauzelle, 1982.

- *Tchad, Opération Manta (août-octobre 1983)*. Lavauzelle, 1984.

In collaboration with Colonel Jean Delmas and Colonel (ER) Paul Devautour:
- *Mai-Juin 40, les Combattants de l'Honneur*. Copernic, 1980.

In collaboration with Horst Scheibert:
- *Les Panzer dans la Seconde Guerre mondiale*. Copernic, 1981.

In collaboration with General (ER) Etienne Plan:
- *La Bataille des Alpes, 10-25 juin 1940 (L'Armée invaincue)* Lavauzelle, 1982.

In collaboration with Jean Mabire:
- *La LVF 1941 (par - 40° devant Moscou)*. Fayard, 1985.
- *Léon Degrelle et la Légion Wallonie, 1941-1945*. Art et Histoire d'Europe, 1988.
- *La Légion Perdue (face aux partisans, 1942)*. J. Grancher, 1995.

Eric LEFEVRE

BRANDENBURG DIVISION

COMMANDOS OF THE REICH

Translated by Julia FINEL

HISTOIRE & COLLECTIONS

INTRODUCTION

Mystery still hangs over the Brandenburg units of the Second World War. Little is known of those who called themselves the *Brandenburgers*, except that they were combatants in the shadow of the German Army, whose appearance, as sudden as it was unforeseen, created confusion among the enemy.

Secrecy was their main weapon. Secrecy in the preparation and until the first stage was carried out. Their ideal was to pass unnoticed and fulfil their mission without using their weapons. They have left few records behind, the majority of which belonged to the Abwehr II [1] — for whom they were the expression of active combat for more than three years — and were destroyed before the capitulation in 1945.

At the end of 1939 they had the strength of just one battalion; in 1944, a whole division. But throughout those years the nature and the task of the unit varied little.

The house unit of Admiral Canaris, in 1943 it passed under the direct supervision of the Armed Forces Operations Staff, which used it essentially in the struggle against partisans in the Balkans.

That Autumn of 1944 heralded the end of the Brandenburg units such as they were and they went on to form a standard *Panzergrenadier* division committed on the Eastern Front. Its tasks during the first years of the war entirely fell to Otto Skorzeny's *SS-Jagdverbände*. [2]

1. See organisation of the Abwehr in the appendixes.
2. Referred to as 'Jagd' or Commando units, administratively attached to the Waffen-SS but used by the Reich's Main Security Office (RSHA).

What was particular about these soldiers was the method and the source of their recruitment. The first nucleus of the Brandenburgers, which gave its particular spirit to a new unit, resembled a very exclusive club which preferred to choose its members itself. A reserve officer of the Abwehr, Yupp Hoven, who was its main recruiter during the 'phoney war' in 1939 and 1940, enlisted a great number of his old comrades from the *bundische Jugend* [3], whose intelligence and character he had had the opportunity of appreciating during their shared experiences, on the occasion of the first manifestation of resistance to the National Socialist regime.

The *Volksdeutschen*, members of German ethnic minorities living outside the political borders of the Reich, and the *Auslanddeutschen*, German citizens settled abroad, would provide the majority of volunteers. They were sought after for their knowledge of the language and customs of the country where they were called to intervene. When the system was running properly and the Brandenburg Regiment formed, those volunteers coming from Transylvania, Banat and from other provinces in south-eastern Europe were sent to the Baden home base near Vienna; those coming from Poland, Russia and the Baltic States were sent to Düren, near Cologne.

Within each battalion, companies were specialised as much as possible and the teams formed for a specific operation were even more so. Preference was understandably given to those who had some knowledge of the target area.

Recruits were often unprepared for the extent of Prussian stiffness or political dogmatism. For them, everything was relative, except their love of the Fatherland, sustained as it was by a long standing nostalgia. Others among them were adventure-seekers, proud men who, in every country, formed the nucleus of crack units. A particular type of officer was sought after to command them. They were found among the former members of the free corps, who had fought, alone and unyielding, on the Eastern Front and in the Ruhr between 1919 and 1923.

3. Collective name given to youth associations after the First World War.

The former soldiers of the free corps and the youth associations who perpetuated their traditions would put their indelible mark on the human cocktail that made up the Brandenburgers. The communal feeling of destiny and of being model comrades-in-arms served, in combat, to unite them.

The task of the Brandenburgers of the Abwehr essentially consisted of entering enemy territory to carry out reconnaissance missions or to prevent the destruction of strategic infrastructure as bridges or tunnels essential to the advance of forces carrying out an offensive, or to carry out destruction missions which were designed to hold up enemy movements.

To reach their objectives without being identified and therby rendered useless, they had to operate in small teams and make use of disguises, of which there were two types. The *Halbtarnung*, or semi-camouflage, consisted of covering the German uniform with an enemy greatcoat and wearing the corresponding headgear. This half-disguise was enough to change the outline and at night or in dull light it proved to be sufficient. But, when they exposed to enemy surveillance in broad daylight, a complete camouflage apparatus was necessary: this was the *Volltarnung*. In this case, the Brandenburgers, as a general rule, wore the enemy uniform over their own. This was not always feasible and considerably restricted their movements.

In both cases, if they found themselves unexpectedly having to open fire, it was not always easy for them to cast off their disguises in a trice to appear in a German uniform. On this point the instructions were clear: if the Brandenburgers made use of weapons in enemy uniform, they thereby contravened the rules of war and if captured were treated as spies.

In actual fact, concealment, deception and surprise have always played a part in the art of war. It is said that the duel-wars of aristocratic times have given way to the butchery-wars of the democratic era. The Hague convention which authorised camouflage of clothing under certain conditions had not been abolished by the victorious Powers; its Article 23f was, on the contrary, supplemented.

This international convention merely accepted responsibility again for the age-old use of commerce destroying battles, which enabled the corsair ship to bear the enemy flag, but did not authorise the firing of a gun until its colours had been struck and its own flag had been hoisted in its place. Otherwise, Surcouf himself would have been hanged in short order for piracy.

Because of clothing camouflage, the Brandenburgers were able to carry out a number of operations with practically no casualties. Throughout the seven raids organised in April 1941 against military posts and bridges on the borders of Serbia, Bulgaria and Greece, the total losses were three killed, two injured and one missing. But occasionally things took a bad turn, when they took off their disguise, the Brandenburgers had to defend the occupied objective against an enemy recovered from its surprise. The 8th Company, which single-handedly held the bridges of Bataisk on the Don for a whole day, lost its commander and 87 men.

If the particular character of the fighting methods of the Brandenburgers was not always acknowledged by conventionally trained officers, their state of mind was even less so. The standard soldier likes to hide behind the hierarchy and looks unfavourably upon the elite corps where initiative and risk are cultivated.

The Brandenburgers caused unrest and consternation, because they had been trained outside the norms.

Editor's note: in certain cases the author has chosen to keep German names, which are, paradoxically, clearer in the context.

PART ONE

THE VON HIPPEL BATTALION
(1939-1940)

Chapter one

An idea born on the Vistula (September 1939)

The Treaty of Versailles remapped the Polish State to the detriment of German territory. Poland made a breach west of the Vistula River, to reach the Baltic Sea and to establish the port of Gdingen, which was later to become Gotenhafen, then Gdynia.

East Prussia and Königsberg found themselves separated from the Reich by a 'corridor' where Germany's only right was to route its trains through Polish checkpoints. The only concession made by the Allies was the forming of the old Hanseatic town of Danzig, at the mouth of the Vistula, into a free city.

Following the seizure of power by the National Socialist Party in Germany, the question of the eastern borders was raised with a passion and with increasing insistence. From March 1939 one thing was certain: the Reich could not draw back from a war that would re-establish the continuity of its territory.

Aware of the consequences of German military action, the great European powers multiplied diplomatic moves over a period of five months, in order to persuade the two neighbouring States of the Vistula to seek an agreement by negotiation.

These steps were not helped either by the inhabitants of Danzig who were proclaiming, with increasing violence, their desire to return to the Reich, or by the Polish Government, which did not seem inclined to give in.

The conviction of the German Government was set. Hitler, after the signature of his pact with the Soviets on the 23rd of August 1939, was assured of having his hands free, considered that a rapid victory over Poland would face the Western Allies with a fait accompli before the conflict could spread. He fixed the date for Wehrmacht operations on 26 August 1939 at 04:30 am.

The OKW [1] was ready. They had prepared the 'White plan'.

A glance at a map showing the borders in 1939 would show German territory taking Poland in a pincer movement which threatened to close in. On the west the nearest German soldiers were 350 km from Warsaw, and in the north 110 km away. In the south, German troops assembled on Slovakian territory could cross over the Carpathians under Warsaw. However, an absolutely essential condition of being able to close the pincer movement effectively was to make sure that its extremities had the necessary potent logistic support. As far as this point was concerned, there was a threat.

At the first sign of German attack, neither of the two main railways that had to ensure the rapid transport of men, ammunition and supplies was sheltered from destruction by Polish engineers.

In the north, the Berlin-Königsberg-Vilna line crossed the corridor, in other words Polish territory, for a distance of 100 km, then, entering the territory of Danzig, crossed the Vistula over the great Dirschau bridge to then re-enter Prussian territory at Marienburg. With this bridge destroyed, only the Graudenz road bridge remained, approximately 70 km further south. Everywhere else, the Vistula River, wide and impetuous, was an impassable obstacle, save for the use of unstable pontoons.

1. *Oberkommando der Wehrmacht*, High Command of German Armed Forces (Army, Navy, Air Force) constituting Chancellor Hitler's staff in his capacity as Commander-in-Chief. General Wilhelm Keitel, promoted to Marshal in 1940, was its chief.

18

In the south, the great Vienna-Warsaw line with its branch-line over Cracow and Galicia, in Polish territory, crossed the Beskid Mountains by a double tunnel under the Jablunka Pass, only 3 km away from the German outposts. If this tunnel was destroyed, there would only be local lines of small output leaving from Upper Silesia, further to the north.

The secret service of the Wehrmacht, *Abwehr II*, had planned three operations in order to hold the sensitive areas of Dirschau, Graudenz and Jablunka.

For surprise, speed and secrecy were the essential elements ; for success, unflawed prepration was the key. Such a programme was very ambitious. Everything had to be improvised, in the middle of a permanent conflict of powers.

An attack from the west, across the Polish corridor, would rule out any element of surprise. An attack from the east was therefore necessary, by crossing the territory of Danzig, which was in friendly territory and a quarter of the distance. The men were to be transported in an ordinary goods train which would not attract the attention of Polish employees in the three stations en route. At the moment when the train was to reach the bridge at Dirschau, a bombing squadron would carry out a bomb strike at the other end of the bridge where an explosive charges firing post was situated. An armoured train was to follow several minutes later to break down any possible Polish resistance.

The plan was not badly formed and the decision not to use paratroops very wise; they would have had to jump quite far from the target and would have jeopardised the effect of surprise.

So that nothing would arouse the attention of the enemy, the Abwehr managed to obtain confirmation from the Kriegsmarine that no action would be undertaken in the bay of Danzig prior to the fateful hour. The order to postpone the offensive fell at the last minute. Exposed to increasing diplomatic pressure, Hitler judged that the futility of the peace efforts must be proved before resorting to arms.

On the 31st of August it was thought that the combined efforts of the Western Heads of State were going to be successful, especially as, at 7.45 p.m, Poland had accepted the principle of negotiations. But the order to attack the following day at dawn had already been given to the German armies.

Those six days of uncertainty were to prove fatal. The Polish, who had an excellent intelligence service, no longer doubted the imminence of a German attack. They had the time to load the mine-chambers on the Dirschau bridge (which, on the morning of the 26th, were empty) with ten tons of trotyl and took measures to cut the line ahead of the bridge in Danzig territory.

The German detachment got moving under the command of an experienced officer, Major Mendem, former free corps commander. However the goods train, properly camouflaged, left a quarter of an hour late. The Polish employees of a station midway along the route, finding this unreported delay suspicious, immediately warned the station at Dirschau by telephone. In order to gain time, they pretended there was a problem with the points, which sent both assault battalions, enclosed in their waggons, onto a siding. When they came out they were half an hour late. Within sight of the bridge, the engineers recoiled in surprise as they realised that the line was blocked by iron joists and the entrance to the bridge obstructed by two armoured doors. The officer accompanying the train shouted:

"Smash through it!"

"It's no good," replied the driver, "it would derail us."

The train stopped.

At the same time the train came under machine-gun fire. The soldiers escaped from the trucks in a mad rush to seek shelter. It was then that the air attack struck Dirschau. However, due to a lack of accurate intelligence, the shower of 250 kilo and 50 kilo bombs spared the engineers' firing post, as well as the wires linked to the mine-chambers. When the armoured train arrived, it could not approach as the line was occupied by the false goods train evacuated by its occupants.

On the stroke of 6, in front of the exasperated Germans, the Dirschau bridge broke in two with a huge roll of thunder and was engulfed by the river.

Further down, in Graudenz, the affair was taking a tragicomic turn. At dawn, a team led by Lieutenant Tanzer and wearing Polish uniforms, succeeded in crossing the first Polish lines. He advanced carefully towards his target, seeking shelter in the woods. But the progress of the German forces was so fast that the infantry caught up with, then overtook him. He then had to cross German lines in order to take the lead again.

Just as he was about to succeed, the party was stopped at gunpoint by an infantry officer of the Wehrmacht. He did not believe a word of these men and was convinced they were deserters or Poles and took them back to the rear after disarming them. The misunderstanding was soon cleared up and the general had the small group transported to the front by car. When they arrived in sight of the bridge, already exposed to the vanguard's fire, the same spectacle as at Dirschau repeated itself under the sorry eyes of Tanzer and the bridge was swallowed up by the Vistula.

When the counter-order reached the 7th Infantry Division HQ, which was on site in front of the Jablunka Pass on the 25th of August, it was nearing midnight. The thirty-four men of the *Kampforganisation*, set up and commanded by the Reserve Second lieutenant Dr. Hans-Albrecht Herzner of the Abwehr, had already left, their mission being to occupy the double tunnel and, a mile further on, the station at Mosty.

So as to be able to dodge in and out of the Polish outposts, the strength had to be reduced. It would have been insufficient to defend its targets if faced with even the slightest Polish counter-attack, but this was not realistic. German forces were in a position to outflank Mosty from the first hours of daylight.

The scouts hastily sent to rejoin Herzner's special unit, through the dense wood that covered the mountain along the border, also had to take precautions so as not to be spotted by Polish sentries. They lost their way in the total darkness which reigned beneath the tall trees and came back having failed completely.

Meanwhile Herzner had taken twenty or so men from his unit to seize the station at Mosty and led the rest towards the tunnel. A little after 3 a.m., he took possession of his target, unguarded, with no more than inconsequential rifle fire, but did not discover the telephone exchange in the basement flat. This allowed the operator to alert Polish military authorities.

Around 5 a.m. the miners who, every morning, boarded a reserved train going to the Cieszyn mines, started to show up. As they arrived they were imprisoned in a hangar.

Around 8 a.m., as he saw nothing coming, except the Polish advanced guard, Herzner ordered an evacuation and sought to get back to the border through the woods. But his unit was soon completely encircled by two enemy battalions who, not knowing quite who they were dealing with and wanting to avoid a *casus belli*, refrained from opening fire.

Polish General Kustron, who had just established headquarters in the station at Mosty, was then informed of events. He learned that another troop of unidentified assailants had failed in front of the well-guarded tunnel. Being master of the situation, he went to the border as a bearer of a flag of truce to obtain explanations from the *Kommandeur* of the 7th German Infantry Division, facing him. He found only a simple staff officer, Dr. Kreisel, who did his utmost to persuade him that his prisoners were Slovak militiamen convinced that the territory of Cieszyn belonged to their country and who believed the time was right to symbolically take possession of it.

"How is it", asked the Polish general, "that some of these Slovaks speak German and their officer is wearing the uniform of the 9th Infantry Regiment from Potsdam?"

The German officer was barely able to stifle his anger. He did not know that Second lieutenant Herzner had made the mistake of keeping his uniform, while all the men in his special unit, German volunteers from the Sudetenland, Silesia or Poland, were in civilian clothing and, at least in theory, issued with an armband supposed to prove they were combatants.

He replied hastily:

"This uniform is worn wrongfully. It has been worn especially to intimidate you."

General Kustron, whose main concern was to hush the matter up, agreed to exchange his 'Slovak' prisoners for Polish engine drivers that the Germans kept on their side of the border. [2]

In the Silesian sector of the starting lines, the problem of rapid advance in enemy territory was settled differently. Here, there were no natural obstacles, but a knot of essential rail communications in a highly industrialised zone had to be secured.

Following the First World War, the coal-basin of Upper Silesia had been divided between Germany and Poland. During the unsettled period which preceded the fixing of the new border, some volunteers were raised and formed into paramilitary formations under the name *Industrieschutz Oberschlesien* to stop the uncontrolled gangs of Polish insurgents from sabotaging industrial plants.

Fifteen years later, the local station of the *Abwehr* at Breslau, largest town of the province of Silesia, drew essentially blast-furnace workers and miners from among the former members of the *Industrieschutz* and from German minority refugees in Poland, in order to constitute in 1938 the *Kampfverband Ebbinghaus*, a 'combat unit' bearing the name of the Abwehr officer who was in command of it. It had to be set up in the form of autonomous parties, known as *K-Trupps* [3], whose mission consisted of holding bridges, tunnels, viaducts etc. ahead of the German forces just before the beginning of hostilities.

It was obviously of the utmost importance for the Reich that the Upper Silesia industrial complex, under Polish sovereignty, be able to contribute fully to the war effort immediately.

Katowice was the vital area that the Wehrmacht had to take up from the very beginning. The lines that meet at that point drain the entire basin and continue towards the oldest Polish industrial zone, towards

2. A detailed and patient investigation undertaken by the Federal Republic military archives resulted in the publication of a first booklet in 1971 and a second in 1979, which collate witnesses from both sides of the border and approximately establish the truth.

3 For *Kampf-Trupp*, combat team.

Cracow and Czestochowa. Katowice is only 12 km from Beuthen, the German border town. Between the two is the town of Königshütte.

The chief actor in this event was Second lieutenant Herzner, who died in an accident in 1942 after having commanded the Nachtigall Battalion formed from Ukrainian volunteers and attached to the Brandenburg Regiment. He was therefore no longer around to confirm or deny the achievements that were perhaps wrongly attributed to him.

Together it formed a conurbation of three million inhabitants. The distance to clear was short, but the terrain offered no cover to a unit that wanted to cross in secrecy.

Reserve Second lieutenant Siegfried Grabert, whose special line had been relations with Germans abroad, had been noticed by the Abwehr. In the spring of 1939, he was recruited to collaborate in the preparation of a possible campaign against Poland.

Grabert, who was dissatisfied with his medical studies in Tübingen, accepted straightaway. He was in charge of finding and enlisting, in the territories of Upper Silesia joined to Poland, former members of the ex-*Industrieschutz Oberschlesien* willing to take up arms again, in order to amalgamate them to those found in German territory.

He succeeded beyond all expectations. If these former German citizens were often racially Polish, they remained German at heart. In the unit that was formed, practically the only language spoken was Slav! But that fitted in perfectly with the tactic that the Lieutenant thought of using after his objective had been fixed: the railway junction at Katowice.

Among his eighty men, chosen one by one and all volunteers, he took care to include several experienced smugglers, who knew all the little paths crossing the border between the inhabited zones perfectly. The bulk of his unit was made up of factory workers, miners and railwaymen.

It was a strange group that slipped between the enemy border posts at 2 a.m. on the 1st of September 1939.

Eighty troops disguised as employees of the Republic of Poland railways marched in column with impassive faces, some carrying rucksacks, others haversacks containing submachine-guns, hand grenades, ammunition and explosives. In a cart track, four lorries were waiting for them. After getting on board, the vehicles turned into the main road, their headlights on. They passed round Königshütte by the south. On reaching the first switching point at Katowice the passengers got off and took shelter in a hangar.

One by one Grabert sent forward teams of ten men who had been trained on a reduced scale mock-up model to find their way in the maze of the marshalling yard. They had to occupy and hold all the sensitive areas until relieved by German forces.

Grabert, accompanied by a German NCO, who spoke fluent Polish, were the last to leave so as to be able to supervise the deployment of his men.

The two men walked towards the lights, stumbling over the sleepers. The sound of rifle fire broke out over the warehouses, 500 metres away.

"What idiot...?" thought Grabert to himself, and then started to run towards the ever-increasing sound of gunfire. He saw nothing. The goods trains stationed parallel to the warehouses blocked his view. While the two men were getting ready to pass under the buffers, a locomotive arrived and stopped just at their height. Behind it, a dozen or so waggons unloaded one or two infantry companies wearing khaki uniform onto the ballast. The second lieutenant and his companion found themselves mixed up with Polish soldiers who, mistaking them for railway workers, paid them absolutely no attention.

Seeing the Polish surround the warehouse where several of his men had entrenched themselves, Grabert knew that he had to keep a good length in front of the enemy, or resign himself to being overpowered by numbers before having been able to fulfil his mission. He returned quickly to the last signal box where he had positioned a team and gave its leader precise instructions. Immediately, the leader detached three men, who were very familiar with the area, to the large railway bridge in the outskirts of the town.

Grabert went back to the train that was being surrounded by several

25

men. All around the warehouse the rifle-fire continued. Almost an hour had passed when a large explosion was heard from afar, followed by several others. The soldiers who were attacking the warehouse surged back to the train. The officers discussed the situation vehemently, clearly in disarray. At that moment three false Polish railwaymen came running and shouting that the Germans were attacking.

Taking advantage of the disorder, Grabert and his three men, one of whom was an engine-driver by trade, occupied the cab of the locomotive and tied up its two occupants.

"All aboard!" shouted the railwaymen at the top of their voices.

The locomotive started off very slowly. Believing it to be following the orders of one of their commanders, the soldiers hurried to get on, with officers leading the pade.

Soon the train started moving at a good speed. Everything was quiet again. Outside the town, Grabert gave the order to stop. The Germans abandoned the locomotive and hid before the Polish, wondering what was happening, decided to get out and ask the drivers why the train had stopped. The first German AFVs coming out of Königshütte, on the road parallel to the track, rounded up scores of dazed Polish prisoners. Katowice station, along with its points, signals, bridges, warehouses, cranes and all its equipment and rolling stock fell into the hands of Colonel-General von Rundstedt's forces intact.

The Polish campaign was to unfold at lightning speed. Within three days, the Polish front was broken through in the north, in the centre and in the south.

In twelve hours the German engineers compensated for the failure of the *K-Trupps* brought into action against the bridges of Dirschau and Graudenz, by launching solid pontoon bridges under the protection of the Luftwaffe, which had complete air superiority.

Motorised columns were spread out in all directions, outdistancing the withdrawing Polish troops who were transformed by the automatic fire and bombing of German combined arms, to a disorderly rabble mixed in with waves of refugees. For the Germans it was no longer a question of pursuing the destruction of the Polish armies, but to advance towards the east as rapidly as possible.

The *Abwehr* at Breslau hastily formed another *K-Trupp* from the *Kampfverband Ebbinghaus* to occupy the great railway bridge spanning the Vistula near Deblin, to prevent enemy engineers from blowing it up. The unit was made up of Upper Silesians who had all done their military service in the Polish Army. The unit, led by a former NCO in the Polish Army named Kodon who impersonated a lieutenant, played to perfection the role of one of the few enemy infantry platoons with drawing in good order. In the night of the 8th and 9th, they crossed over German lines.

Sunrise found them mixed up with a column of refugees and soldiers. In order to gain ground they got free from it every time they were able. To inspire them with confidence, they broke into Polish marching songs, keeping step. But by nightfall they had only covered two-thirds of the route. Congested with lorries, waggons, artillery guns and cars, the column came to a stop. It became an impassable obstacle in the darkness.

The *K-Trupp* attempted to continue on its way across fields, but the soft ploughed earth proved such a test for the men, already exhausted by a hard forced march. Kodon decided to have a break until daylight.

The men lay down where they stood, tight against each other, and fell straight asleep. They needed to wait for dawn to be able to carry on their way. They were able to reach the head of the column and make swift progress on a road that was practically deserted.

Around midday, they spotted the distinctive outline of the steel bridge on the horizon. The entrance to it was blocked by massed vehicles that forced pedestrians to make detours round them. It took Kodon's troop more than an hour to cover 500 metres in the midst of all the shouts, scrambles and curses. They at last reached the bridge, where the human tide was so thick that those who stopped or fell were mercilessly trampled underfoot.

Kodon, arriving from the eastern bank, located the guard of the bridge. They had erected their tents on one side of the route. They were a platoon of engineers, clearly under orders to destroy the bridge as soon as the last military detachments had gone past. Kodon, with great self-assurance, shouted at the Polish second lieutenant:

"I have orders to relieve you."

The young officer did not understand the reason for this order. He demanded confirmation and went over to the field telephone in his tent, without having seen that one of Kodon's men, who had moved away with the excuse of answering a call of nature, had cut the cable 50 metres away. The second lieutenant turned the handle in desperation;

"Typical Polish equipment! If only we had bought German equipment!"

But he had absolutely no intention of leaving. Kodon hesitated to confront a troop greater in number and outfitted for combat. It was at that moment that a flight of Stukas with their sirens screaming dived towards the bridge and released their bombs, opening bloody gaps in the crowd. Kodon's men spotted the black crosses on these planes as they approached. They had run as far as they could and then thrown themselves on the ground.

There was not one injured among them. It was not the same however for the bridge guard who suffered losses. The second lieutenant had splinter wounds in his arm. Kodon advised him, in a fatherly way, to go and get his wound dressed and to remove the wounded at the same time. He would bury the two dead and ensure the bridge was destroyed. Demoralised, the Poles left.

The initial worry for the Germans was to defuse the charges on the abutment and the first span, but it was impossible for them to reach the western end of the bridge, against the current of runaways, to carry out their task. Even by using their weapons, they would not be able to do it. They examined the banks. The Polish had sunk all the small boats. As for swimming across the Vistula, the strength of the current and the eddies on the water were enough to stop any swimmer from even thinking about it. They would have to wait, therefore, for the human tide to move on.

They waited five hours. In the distance the first Panzers were beginning to appear. Kodon trembled at the thought of a well-aimed round hitting the two chambers fitted with explosives. He feared also that the Polish troops still on the other bank several companies strong would have the unfortunate idea of setting up a bridge head, by bringing the two antitank guns, abandoned in the confusion, into action. He desperately sought a way to evacuate civilians from the area. All of a sudden he shouted:

"The bridge is going to explode in five minutes. Let everybody know!"

A clamour ran through the crowd from one end of the bridge to the other: "The bridge is going to explode!"

There was total panic. A number of civilians and soldiers threw themselves into the river where they simply disappeared fighting against the current. When the grey and brown Panzers with their turrets bearing white crosses arrived at the entrance to the bridge, there was a mass of entangled vehicles on the deck, obstructing the way. The tanks pushed any obstacle they met on to the sides and even over the parapets.

After stripping off their Polish uniforms, Kodon and his men emptied the dangerous mine-chambers on the western bank without being disturbed. Nearly the entire 10th Army under Colonel-General von Reichenau crossed the bridge at Deblin over a period of three days. From there they reached the Bug River behind which Soviet forces were preparing an offensive.

Chapter II

Old barracks
in Brandenburg

The rapid growth of the Abwehr, parallel to the German rearmament undertaken by Hitler after his seize of power in 1933, had made the recruitment of a new cadre of officers necessary. Ex-service men of the First World War having some knowledge of subversive warfare or matters of intelligence were the first ones contacted.

Captain Dr. Theodor-Gottlieb von Hippel was one of those who wore the feldgrau uniform once again with the great satisfaction. Did he not win fame in that war where General von Lettow-Vorbeck joined battle from 1914 to 1919 against the British in German East Africa, modern day Tanzania?

Subsequently entering the world of business, he found his new occupation rather monotonous. He had lived through an extraordinary adventure when, with 15,000 Askaris led by several hundred Europeans, he held off enemy forces nearing 250,000 men, the majority of European origin and better-equipped.

He was a firm believer that a 'little war' led by small, highly mobile groups, disguised and operating at the rear of the enemy, was capable of causing immense damage. By reinstating the secret service, he had an immutable idea, to provide the German Army with what he considered to be an irreplaceable success factor, particularly when swift progress is the necessary condition of victory.

31

He had been posted to Department II of the Abwehr which was in charge of sabotage and subversive action at the rear of the enemy. Its commander was Major *i.G.* [1] Helmut Groscurth. A tall, bespectacled fellow, the Major was a remarkable organiser, but had no experience in the operations that he was to prepare. He was very happy to be joined by a person such as Hippel, an officer who possessed experience in the field that he lacked. He listened to him willingly and tolerated his frankness. The two men complemented each other, the sense of reality of one balancing the imagination of the other. Von Hippel had a very fertile imagination and his daring ideas knew no limits.

He was a 'poet of action'. From 1938, during the crisis in the Sudetenland, he welcomed, lodged and organised, from the Abwehr Dresden station, young people who were leaving Czechoslovakia in order to work in the Reich for their territory to be united to the German Fatherland. Drawing from a pool of several thousand refugees, he trained half soldiers, half secret agents, who made incessant raids into Czechoslovakian territory to foster an atmosphere of instability, gather military information, carry out acts of sabotage and to stir up politically exploitable discord.

Strengthened by the results obtained in Czechoslovakia, Hippel confided to his commander one evening his idea of small camouflaged units, integrated into the army, yet independent.

"So that my *Kommandos* [2] can seize bridges, occupy dams and power stations in order to stop the enemy from blowing them up, they must cross borders before indisguise any declaration of war."

"But my dear fellow, the Abwehr does precisely that. Our stations at Königsberg and Breslau in the East, Aachen and Hamburg in the West have the job of organising, in the time required, such *Kommandos*. Yourself, in Dresden..."

1. Major of the General Staff Corps (im Generalstab).
2. The captain's African past obviously led him to use the term 'Kommando'. It was with this word, of Portuguese origin, that the Boers, at the beginning of the Twentieth Century, named troops of one hundred men commanded by one officer. The British were to keep it to name their units responsible for tasks similar to those of the Brandenburgers during the Second World War. As in German military

"I know" interrupted Hippel, "but these attempts are made in the scope of the secret service and not the army. Because they are totally improvised, the personnel lack training and military aptitude. Units that they should collaborate closely with ignore them, yet they help to facilitate their advance. Chaos, misunderstanding, inefficiency and bitter defeat, as we have seen, is the result. My *Kommandos* must constitute a real part of the Wehrmacht. Nonetheless, I believe it necessary that they depend exclusively on the Abwehr for their recruitment and instruction."

"That stands to reason. But I doubt that the higher authorities in the army will accept your proposition. There is no provision for it in any handbook and it is not taught at the *Kriegsakademie*. [3] The idea of irregular soldiers is traditionally abhorred by our officers."

"Of course. That is why everything must be done outside the official framework of the army, almost behind their back, at least as long as our point will not be carried by the results obtained. Only the Abwehr, which is answerable to nobody concerning the methods that it uses, has enough elbow room to take it on."

Groscurth was struck by the judiciousness of the argument. He remained hesitant however.

Hippel continued:

"The *Kommandos* and every man who is part of them must have a great potential for using their initiative and for taking responsibility, completely the opposite of Prussian style drill where the soldier is nothing more than a perfectly prepared automaton. This demands an exploitation of an innate skill rather than training, careful selection rather than blind recruitment. I believe, in this very specific instance, in a military individualism, the same way as I believe in a social individualism, by that I mean an individual's qualities cultivated for the benefit of all."

parlance the word Kommando applies to a command of a superior officer given to a subaltern, to a level of command or even to a party created with a particular aim (Wachkommando, guard party, etc.), the Brandenburg 'commandos' were called Einsatzgruppen, Kampftrupps, etc.

3. The Berlin equivalent of the Staff College in Surrey.

"Hippel you have already developed your theories on this subject for me. Let's leave it there. I will speak to the Admiral about it when I judge the time to be right."

Several weeks later, the Reich was at war with Poland, Great Britain and France. The streets of Berlin were filled with the sound of brass bands. Red flags embossed with the swastika flapped at the windows, even on the austere facade of the building which housed the offices of the Abwehr on the Tirpitzufer. [4]

Following a telephone call from the Admiral's aide de camp, Captain von Hippel hurried towards his office half an hour earlier than usual. There could be no doubt that Groscurth had spoken. Joy shone in his eyes when he responded to the salute of the *Schupo* [5] guard. Had the great day arrived? Up until now his suggestions had fallen on deaf ears. Improvisation had reigned, so heavy with disappointment.

Has the Admiral managed to overcome his repugnance for crude guerrilla methods? Has he had enough of letting himself being talked into things instead of taking control, he the born commander? The captain had a premonition that this was indeed the case.

He was immediately shown into the office of Canaris, a place that was not very military in appearance and he felt no particular attraction to it. With its bare, shiny parquet floor, its chairs all lined up, it had the atmosphere of a parlour, were it not for the maps and military portraits which covered the walls. He took a step back when he saw the Admiral coming towards him holding one of his famous basset hounds, the other one butting against his feet. Hippel liked his horses in stables and his dogs in kennels.

"Come in, come in Captain, I have something in mind for you. But, beforehand, we must be in total agreement on one thing. No interfering with politics. All opinions, as you know, are represented in this establishment, even those which are in favour. Our strength is the esprit de corps. Nothing must divide us..."

4. Tirpitz Quay.
5. Policeman of the Schutzpolizei, town police.

"I quite agree, *Herr Admiral*."

"Good, that's enough of that. Let's get to the heart of the matter. Your story is beginning to take shape. Putz, from the station at Vienna has set up a unit that I have baptised *Bau-Lehr-Kompanie zbV*[6] that he wanted to entrust to Captain Verbeek. There is a certain Lieutenant Siegfried Grabert, if you remember, he carried out the raid at Katowice without a hitch. I am going to send this company to Slovakia, so that it will be ready to operate in Rumania. They are needed to keep an eye on the oil at Ploesti."

"Forgive me, *Herr Admiral*, but unless I am mistaken, Slovakia is a sovereign State. How..."

"Yes appearances must be respected. Consequently our chaps will go there in civilian clothing, members of some kind of sports club no doubt. I'm leaving the details to the Viennese. The important thing is to be in agreement on the essentials. The point where I encountered the most reticence is on the principle of camouflage clothing. A number of our comrades maintain that it is an act of cowardice and treason to approach the enemy with a disguise. That shows a certain ingenuousness. The same people would not hesitate to transform their tanks into green bushes so as not to be spotted by the *Pak*. [7] They will understand eventually. I was convinced by what happens in the Navy. The Hague convention is very clear. A war ship is authorised to approach the enemy bearing colours other than its own, on condition that it raises its own colours before opening fire.

The colours of a warship are its uniform. We will do the same.

"I have explained my point of view in two articles. The role of these soldiers does not consist of fighting in enemy uniforms, but simply to prevent the destruction of important objectives and to defend them

6. Special Purpose Training Construction Engineer Company. Name retained on account of the officers of this unit belonging to the engineers. The abbreviation zbV (*zur besondere Verwendung*, special purpose) applies to independent units and command levels of all branches of service, without any links with secret or subversive action.

7. *Panzerabwehrkanonen*: antitank guns.

35

while waiting for the arrival of the main forces. But they must only wear foreign uniforms in order to penetrate, without combat, enemy territory and to be able to approach objectives without being recognised. In the event of a combat situation becoming inevitable they must identify themselves as German soldiers before opening fire."

"Yes, *Herr Admiral*", said von Hippel, "that is all very well in theory. But in practice it is only possible if they wear what I would call 'semi-camouflage'. In the case of an all over camouflage, when our men are dressed as, let's say, French soldiers, I can't see them undressing, opening their haversacks and getting dressed again in *feldgrau* under bursts of machine-gun fire! It's obvious that they will use their weapons without always having the time even to slip on an armband. What will happen to them then if they are taken prisoner? They will be slaughtered like dogs. Our men must know that fact before putting on any disguise and must be free to accept or refuse. If this point of view is not accepted, then, with regret, I will not be able to be a candidate for the command of one of these units."

"Don't get on your high horse, Captain. It has always been like that in our operations. Where have you seen other than volunteers?...Well, here is my proposition: I'm giving you responsibility of mustering a unit of about 900 men for the western offensive which will happen one day and in any event must be prepared for. Recruitment sources are numerous: agents and *K-Trupps* from the Abwehr, reserve officers, free corps of the Sudetenland and, of course, volunteers from all German regiments, with, as always, preference given to personnel qualified for this type of work. In addition I will put those of my officers that you will need at your disposition, as far as the demands of the job will allow."

"Thank you, *Herr Admiral*."

"One more thing. You will have your quarters at Brandenburg-an-der-Havel. We will keep in touch easily, as it's a one hour journey away. I have in mind large, very pratical barracks, which are available. They housed the '*Generalfeldzeugmeister*' No. 3 Prussian Artillery Regiment before the other war. I'm thinking of making it the home station of the unit that your company will be the nucleus of.

Your orders are ready. Go and receive them from Colonel Oster." [8]

During the winter of 1939-1940, the unit took shape. Even though it was still designated as a company, it reached the strength of a battalion with an HQ company. Half of the units were at Brandenburg.

Hippel was very careful with the training of his officers. An esprit de corps was beginning to emerge. Soon, Colonel Oster visited Brandenburg/Havel. He listened, observed and then left.

The following day he was in the Admiral's office.

"You wanted to speak to me?"

The colonel cleared his throat. Canaris carried on tidying his papers.

"*Herr Admiral,* I have been giving much thought to the question that the existence of von Hippel's company gives rise to. I think, at last, we have some extraordinary possibilities."

"I don't doubt it. We are going to see something other than the improvisations of the beginning of the invasion of Poland, and which did little for our prestige."

"I am not referring to that, *Herr Admiral,* but to the idea that all of us have in the back of our minds."

The preoccupations of his subordinate were well known to the Admiral, they were slightly worrying rather than outrageous. For the Admiral, it was not the moment to attempt anything against the regime, whose recent political successes and victories in the East had assured popularity. He felt, in addition, closely watched by the SD [9] and feared that what he considered to be Oster's carelessness would attract major problems to his departments.

"Let's say rather 'your' ideas, Oster, those which are doubtless the subject of your private conversations with a certain military attaché."

"You know that, *Herr Admiral?* Captain Sas is only a good comrade. And isn't the task of an intelligence officer to worm the information

8. In charge of the Central Department of the Abwehr.

9. Sicherheitsdienst, Security Service - in fact espionage and counter-espionage - operating like the Abwehr on the territory of the Reich or abroad, but outside the framework of the military. It was integrated in the Reich's Main Security Office, headed by SS-Gruppenführer Heydrich, and its members wore the uniform of the SS.

out of his foreign colleagues?"

"That is of course what I will say to my friend Heydrich, the next time we have lunch together, if he mentions the Dutch captain's kepi in whose shadow you have been seen perhaps more frequently than is desirable. You know that I consider that if an officer opposes the regime, which is his right and I would even say his duty, that opposition knows a limit. And that is called treason."

"That is a hard word, *Herr Admiral*. May I explain myself to you frankly?"

Canaris nodded his head.

Oster continued:

"I think all methods are justified to bring down this harmful man, leader of a gang of cranks, hoodlums and criminals."

He looked at the Admiral who didn't bat an eyelid.

"We know here better than anyone in the world that Germany does not have the means to win the war with the entire world that this visionary is dragging us into. When operations start up again one day soon, they must not succed because that would give this Austrian corporal glory on a national scale and would entwine his fate with that of Germany's. Our neighbours in the West must be able to drive back their aggressors."

The Admiral lifted his head and gave his interlocutor an icy stare:

"Oster, the foreigner does not know our country. He is ignorant of the internal conflicts. He supposes that, apart from a tiny minority, every German is behind our leader. They will make no distinction and there will be no peace until they have destroyed the Reich along with its Führer. That is why it is not possible, from the moment that we are at war, for us to betray the regime without at the same time betraying Germany. I beg you Oster, forget what you have learnt in this department when you speak with a foreign military attaché. You do not have the right to work for a German defeat, even for a motive which is honourable in your eyes. Do not have the bodies of German soldiers on your conscience."

"Those who leave this maniac to get sucked into a Second World War will have more on their conscience than I."

"Colonel, enough of this subject, we will never agree. While Germany is at war, our duty will be to obey the government. I will leave it there. But, if I remember correctly, you wish to speak to me about von Hippel's company?"

"Indeed. And here, I am perhaps going to play a part in your plans. In the Wehrmacht, there are but a few officers who have not fallen under the charm of this house-painter. What can we do, militarily speaking, when we have the Armed-SS [10] in front of us which already forms several divisions? Nothing. We need a unit which belongs to us. Let's make the Hippel Battalion the heart of this force which will be capable of entering into action when the situation has developed."

"I am not unsympathetic to an idea of an Abwehr's house combat unit. But I'm worried that you are being carried away by your imagination. I see two major objections: first, the composition of this unit. It's not a rounding up of anti-Nazis, but of Germans from every horizon, a lot of whom are indifferent to politics and who have been chosen for other reasons. It is by no means certain that, when the time comes, they will accept the role that you hope they will play. Secondly, this unit, because of its purpose, will never be regrouped. Therefore it will be inaccessible and unusable at the same time. Besides, this is already true. There are two companies at Brandenburg, one other in the Wienerwald."

"No doubt, but there will also be periods of regroupment that we will be able to profit from. Troops which have been at the front under the orders of good officers afterwards follow them blindly. Both of us have seen that with the free corps in 1919."

"Come on, Oster, once again I repeat that I do not agree. That is my final word."

With a frowning air, and a stubborn expression Oster made a slight bow, turned back perfectly and left the room.

Canaris ran his fingers on his forehead. His basset hound came up against his leg. He patted it on the head:

10 The *SS-Verfügunstruppe* and the *SS-Totenkopfverbände*, joined together at the end of 1939 under the name Waffen-SS.

"Don't you see, Hannibal, this man is led astray by his passion. He's going to create difficulties for himself, and moreover for us as well. I should get rid of him. But sometimes the best thing is to be deaf and blind, that's not bad for the head of an intelligence service!"

The orderly knocked at the door.

"Will the Admiral be taking his horse ride tomorrow morning? The groom is awaiting orders."

"Of course Kurt, serious matters above all."

Every day, from the window of his office, Captain von Hippel saw volunteers arrive in small groups. The groups were too small... An orderly led them one by one before a *Spiess*.[11] A simple routine questioning: name, family address, unit of origin etc. From the reception office, they reached the barrack-room which had been assigned to them. One day there were six of them. A jovial *Gefreiter* introduced himself:

"I'm here to take charge of you. No duty until tomorrow. After supper, we'll have a chat."

The soup was spartan. A clear stock with boiled mashed potatoes in it. A few slices of sausage with two pieces of rye bread.

They got used to it, it was war. The rain led them back to the barrack-room well before nightfall. They started smoking, already bored. Two of them started a game of skat. Others swapped banalities without finding a subject of common interest.

The lance-corporal entered and introduced himself.

"Steiner, Otto. I come from Cologne, the land of the carnival. That marked me out for coming here, to the company of disguises!

"I was one of the first volunteers. And you?" he said turning to one of the new arrivals, a tall, brown-haired lad with dark eyes.

He shrugged his shoulders. "I've written my name on my locker: Heinrich Torpf. I was preparing my history doctorate in Graz."

"What brought you here?"

"My platoon leader appointed me. He told me I was very suitable.

11. German military slang for company sergeant-major.

That's all."

The man on the second bed, seeing his turn was next, introduced himself spontaneously:

"Paul Gross from Pankow. When I learnt that it was 'special' here, I liked it. In the engineers, all we did was dig over the earth or transport planks. I like action, and freedom."

The lance-corporal smiled.

"The freedom I can guarantee you is the freedom to obey the orders you will be given. Have you heard of the *SS-Verfügunstruppe*? Here it's just as tough. And certainly more difficult."

With a nod of the head, he questioned the next one.

"Himmelmann, Fritz from Okowakuatjiwi. It's not in Pomerania, nor in Wurtemberg. It's in Southwest Africa."

"But", said the Berliner "that hasn't been German since 1919. Are you South African or something like that?"

"I'm a German, that's enough. I asked to come here, because it was pointed out to me that I could be useful in a special unit because I speak English and Portuguese. I didn't ask to understand. And then I heard that the radio sets are so bad here that Adolf's speeches cannot be heard."

With these words he looked around at his comrades. There was no smile, but a glimmer of complicity in the eyes of some.

The fourth was born in Château-Salins, in Lorraine, and spoke French like a pure-bred *Welsch*. [12]

"We were even taught it at school at the same time as German. Which means that I am not the youngest. Thirty-five! Nobody appointed me. I have a cousin here. He did some advertising. He told me that in the Brandenburgers, it's not the shoulder straps which count, but guts and intelligence. I like that."

The *Gefreiter* was enjoying himself.

"My dear little Frenchman, if you think that the shoulder strap does not count here you are in for a nasty surprise. The German Army is every bit as indelible as the ink on your *Soldbuch*. I'll say no more so

12. German name for people of neo-Latin language.

as not to shatter your illusions on the very day of your arrival."

"And you last two?"

"Well" said one of them, a tall blond, "I have an uncle in the Abwehr. He told me I have an astonishing visual memory and that it could be useful here. *Zur Sache!* My name is Kramer, August. My trade? Good for nothing, other than watching what the others do."

"We will know how to take care of any slack periods" the *Gefreiter* slipped in. "From six in the morning to six at night, never mind the night alerts. I swear you won't have the time to watch what the others are doing."

All eyes turned to the last one. He was the smallest. Broad shouldered and very muscular. He spoke without looking at anybody. His hard grey gaze passed above their heads:

"Bohmer, Anton. Brunn, Moravia. Formerly in Czechoslovakia. I speak Czech and Slovak and even Hungarian; I lived in Munkacevo, that's completely Magyar. I want to fight. I have been part of the *Sudeten Selbstschutz*, the Free Corps Heinlein. [13] I've got scores to settle with some bastards. Anyway I don't like anonymous war. Have I come in the right door *Herr Gefreiter?*"

"Without betraying any military secrets, I can say yes. When you know precisely what our role consists of, you will be free to return to your original unit if you have not found what you are looking for. But men like you always stay."

The 15th of December 1939 marked the official birth of the *Bau-Lehr-Bataillon zbV 800.* Only the staff and the equivalent of three companies were maintained at the *Generalfeldzeugmeister-Kaserne* at Brandenburg. The 1st Company under Lieutenant Kniesche remained in Austria and the completely new 3rd Company under Captain Rudloff in Münstereifel, near Cologne. But the commander of the new *zbV* battalion was anxious. Half of his barrack-rooms were still empty. Conscription was not an option: all Brandenburgers had to be volunteers. Many came through personal relations or by word of mouth, but this source rapidly dried up. Group training started in a

13. More familiar name for the German Sudeten Free Corps.

week's time, they would have to resort to drastic measures. Consequently the order arrived from Berlin to name a recruitment officer for each unit and to send him to raise volunteers in the neighbouring garrisons, starting with the one in Brandenburg itself.

Lieutenant Klein, accompanied by a Feldwebel and two lance-corporals consequently went to the depot unit of the 230th Infantry Regiment. They entered the barrack square under driving rain. The *Ersatzbataillon* [14] was assembled in the training room.

Klein was faced with hundreds of curious eyes staring at him.

"Let me introduce myself: Oberleutnant Hugo Klein, 800th Special Purpose Training Construction Engineer Battalion. I am here looking for volunteers, men with guts who are not afraid of hard work. Men for whom close combat would be a sort of favourite pastime. You know that when a troop advances, it is preceded by a vanguard. Well, we precede the vanguard."

"Shock troops for heaven?" said a recruit.

"Something like that", replied the lieutenant laughing. "In any case where we are going, Iron Crosses, even Knight's Crosses, are lying thick on the ground."

The shiny new 1st Class Cross on his left chest pocket corroborated what he was saying and attracted some interest.

He paused so that his words would have time to take effect, then he continued:

"Well, I have never spoken as long as this in my life. Those who are interested come forward immediately. But careful, no heart, sight or hearing defects. Is that clear? You have ten minutes to make up your mind. *Weggetreten!*" [15]

The assembly dispersed and split up into little groups where the men discussed amongst themselves vigorously. When the time was up, the gathering re-formed spontaneously.

"Volunteers, leave ranks and line up in front of me!" ordered Klein.

Twenty or so men moved forward immediately. "The most sure",

14. Battalion supplying drafts to a mobilised regiment.
15. "Fall out!"

thought the lieutenant. He did not let them out of his sight. "Take down the names of those on one side."

"Is that all?" he asked. "Only those who want the quiet life left?"

In the midst of laughter, some other volunteers broke away from the ranks, sometimes one by one, sometimes two or three together. Eventually there were nearly forty.

"Nobody else?"

A hand was raised very reluctantly.

"*Herr Oberleutnant*, I have a conviction."

"Motive?"

"A brawl. I bashed someone's face in."

"Excellent. Come on board! And you?" he said, looking at another raised hand.

"Five years in the Foreign Legion with the *Franzosen*. Eighteen fights, including five hand-to-hand. Military medal. Two injuries. Participated in three special missions in dissident territory."

The lieutenant let forth a whistle of admiration:

"I don't know how we've been able to do without you up to now. Come forward!"

There remained only one more raised hand.

"*Herr Oberleutnant*, could I speak to you privately?"

Klein listened to the tall blond boy, with a determined appearance.

"*Herr Oberleutnant*, I have a Jewish mother... Nobody here knows that..."

"If nobody knows it then I don't know it either. That concerns the recruitment branch, not the single units. What's your name?"

"Wolfram Koppenwalner."

"That's better than Isaac Schweinkopf. Go and enlist."

The volunteers now formed two rows of twenty-six men, fifty-two in total. Lieutenant Klein inspected them. He considered he had creamed off the best of the battalion. A greater number would not be desirable. But he noticed that apart from two or three lance-corporals, there were scarcely any non commissioned officers.

"Where have all the NCOs gone?" he asked with a touch of irony.

He had seen them perfectly, right from the beginning, grouped together on the right. He walked over to them casually:

"I must, gentlemen, make up for my lapse of memory. I did not inform you that my speech was addressed equally to NCOs."

Then he added curtly:

"Who amongst you are regulars? Raise your hand."

They all raised their hands.

"Oh? Some compelling vocations? No vulgar amateurs like the fifty-two men over there? So, what is holding you back?"

A *Feldwebel*, with a furrowed brow, replied in a flat voice:

"We are infantrymen, not engineers."

"Aha! A lovely objection. But, you know, we are not engineers like the others. Well, it's your business. We are not going to force anybody. I will leave you to the delights of garrison life."

The captain in command of the battalion, who had witnessed the whole scene from the very beginning without turning a hair, approached the lieutenants who had presented the unit to the visitor:

"He has taken the best of our men. We should consider ourselves lucky that he left leave the cadre."

Chapter III

We will go and get the Devil in Hell itself (winter 1939-1940)

The order of the day stated: 7 a.m., training at Quenzgut.[1] Working dress.

It was still dark on this January morning when the section left the barracks, as usual marching in step, under the command of Corporal Winzel. As they left the town they 'marched at ease'.

"Where are we going, *Herr Unteroffizier?*" enquired several voices.

"We are going to pay a visit to Hell's kitchen, Kinder. But remember the paper you signed. You'll be a lot wiser soon enough."

The Quenzgut was a vast area, bordering Lake Quenz, that had a thick curtain of trees and a ring of barbed wire to discourage indiscreet glances; there were several huts and some installations that were difficult to make out at first sight. The volunteers were shown into a sort of class room. An old NCO from the engineers with greying hair, representing the least war-like specimen that it was

1. School set up by the Abwehr at Gut Quenzsee, several kilometres from Brandenburg, to train its agents. The *Bau-Lehr-Bataillon* made its men follow several courses there.

47

possible to imagine in a *feldgrau* uniform, entered the room and positioned himself in front of the blackboard.

"Young men, I am simply your technical instructor. The knowledge that you acquire here will be, in certain situations, indispensable to you. I see on your training syllabus..."

After putting on a large pair of glasses, he lifted a sheet of paper to his eyes: "...that you are already familiar with the explosives of the engineer range. But it's the sappers who have done all the work. Here, the difference is that you will do it yourselves. Let's go and visit Hell's kitchen!"

The section was shown into the neighbouring hut. After making a presentation of the different explosives used by the engineers of the army, just like those available on the civilian market, the instructor moved a little further away and took a small black fuse from a table.

"This is a safety fuse. It's a small cable made waterproof by the use of tar, in its core there is a black powder. It is lit at its free end. Here, I'll do it."

Instinctively, all the students took a step backwards. Winzel and the professor smiled:

"No, *Jungen*, a safety fuse burns and does not explode. It burns at the rate of a metre in ninety seconds. Use one three metres long and you have four and a half minutes to take cover. I will show you later how it is mounted on the primer, and the primer on the charge.

"Now, there are two other ignition options. First the detonating cord. As you can see, it is in nickel silver, therefore malleable. Inside, it also has a core, which is filled with high explosive. It explodes from one end to the other, practically at the same moment. We shall see under what conditions it may be used. The last method with electricity using an exploder. Today this is the most widely used. This little box contains a dynamo and this key turns it round. The current is transmitted by this double cable, the end of which is in contact with the explosive charge by the switch which creates a spark... there you have it..."

The training continued the next day and over the following two weeks. They learnt how to make the charges, then how to defuse

48

Below:
Admiral Canaris, who was head of the Abwehr from 1935. The idea of creating Brandenburg type armed units was not his. He accepted it but despite his ambiguous personal position, he did not use the unit as an instrument of a plot against the national socialist regime. *(Bundesarchiv)*

Two German formations created between the wars served as a 'catch basin' for the first special fighting units of the Abwehr formed in 1939:

Above: In 1919, following the occupation of the industrial areas of Upper Silesia by Polish forces, a German self-defence movement was organized and set up a free corps, the *Industrieschutz Oberschlesien,* made up of armed volunteers who fought relentlessly to reconquer their land. *(Bundesarchiv)*

Below: Formed in 1938 in Germany from the protection service of Konrad Heinlein, the political leader of the German Sudeten population, the *Sudetendeutschen Freikorps* actively helped the Wehrmacht to invade these territories in the following October. *(Bundesarchiv)*

Below: In 1939, with a view to the inevitable German-Polish conflict, the Silesian station of the Abwehr set up a *Kampfverband Ebbinghaus*, made up of several special units called *K-Trupps.* One of them was entrusted to reserve Second Lieutenant Dr. Hans-Albrecht Herzner. *(Private Collection)*

Above: This *K-Trupp*, amongst which Herzner is seen in uniform, was especially made up of Polish-speaking Germans from Upper Silesia, some of whom had fought within the *Industrieschutz Oberschlesien* twenty years earlier. *(Private Collection)*

Below: The mission of Leutnant Herzner's special unit consisted of occupying a tunnel and a railway station off the Jablunka Pass, on the Slovakian-Polish border, south of Cracow, to open the way for the 7th German Infantry Division. It was carried out in the night of the 25th and 26th of August 1939 and crowned a success. However, operations against Poland had been postponed several days: Herzner's volunteers had to turn back and some were captured. On the 1st September, infantrymen of the 7th ID finally crossed the Jablunka Pass. *(Private Collection)*

Right: Captain Dr. Theodor-Gottlieb von Hippel in his office at Brandenburg/Havel. Having fought in East Africa during the First World War, this officer became a salesman before entering the service again in the *Abwehr II* after the creation of the Wehrmacht. An innovative military strategist, but a difficult subordinate, he can be considered as one of the founding fathers of the Brandenburg units. In 1939, he was in command of the *Bau-Lehr-Kompanie zbV 800*; it became a battalion at the end of December and he was maintained at its head until 1940. *(Col. WA)*

Above: The Brandenburg *Generalfeldzeugmeister-Kaserne* where, in October 1939, the small unit which was to become the *Bau-Lehr-Kompanie zbV 800* barracked. It was soon expanded into a battalion and was to take the name of the garrison. When it became a regiment, the unit maintained the home base of its I Battalion at Brandenburg, just like the division created in 1943 did with that of its 4th Light Infantry Regiment. *(Col. WA)*

Right: In 1940, in the barrack square at Brandenburg, Admiral Canaris reviews the Brandenburg volunteers. On his left, wearing a helmet, is Captain von Hippel commander of I Battalion. On the Admiral's right, Colonel Lahousen Edler von Vivremont, head of the *Abwehr II* which, at that time, the 'zbV 800' units were dependent on, in other words the Brandenburg Regiment. *(Col. WA)*

Above: In the night of the 9th and 10th May, Lieutenant Herrmann Kürschner's *Westzug* took four bridges intact over the Juliana Canal, in the Netherlands, to open the way for the 7th German Infantry Division. The Brandenburgers who performed this task were clothed in Dutch uniforms and one of them can be seen here at the conclusion of the operation, before changing back to the *feldgrau* uniform of the German Army. *(Private Collection)*

Above: Brandenburg, 1940. Second Lieutenant Johannes, an officer of the Luftwaffe, adjutant of Captain von Hippel at the I Battalion's Staff. Opposite him, Lieutenant Weiner, commander of the 3rd Company. *(Col. WA)*

Right: On 10th May 1940, the missions assigned to the Brandenburgers were mainly the seizure of large bridges, such as those over the Meuse as well as the Rhine and the Juliana Canal, which allowed the mobile formations to advance towards the Netherlands and Belgium. As shown by this collapsed bridge south of Rotterdam, in certain cases the destruction of some infrastructure could not be prevented, because Brandenburg units were not deployed. *(ECPA)*

Right: In the square of the Brandenburg barracks, during the Summer of 1940. From right to left: Lieutenant Weiner (in white tunic), commander of the 3rd Company; Second Lieutenant Johannes, adjutant of I Battalion; Captain Dr. von Hippel, battalion commander; Second Lieutenant Dlab; Lieutenant Ahrens; Second Lieutenant Kneissl. *(Col WA)*

Left: In the company of two other officers, Colonel Haehling von Lanzenhauer (on the left), who was to command the *Lehr-Regiment Brandenburg zbV 800*, which became the *Sonderverband Brandenburg*, from October 1940 until his death in a hospital in Germany in February 1943. *(Private Collection)*

Below: Oberleutnant Wilhelm Walther was one of the most famous officers of the Brandenburgers, the first to be awarded the Knight's Cross of the Iron Cross. On the 10th May 1940, he was in command of the 4th Company, *Bau-Lehr-Battalion zbV 800*, the platoons of which seized several bridges over the Juliana Canal and the Meuse near Gennep; he participated in the operation, playing the part of a German prisoner. *(Bundesarchiv)*

Above: Between 1939 and 1941, men from the Brandenburg Battalion then Regiment detached in Rumania to thwart the British secret service, succeeded in preventing the destruction of many oil wells in the famous Ploesti oilfields north of Bucharest. *(ECPA)*

Right: In Zakopane, in the High Tatra, men from I Battalion prepare for the attack of USSR in the Spring of 1941. Left, *Oberleutnant* Oskar Schatz, of the 2nd Company; right, Second Lieutenant Fritze, of the 3rd. *(Col. WA)*

Below: In France and Belgium, the period which followed the campaign of May-june 1940 was devoted to the preparation of Operation 'Seelöwe', the landings in Great Britain. The new *zbV 800* Regiment's I and III Battalions were wholly involved in this hastily prepared operation using makeshift assets. *(ECPA)*

Left: Oberleutnant Siegfried Grabert, the most famous and engaging officer in the Brandenburg Regiment.
In May 1940, he was the leader of a platoon of the 4th Company with the task of taking the bridges over the Juliana Canal intact and preventing the destruction of the locks at Nieuport. He then commanded the 8th Company and, during the Yugoslavian campaign, seized the bridges over the Vardar on the 6th April 1941.

This success brought about the awarding of the *Ritterkreuz* of the Iron Cross the following June 10th, the second in the regiment. Siegfried Grabert fell the following year at the head of his company in Russia.
(Bundesarchiv)

Below: The April 1941 offensive in Yugoslavia and Greece was once more led following the principles of the *Blitzkrieg*, with the armoured formations leading the van (here, a unit of the *Pz.Gruppe* 1 in Serbia). Only the Brandenburg Regiment's II Battalion took part.
(ECPA)

Above: 22nd June 1941, like these engineers of the Wehrmacht, almost the entire Brandenburg Regiment, divided between the three German army groups, took part in Operation 'Barbarossa', the largest offensive operation ever organised. *(ECPA)*

Right: Almost all of the targets of the Brandenburgers were still bridges that had to be taken intact to enable motorised units to advance. Here, one of the road bridges on the Dvina River, in Latvia, seized the 26th and 28th June by Lieutenant Grabert's 8th Company to open the way for the *Panzergruppe Hoepner.* *(Bundesarchiv)*

Above: One of the very rare photos showing Brandenburgers wearing the clothing used for the majority of their special operations between 1939 and 1942: the enemy uniform. These are wearing complete Soviet uniforms. *(Private Collection)*

Left: Schönwalde (East Prussia), several days before the start of Operation 'Barbarossa' in June 1941, officers of the 10th Company are getting prepared. In the background, Lieutenant Aretz, unit commander; in the foreground, Second Lieutenant König, who was killed on the 22nd June taking a railway bridge north of Augustovo with a combat team of twelve men. *(DR)*

Right: At Dunaburg (Latvia), the cross marking the place where *Oberleutnant* Wolfram Knaak, acting commander of the 8th Company, fell with several of his men on the 26th June 1941, attempting to seize bridges over the Dvina. The insignia of the Brandenburg Regiment, uniting the sword and the question mark, is also engraved on the wood. *(Col. WA)*

Left: The most spectacular operation organised by the Abwehr in Africa, named 'Salaam', had the aim of bringing two agents on the Nile across the desert by means of captured transport vehicles. It was carried out with success in May-June 1942 by several NCOs and soldiers of the Brandenburg Regiment headed by a Hungarian aristocrat familiar with the desert, former officer of the imperial and royal army commissionedin the Luftwaffe with the rank of a captain : Count Lazlo Amàlsy. He is shown here on the left with Major Ritter, an officer in the Abwehr. *(PC)*

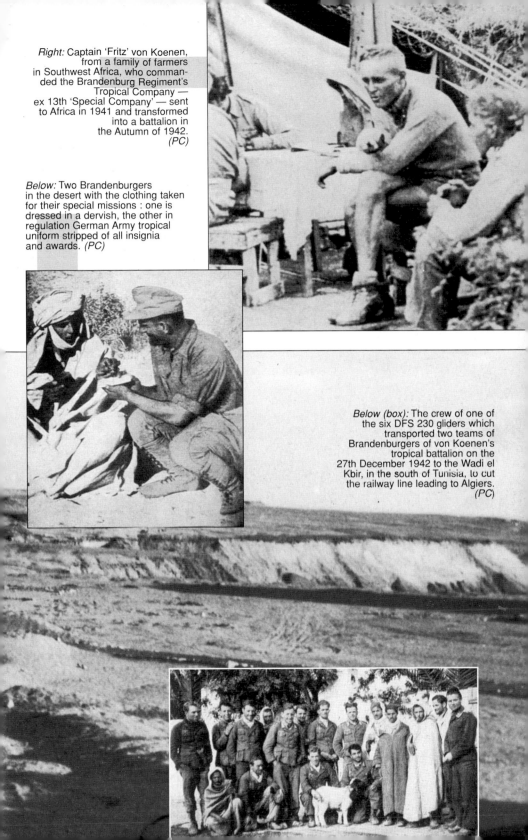

Right: Captain 'Fritz' von Koenen, from a family of farmers in Southwest Africa, who commanded the Brandenburg Regiment's Tropical Company — ex 13th 'Special Company' — sent to Africa in 1941 and transformed into a battalion in the Autumn of 1942. *(PC)*

Below: Two Brandenburgers in the desert with the clothing taken for their special missions : one is dressed in a dervish, the other in regulation German Army tropical uniform stripped of all insignia and awards. *(PC)*

Below (box): The crew of one of the six DFS 230 gliders which transported two teams of Brandenburgers of von Koenen's tropical battalion on the 27th December 1942 to the Wadi el Kbir, in the south of Tunisia, to cut the railway line leading to Algiers. *(PC)*

Left: Major-General Alexander von Pfuhlstein - shown here with the badges of a colonel - took the command of the Brandenburg Division created on the 1st April 1943 and kept it for a full year. Linked from peacetime with the military plot against chancellor Hitler following his contacts with officers of the Abwehr, he nevertheless obtained the *Ritterkreuz* of the Iron Cross in 1942 after having fought in the Demjansk pocket at the head of the 154th Infantry Regiment. *(PC)*

Below: For most of the units of the Brandenburg Division, the years 1943-1944 were marked by battles fought in Yugoslavia against the Titists alongside elite Wehrmacht units, notably the mountain and light infantry divisions, a unit of which is shown here on operations. It was more a real war than a guerilla war, both cruel and unrewarding. *(ECPA)*

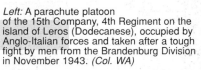

Left: A parachute platoon of the 15th Company, 4th Regiment on the island of Leros (Dodecanese), occupied by Anglo-Italian forces and taken after a tough fight by men from the Brandenburg Division in November 1943. *(Col. WA)*

Right: Captain Konrad Steidl, decorated with the Knight's Cross of the Iron Cross in January 1944 as reward for the success obtained in Bosnia, against the Titist gangs, by his unit, I Battalion, 2nd Light Infantry Regiment. *(Col WA)*

Below: Another photograph taken in November 1943 on the island of Leros, just when III Battalion, 1st Regiment was preparing to carry out a landing by main force on the island of Samos. On the left, Captain Max Wandrey, commander of the battalion. *(Col.WA)*

Below: Titist partisans taken prisoner by German forces in Yugoslavia. A formidable enemy who knew no pity and to whom none would be shown. *(ECPA)*

Above: Major Wilhelm Walther in Greece, 1943. The first *Ritterkreuzträger of the zbV 800* Regiment in 1940 was in command at that time of the Brandenburg Division's 1st Regiment, with a dual responsibility: protect the Athens route and watch over the coastline of the Aegean Sea, where an allied landing was possible. *(Bundesarchiv)*

Right and following page right: Not even the Brandenburgers, the mountain infantry and the German *Jägers* managed to bring down the Serb partisans. *(ECPA)*

Above: Lance-corporal Fred Brandt (front view) during his first meeting with the British Colonel F. Maclean (left), which took place on the 20th May 1944 at the base of operations of the intelligence service set up north of Dibra (Albania). The German succeeded in dealing on an equal footing with his enemy and concluded a surprising agreement with him. *(Col WA)*

Above: The Anti-Partisan War Badge was instituted on 30th January 1944 as a military reward but was delivered by the Personal Staff of Reichsführer SS Himmler. It was widely won by the Brandenburgers, continuously committed against 'bandits' on the Eastern Front and in the Balkans. *(PC)*

Below and bottom: In 1945, all forces of the Wehrmacht and the Waffen-SS deployed on the Eastern Front fought a desperate battle against an enemy with a crushing superiority, impervious to its losses in both men and combat tanks.
The Brandenburg Division, alloted to the prestigious Grossdeutschland *Panzerkorps,* came into action in the Warthegau, then in Lower Silesia and in Saxony. *(PC)*

Left: After serving in the *zbV 800* Regiment from 1941, Lieutenant-Colonel Karl-Heinz Oesterwitz commanded the 2nd Light Infantry Regiment of the Brandenburg *Pz.Gren.Div.* during the fighting of 1945. *(Col WA)*

Below: The cuff-title worn in 1944-1945 by men of all branches of service and all ranks of the Brandenburg *Panzer-Grenadier-Division.* *(PC)*

and dismantle them. Their instructors were two old corporals from the engineers, who handled the explosives with an impressive casualness.

Next came the practical exercises. They learnt how to cut steel track with a counter-force charge, involving two explosive charges placed in a staggered position on either side. They also learnt how to fell a tree, breach a wall and force entry into a pillbox with explosives.

Afterwards came the mines. They got used to laying and camouflaging them, then detecting, defusing and removing them. They were shown the quickest ways to destroy car, ammunition or fuel depots.

One morning, they were taken back to Hell's kitchen. The instructor was waiting for them. He was rubbing his hands together.

"Now, *Jungen*, we are going to make you the cooks in this infernal kitchen. You are going to learn to make explosives yourselves with the means available. Imagine that you are undercover in enemy territory with the mission of destroying a certain objective. Unfortunately you have lost all your equipment. How are you going to carry out your mission? It's very simple: by going to the local hardware shop. By taking the necessary precautions you can make a very suitable explosive, in a garage, or in a hotel room. Obviously a safety fuse must be used. You will not be able to make a real one, but you can quickly make one up with powder from a hunting rifle cartridge, cotton padding and insulating tape. A quick trial will give you the combustion time. It will be fairly short, but making the fuse long enough will allow you to get far enough away in the time required."

Sabotage training ended with an excursion to Tegel, the laboratory which worked for those Abwehr agents abroad. When they entered they found themselves in a veritable storehouse of many and varied articles arranged by categories in departments. At first glance, there was nothing particularly special, but it was only an appearance. A fellow in a grey overall and pince-nez greated them and provided them step by step with precise information, while he moved slowly between the shelves.

He covered such items as false-bottomed suitcases with secret compartments, propelling pencils which were igniters, shoes with hollow heels, wigs and false beards, make up cases, invisible ink and special paper, miniature cameras and microfilms, etc.

"There is no point in showing you everything, you won't need all this because you have not been brought here to become secret agents. But you should have an idea, because some day one of these things could be useful. What I must show you above all are the disguises. This involves uniforms, but not only uniforms. When you want to pass for authentic soldiers of an enemy army, everything that you wear, right down to your underpants and personal items, from your cigarettes to the letters from your parents in your wallet, must confirm your identity. We cannot, of course, provide you with a mother and a fiancee in Nizhni Novgorod, but we can give you letters in Russian and autographed photos, which will appear authentic. And you will know, for example, that this town, which is between Moscow and Kazan, is now called Gorki. Here you will be shown only an assortment of clothing."

"This is the complete uniform of an officer of the NKVD, summer dress. The camouflage is a lot easier in winter, with the fur-lined coat and the fur caps. This is a uniform of a chasseur ardennais, the rank of a corporal..."

"We learned," interrupted Lieutenant Forster, "that the best disguise is that of the NCO. The NCO does not attract attention and inspires confidence. On the other hand, the ordinary soldier is considered run-of-the-mill, therefore closely surveyed and held in check. The uniform of an officer is, of course, ideally the best, but the part is more difficult to play. Should someone impersonating an officer come under scrutiny and be forced into a conversation, he is on very dangerous ground. He will have to exhibit not only a perfect command of the language but of military vocabulary and regulations, not to mention the home affairs of the country he is representing. Very few of our men can meet such high expectations."

Wiesenmeyer, always the curious one, put his hand out towards a shelf.

"Hullo, a packet of Camel, some Navy Cut, some Gauloises..."

The stores manager with the pince-nez leapt up, as red as a beetroot.

"Keep your hands off the merchandise! If there's even a single packet missing, I shall go before the *Kriegsgericht* for theft. I am a soldier too!"

The lieutenant snapped:

"Private Wiesenmeyer, you are confined to barracks for two days. This is not a playground."

The practical lessons of the morning were followed in the afternoon by additional courses. Posters showing uniforms, weapons, combat aircraft and military vehicles of all sorts were fixed to the blackboard.

"You see a man dressed like in this picture, getting out of a vehicle like the one second from the top of this illustration. Question: type of vehicle, nationality, weapon and rank of the individual. Who can answer?"

Emmerich, whose comrades mocked him because he spent all his free time swotting over the handbooks instead of bistro-crawling in town, raised his hand triumphantly:

"It's an English Mamouth. The man is a Captain of the Royal Engineers."

"Correct."

At Brandenburg, after two months of basic military training, it was time for technical training, which started with driving practise.

Every Brandenburger was meant to be capable of jumping into the first vehicle which comes along and carry out every possible manoeuvre, on every type of ground and at maximum speed. In January 1940, after two days of rain, the range was the ideal place to learn how to avoid getting stuck in the mud and, when it did happen, how to get out of it.

"You have two minutes to get yourselves out of there", shouted the *Feldwebel*. "If you take longer than that, I'll spray you with my *Maschinenpistole!*"

The two men who were driving the Mercedes-Benz *Kübelwagen* [2] started to dig up the earth like mad to free their vehicle. They threw

2. 'Bucket' car. Refers to medium, cross-country, open-body vehicles of the army, fitted with 'bucket' seats.

anything that they could find under the wheels, bits of wood or pieces of canvas. When they thought they had finished, they stood up, dazed, covered in mud right up to their shoulder straps. At that moment that the submachine-gun rattled. In front and behind the bullets went 'plof' into the wet earth. The two soldiers threw themselves into their seats and the car tore away from its muddy grave with a roar of the engine and an assortment of cracks, tears and spits.

"Now," continued the *Feldwebel* "that you are fresh and fit for work, go over to the tarmac surface, to the right of the ground, to learn how to carry out spins on a slippery surface. First attempt at 40 kph, second at 60, and so on up to 110. For the bright sparks amongst you it should be a piece of cake. *Los!*"

The spins started with some impressive screeches of tyres. Suddenly the Kübelwagen, arriving at great speed, overturned and slid on the asphalt as if it were a flat-iron on a skating-rink. When it stopped, the two men got up unsteadily. One of them clutched his painful shoulder. The NCO was already on the scene.

"Nothing broken as far as I can see, we'll go and stand the vehicle up again. It doesn't seem to be damaged, that's the main thing. And you, driver, your last run was at 60, what speed was that one? More than 90 in my opinion. That is not how I said to do it. You turned the steering wheel too quickly. You'll do one extra hour of exercises this evening. Now, we'll go back."

A surprise awaited the training company at their quarters. Under the eaves of the company office, there was a small notice: "*Volunteers for the parachute jump must obtain a physical aptitude certificate tomorrow morning and register before noon.*"

Everyone volunteered to become the very first paratroopers in the Brandenburg units. The medical examination eliminated three. Those remaining were assembled for departure at 7 a.m. They were from different barrack-rooms. They were entrusted to a *Feldwebel*, wearing the grey-blue uniform of the Luftwaffe, who they knew only by sight.

"My name is Löber. I am taking you to Spandau, to a Luftwaffe airfield. A lorry is waiting for us."

The first three days were reserved for ground training in the gymnasium of the air station. The students learnt how to land properly, they practised forward and backward rolls. Not everyone was equally successful, but everyone gained from the training.

The following three days were devoted to jump simulations. The student jumped from a tower of scaffolding which had different levels. He jumped from ever higher levels and landed on an inflatable mattress. The last exercise consisted of jumping with a parachute in the air current of a wind-tunnel from a height of 20 metres and to remove it using the chest buckle in one rapid movement.

The exciting week went by: sunday was not a day of rest as the jumps from a plane were to begin the following day. Hearts were beating fast when the candidates for the Parachutist's Badge climbed into the Junkers W 34 training plane. A warrant officer opened the door of the aircraft. After flying in a large curve, to accustom the troop to flying, the plane headed back to the airfield at Spandau. The instructing officer spoke:

"You are about to jump. There's nothing extraordinary about that. I accompany beginners like you every day. There is never any problem. You are lucky, today there is not a breath of wind. You will not be blown off course. Listen sharp fo the signal horn. Keep your eyes open, count up to ten..."

Feldwebel Löber went first. Although it was only his second real jump, he was full of confidence and he wanted to communicate it to the young soldiers. At the sound of a horn then, "*Fertig...Los!*" He disappeared into the emptiness. Everything went off as planned.

Only once, the lieutenant had to tap the back of somebody who was a little hesitant. The following day, jump at 1,200 metres. Everybody was in a good mood. While waiting for the signal, the men, seated on benches, checked their straps calmly. Just like the first time, *Feldwebel* Löber was the first to jump.

But something happened. The Leutnant held his arm out to stop the movement towards the door. He leaned over and turned round, his face as white as a sheet.

"Keep calm. We have a problem. I don't know how it happened, but the parachute of your *Feldwebel* caught on the tail wheel of the aircraft.

From here, we can't do anything for him, but we'll save him."

A shiver of fear ran up the spines of the young men. The second lieutenant closed the jump hatch and went towards the pilot. Two words and, immediately, the plane changed its direction and its speed was reduced to the minimum. Shortly after, the shiny silver ribbon of a canal could be seen. The Junkers dived over it and followed its course.

Löber knew that it was a resistance of the static line and an unexpected gust of wind that had caused the accident. He was aware that another gust could very easily tear the parachute away from its point of suspension, as precarious as it was fortuitous. He knew immediately that the pilot was slowly heading for a nearby canal in the hope that Löber would cut himself free in time to drop into it. He tried desperately to extract his gravity knife from the thigh pocket of his trousers to cut through the rigging lines. The squeezing harness paralysed his movements. Just when the plane was about to climb for a second pass, he freed himself in one go. He fell like a stone into the water just a few feet away from the bank and a bridge. A car from the barracks and an ambulance from the air station arrived just when some men, who were working on board a dredger, were pulling him out of the water, dripping wet.

His lieutenant rushed forward:

"Löber my dear fellow, you got out of that magnificently. You gave us one hell of a fright. Get in the ambulance..."

"Ambulance, *Herr Leutnant*? Are you joking! I'll go back to the airfield with you to carry out the jump as programmed."

During the journey, he explained:

"The lads have been disheartened by the accident. I have no choice. It's the only way to give them back some confidence."

A half an hour later, Löber made an outstanding jump, followed by his twelve trainees.

The last jump was also to have taken place at 1,200 metres, but in fighting dress, with weapons, ammunition and assault pack. The trainees were a little ill at ease. Such a load greatly accelerates the speed of the fall and the contact with the ground would be violent. The platoon leader insisted on being present in the plane, which had taken off in spite of a threatening sky. At a thousand metres, it was in the middle of a snowstorm, visibility was very poor.

The officer could not hope for such conditions to improve. Only a war mission would give him the authority to risk losing these men. He cancelled the jump. As the course was approaching its end, a new attempt would be impossible.

A short while after, *Feldwebel* Böhme accompanied a group of Upper Silesians to Oranienburg so they could have their chance at earning the Parachutist's Badge. It was not until 1941 that a fully qualified airborne company was formed.

In his office in the Brandenburg Battalion barracks, Captain von Hippel was leaning over a decoded message that he had just received from Colonel von Lahousen, his superior and the head of the *Abwehr II*. He called his battalion's adjutant who still wore the grey-blue uniform of an officer of the Luftwaffe where he had served in the Flakartillerie.

"Johannes, gather together all the officers as soon as the companies have gone back."

At 5.30 p.m., the Leutnant reported himself:

"*Herr Hauptmann*, all the officers are here, I even had Grabert informed, who was keeping to his room."

"I'm coming."

The battalion commander entered the orderly room and gestured amicably to his subordinates to sit down.

"Gentlemen, I have just received a message which, once again, sets the date when we have to be ready. It could be the start of the Western Offensive. I don't know any better than the last time whether it will be maintained. If the weather stays bad, the Luftwaffe will remain grounded. However we must still prepare our men for their missions. My information confirms that they have remained scrupulously and unanimously faithful to the oath they took. I think, therefore they can be informed without any risk."

Second lieutenant Grabert returned to his new company. It was the Lieutenant Walther's 4th Company. This unit had just been formed with training personnel who came from the 2nd and gathered together the following day in the honour room which had become the classroom, underneath a plaster statue of a helmeted Germania which dated back to at least the time of Bismarck. The men were seated, the NCOs were positioned along the wall, their hands behind their backs. The second lieutenant waved to them to occupy the seats in the first row and added under his breath:

"They looked like prison warders!"

Then he began:

"We are soon to take the field, in one month or ten, I don't know, but you must know what is expected of you and how you will be employed. I have gathered you all together to tell you. You, over there, don't take notes, just commit what I tell you to memory.

"I would like to talk mainly about operational clothing, something that is never the same in different countries and circumstances. In Silesia, last year, we had the advantage of a bilingual population whose fidelity to Germany was established. But a lot of these Upper Silesians who devoted body and soul to the Reich, spoke little German or spoke it very badly. We were able to produce a Polish speaking unit and to make it act a part rendering its presence plausible in the marshalling yard at Katowice. Several options were possible. Who can say what we did?"

"You were disguised as workers on their way to work?"

"That's not a bad answer. However, workers entering a station are meant to take a train. The first train left far too late to enable us to attack, as planned, ten minutes before our forces could cross the border.

"That's why we chose to disguise ourselves as railwaymen. It went very well. The few non-Polish speaking officers and myself remained in the background."

"We can't do that in the West. We do not have a French speaking German population," one man pointed out.

"You are forgetting Eupen and Malmédy. It is true that these French-speaking Prussians were annexed by Belgium in 1919, but they have remained faithful and already a number of young servicemen have deserted in order to come here. In our company there are three of them. The ex-Belgian citizens, raise your hands!"

Three hands went up and all heads were turned on them.

"But I recognise that no comparison is possible with Upper Silesia. To enter France we'll need another idea."

Over the following days, new questions relative to the employment of the Brandenburgers were dealt with. The use of weapons gave rise to a lively discussion.

"Who can tell me when we are authorised to use our weapons?"

"Never" said a voice from the back. Everybody laughed.

"And why?"

"Because, otherwise, we would not be Brandenburgers."

The interpolator seemed very proud of his answer.

"I see," resumed Second lieutenant Grabert, "that this question must be looked at more closely. As soldiers, we have, in the time of war, the right to use our weapons at any time, but as Brandenburgers, we are enjoined not to use them in two definite circumstances: firstly, when we are committed in enemy territory before the outbreak of hostilities; secondly, when we are wearing the uniform of the enemy. We must not fire before removing this disguise and revealing clearly the fact that we are German combatants."

A hand was raised.

"That can't be easy. It seems to me that it's better to save your life wearing an enemy uniform than to die in our shirt-sleeves because we were following orders."

"That is indeed the prevailing opinion. But don't forget that you mentioned a borderline case which rarely happens."

"If we are captured wearing a foreign uniform, will we really be shot as spies?"

"I have to say that it can happen. You volunteered with full knowledge of the facts. It is your right and you are still free to refuse to take part in an action if it goes against your conscience or if you don't feel capable of putting up a good show, on condition that you inform your direct superior in time. Anyone who withdraws during an action will be considered a coward and a deserter."

At the end of the course, one man out of 183 asked to be sent back to the engineers.

Both platoons of the 4th Company left Brandenburg almost immediately afterwards, in order to move to their starting lines in the Reichswald.

Together once again with the commander of the battalion, the officers gave an account of their discussions with the men. Von Hippel asked many questions. He concluded:

"Continue to study each man individually, so as to take the best and use the maximum of his capacities and to avoid using unqualified personnel in certain operations. We are not all equal when it comes to daring, sangfroid, intelligence and resistance to fatigue and suffering. When you are preparing a raid, you will know how to make up your team like you judge the ingredients in a good stew. Whether they are tall or short, blond or dark, educated or illiterate, if you have put a fire in their belly, I don't care! With them, we'll go and get the Devil in Hell itself!"

Chapter IV

Bridges over the Meuse
(10th May 1940)

By mid-March 1940, the *Bau-Lehr-Bataillon zbV 800* was at last set up. The Staff, the HQ Company under Lieutenant Kotschke and the 2nd Company under Captain Hartmann were quartered on the barracks at Brandenburg. Lieutenant Kniesche's 1st Company was kept at Innermanzig, in ex-Austria, and acted as a processing unit for the newcomers. The 3rd Company under Captain Rudloff was garrisoned at Münstereifel, in Rhineland, a province where the Lieutenant Walther's 4th Company also kept itself in readiness.

Between March and April, the Abwehr II formed a regimental operations staff in Berlin for von Hippel's unit and entrusted it to Major Kewisch. This staff was preparing itself for Norway. Indeed it was there that the Brandenburgers were to receive their baptism of fire.

In April, even though German forces had already joined battle in Scandinavia, a *Nordzug* (North Platoon) was rapidly set up at Brandenburg. This unit was company sized and made up of Polish speaking Upper Silesians who were intended for use against the brigade of Polish riflemen at Narvik, English speaking Germans from Palestine, South Tyrolians familiar with mountain operations and the inevitable Germans from the Sudetenland. The *Nordzug* left Brandenburg on the 20th of April for Oslo.

The offensive on the West had quite a different significance. The Führer immensely liked the idea of camouflaged detachments and ended up adopting it. The Netherlands, whose Army was small compared with the Wehrmacht, flooded large areas of land and blew up all the bridges in the border region, along with those giving access to vital areas, in order to block the way to the invader.

Belgium counted on the formidable obstacle of the Albert Canal whose key was the fort of Eben-Emael, thought to be impregnable. South of the Liège gap, the Ardennes formed a natural obstacle to the rapid advance of a modern army, whose motorised units could not theoretically take many risks in such undulating terrain. France also felt itself to be temporarily sheltered behind its powerful Maginot Line and planned to push its battle force into Belgium to go to meet the German Army. For this manoeuvre to be successful, it was indispensable that the invader mark time for a certain period in front of the obstacles amassed at it at the borders.

For the Wehrmacht the solution was the reverse. It was a question of rapidly overcoming all these obstacles and to push towards the sea across the Ardennes, after securing the Netherlands on its right wing to isolate the French and British in Belgium; this was also a way of taking the Maginot Line from the rear. Throughout the winter, horse drawn batteries hurried down the wooded slopes of the Black Forest, without worrying about breaking the legs of the horses, and tanks practised crossing over ravines.

On the training area, the Ardennes had already been defeated.

The initial presence of the Brandenburgers was hardly noticeable. In a clearing, between two thickly wooded hills several kilometres from the German border with the Netherlands, in the extreme north of the Rhineland, the military authorities had enclosed several hectares of meadow with barbed wire and had erected several huts.

Above the entry-gate there was a board: "*K2-Lager - Entrance forbidden to civilians and military personnel*". Then lorries brought in the soldiers. They could be seen drilling in the distance, but, in the evening, none of them left. The locals who, in the neighbouring cafés, liked to make them talk, never got their money's worth. Many rumours were in circulation. For some, it was a sports training centre subject to very strict regulations; for others, it was quite simply a disciplinary camp. They were very far from the truth. It was the secret training camp of the 1st Platoon, 4th company under the command of Leutnant Witzel and several *Feldwebels*.

Every precaution was taken so that nothing leaked to the outside world. Those on Saturday night leave were taken in lorries to a town situated a good distance away and were never left alone. It was imperative that they remained in groups of at least two, to prevent any possible confidences being imparted on the pillow of some girl they had just met. Every week, they changed town. It was Cleve, Emmerich, Wesel or Geldern. In that way no romance could begin.

At the beginning, the military training of the recruits left a lot to be desired. The majority were Germans from abroad who had come running to answer the call of the Fatherland, when several weeks earlier they had stepped over the portal of the barracks at Brandenburg/Havel, they saw soldiers dressed in a line for the first time in their lives. Little mattered to their leaders. They did not need automatons, but 'wolves', with exceptionally strong nerves and hearts.

The officers of the *K2-Lager* acted in this way. Like all regular troops, the Brandenburgers trained in close quarters combat and firing. But this was not the main thrust of their training.

They were drawn up in a line, three paces apart, bare-headed, in uniform and in order of height. In front of each one of them, folded on the ground, there was a greatcoat with no insignia, an old Adrian French Army steel helmet, a sumachine-gun with seven magazines, a 9-mm pistol with three magazines, four egg-type hand grenades, two stick hand grenades and a trench knife.

The instructor spoke:

"You must put on this armament in such a way that once the greatcoat is on — without buttoning it up of course — nothing is visible and — pay careful attention — that it is placed on you in such a way that you can throw off the helmet and greatcoat and fire simultaneously. When you hear the first whistle, put it on. Slowly, you can take your time. When everybody is ready, I will blow the whistle again. Then it must be done quickly. I will time you and we will do it again until your reflexes are automatic."

When the whistle blew the nine lads got busy. The submachine-gun had to hang under the left armpit, with a round in the chamber and the safety on. The remainder of the weapons was slipped into the pockets or stuck in the belt. In addition, one carried a pair of wirecutters under his right arm, the other an explosive slab suspended by a string. With the greatcoat, each man was carrying about thirty kilos.

"Now," said the second lieutenant, "*Marsch! Marsch!*"

He led the others at the double, after putting a machine-gun over his shoulder so as to be in unison with them. A very tiring period was about to begin. Not a single word was spoken. The officer stretched out his arm: everybody threw themselves on the ground. He got up, everybody started at double time. Sweat was running down their faces. Even though the April air was chilly, their faces were drawn by the effort. When the second whistle blow rang out, the young men once again stretched out. One of them got up in order to remove his greatcoat more easily. The Leutnant roared:

"Get down! Who gave you the order to get up?"

The men were rolling on the ground trying to get their arms out of the sleeves; they freed the submachine-guns. A first burst of fire was heard.

"Twenty-two seconds!" exclaimed the officer. "Forty-one seconds", he noted with a note of disgust when the last one rang out. "The record is ten seconds. *Verstanden?* We'll do it again."

Another exercise consisted of shedding the greatcoat, simultaneously throwing a grenade and hitting the dirt, then removing the remaining grenades form the coat pockets pulling the caps off the friction igniters as cautiously as possible. Immediately afterwards a second grenade was thrown.

Following these exercises, of which there were many variations, the men were divided into four teams. Lieutenant Walther had planned the following tactic for his own one: he would approach his target, with several of his men acting the part of German prisoners, escorted by Dutch gendarmes.

But for this situation to be credible, it was indispensable that the gendarmes be real Dutchmen. The local NSDAP [1] organisation, consulted concerning the possibility of recruiting young people "*to possibly work together with the German Army in case it has to protect the Netherlands against any foreign aggression*", replied that the question raised no difficulties.

There existed, in the Netherlands, a national socialist party, whose Führer was called Mussert and who led numerous resolutely pro-German elements wishing to actively contribute to the German victory. Agents form the Abwehr set to work. Forty or so volunteers, with the required physical and moral qualities, were discreetly brought to the Reich and billeted separately in the Rhineland region. This number was relatively high because there would naturally be a certain attrition rate amongst the candidates.

Officially, they had been recruited as *Kampfdolmetscher* or combat interpreters. They were photographed and their measurements were taken without any explanation to preserve secrecy. At the camp, a *Feldwebel* was dressed in the tunic of a Dutch gendarme and he also was photographed. Many copies were made of his picture. Then, in Berlin, the head of one of the young Dutchmen was stuck onto each picture. The photos were then attached to excellent imitations of identity cards of the Dutch gendarmerie.

Not less than a hundred targets were assigned to the rapidly expanding Brandenburgers, who went from a company and a battalion size to a regiment almost overnight. Targets included bridges that had to be seized in advance of German troops, roadblocks on routes that had to be freed in time and various facilities to be knocked out of commission.

The 3rd and 4th Companies were now deployed from Lorraine to the Netherlands. Their platoons enjoyed the greatest freedom in preparing their operations. The leaders of these platoons had built

---

1. *Nationalsozialistische Deutsche Arbeiterpartei*, National Socialist German Workers Party.

teams of rarely more than a dozen men strong, each one responsible for a specific objective.

In the north, Lieutenant Walther had planned to dispose the teams of the 4th Company from the point where the Rhine penetrates into the Netherlands until the town of Roermond, 80 kilometres further south, down by München-Gladbach. After the beginning of March, training was greatly intensified: night marches, map courses, live firing exercises in every possible situation, explosives, photo interpretation of targets and exercises on the sandtable and subsequently on the terrain. Some mysterious padlocked boxes had arrived, to which only the company commander had the keys. They were placed in a carefully locked room. It was an open secret, everybody knew that they contained Dutch uniforms.

2nd Platoon was a wilful unit led by the motivated and well-known Lieutenant Grabert. His men no longer asked themselves whether they had the right to enter foreign territory by force. Their spirit had been steeped in the absolute and their faith in the mission of their people was unshakeable. Their officers had told them that the British were ready to invade the Netherlands to attack the Reich at its vulnerable point, the Ruhr, and they believed them. Had they not seen, a month earlier, that the British were the first to violate Norwegian neutrality?

Grabert insisted on gathering all possible information on the targets assigned to his platoon before X-Hour. [2] He bribed several smugglers, without gaining very much; they were not soldiers and did not want to take too many risks. It was vital to send a reliable and competent man. The officer finally came to a decision. Although it was strictly forbidden to send a member of the German Army in foreign territory before hostilities, he offered the mission to Lance-corporal Hüller, a very competent student from the Sudetenland. He was educated, intelligent and knew what interested his leader. In addition, his innocuous appearance served the purpose. Nobody would suspect a young botanist with gold-rimmed glasses and a cumbersome white

2. The Germans say '*X-Tag*' and '*X-Zeit*' and not 'D-Day' and 'H-Hour'.

metal herborisation box, of being an elite soldier of the proud Wehrmacht.

Hüller went, returned and left again. Each one of his journeys brought back vital intelligence concerning Dutch layout for surveillance and destruction of bridges over the Meuse.

One evening he did not come back. In his place, a Dutch *V-Mann* [3] showed up in the night who had secretly crossed the border to announce that Hüller had been arrested that day and locked up in a surveillance post a short distance from the border.

Grabert felt responsible for the acts of his men when it was he that had given the orders. If he could bring his man back without casualties, there would never have been a case of disobedience!

The affair naturally had to take place at night. Grabert selected six men and dressed them in navy blue Wehrmacht sport training suits. At their head, he placed the *V-Mann*, rigged out in a Dutch captain's uniform. Arriving at the target, the Germans disappeared to leave the starring role to the false captain, who in reality held the rank of corporal in the Dutch Army. He entered the post and inspected it, finding some peelings in a corner and a pair of dirty ankle boots while he severely railed. Meanwhile, Grabert and four of his men approached and, at the call of the V-Mann rushed forward, pistol in hand, while the other two were watching outside. The Dutch soldiers did not understand what was going on and wisely put their hands up. Hüller was handed over and as they left, they warned the Dutch not to move or the building would explode. This gross bluff gave them the precious minutes they needed to slip away into the night. The alarm reached the other border posts too late and their reactions were ineffective.

The lieutenant was particularly happy to bring together, the following day, the full complement of his men. The 'father of the Brandenburgers' car came to a halt at midday in front of the quarter of the 2nd Platoon. Captain von Hippel tapped the young officer on the shoulder.

---

3. Abbreviation of *Vertrauensmann* : 'Man of confidence', in other words an intelligence agent.

"My dear Grabert, are you, this time, going to throw your laurels of Katowice into the shade? We will speak about your operation plan later on. In the meantime, I would like to talk to your boys. They must have finished their meal. Muster them."

"*Herr Hauptmann*, we have been on alert since the day before yesterday. Does this mean...?"

"Yes, the die is cast. We attack tomorrow morning at 4.45 a.m."

The news did not provoke any particuliar emotion within the lieutenant. He had discovered that the execution of a mission, so many times rehearsed during exercises, seemed to him to be something almost routine.

The men, curious, were assembled. The *Spiess* put them to attention. Hippel came forward and gave the order: "*Rührt Euch !*" [4]

"Men, this is not an inspection. I just want to wish you good luck for the mission that you are to carry out tomorrow morning, before the cock crows..."

He paused, to allow the men to assimilate the news; a wave of murmuring passed along the rows.

He continued: "You know as well as I do what it is about. There is very little left for me to say to you. You have been well trained and you must succeed. Don't let your imagination carry you away. Perhaps you will be hit by a bullet, but those that follow you will certainly have a lot more trouble. I don't think that you risk being taken prisoner, because we are going to occupy the whole of the Netherlands and I don't know where they would keep you! Now, I repeat, I want only volunteers in the Brandenburgers. If there is one amongst you who is still hesitant to give your all, then take one step forward now, turn right, straight on and disappear. It is not only your right, but also your duty towards your comrades, who could be put in danger by your lack of conviction..."

"Nobody?...I thought so. So, it only remains for me to say 'See you soon' for the distribution of the Iron Crosses and above all: '*Hals- und Beinbruch!*'" [5]

4. At ease!
5. "Break a leg!" meaning "Good luck!"

The same day, the 9th of May 1940, a group of young Dutchmen chosen from the best candidates for acting as enemy gendarmes, arrived at the camp. They assembled in a hut.

Second lieutenant Witzel explained the situation and what was expected of them.

"You have been brought here because the hour has arrived. At this very moment, the British are landing in the ports of the Netherlands to occupy your country and attack National Socialist Germany. Are you sincerely ready to help us, tomorrow morning, to penetrate Dutch territory to push back this aggression? You are aware that we do not want to harm the Netherlands in any way, on the contrary. We are all of Germanic blood. You will not, in any case, fight against your compatriots, only talk to them, that's all we ask of you. Agreed?"

The sound of cheering answered him. Worked up by several weeks of waiting and confinement, the young Dutchmen were impatient to act and to show their mettle. However, the keen eye of the second lieutenant, used to gauging men and to sounding out their hearts, noticed that three or four of the boys had not shown the same amount of enthusiasm.

The young officer went over to them and assured them that, if they wished, they would be sent back to the Netherlands without delay. He had a *Feldwebel* take them away, where they were lodged separately in the NCOs hut, to avoid them contaminating the others. For the six Germans and the three Dutchmen of Lieutenant Walther's assault team a detailed briefing of the following day's mission began. Up until then, apart from the highest ranks, nobody knew precisely what was being prepared.

Gendarme uniforms were distributed to the young Dutchmen which, to their great surprise, fitted them like a glove. Wake up at 1.30 a.m. and after dressing, a solid *Frühstück*. [6] Starting in column at 2.30 a.m. It was expected to take three hours to cross the eleven kilometres between the camp and the objective.

6. Breakfast.

Just before the border, the first hitch took place. One of the three false gendarmes, a tall blond whose particularly intelligent air had struck the officer, asked to speak to him alone.

"*Herr Oberleutnant*, I don't know how to tell you this, but there's something wrong. I can't do this. Instead of causing you any problems, I'd rather go back."

It was neither the time not the place for any exchange of views. Walther immediately judged the situation and called his second NCO. He gave him the order to take the false gendarme back to the camp, stop him from escaping even if it meant shooting him and to stay locked up with him in his own room until the operation was brought to its conclusion.

A smuggler was waiting for them at a rendezvous point situated very near the border. He got them accross unobserved by the authentic Dutch gendarmes between two patrols.

They progressed without incident towards the bridge. Around three hundred metres from the bridge, he stopped his unit and asked several last questions to check that there would be no hesitation when the moment came to act.

Then he gave the signal to continue the march, the gendarmes standing bolt upright, self-assured, the defeated prisoners dragging their boots.

The night of the 9th and 10th of May 1940 was particularly dark. Under the great Gennep railway bridge, the Dutch sentry who was leaning over the railings could not even see the waves of the Meuse, whose powerful rumbling was the only sound amid the silence. He kicked against the rails which linked Westphalia to Brabant.

"Wildiers!"

The soldier heard somebody whisper his name. He crossed the few metres to the entrance to the bridge. His NCO, craning his neck, examined the darkness in front of him in vain. Next to him, another soldier tried to do the same thing.

"What's the matter, Sergeant?"

"Don't know, I heard somebody walking over there. Now, there's nothing. Wait! There it is again... Chamber a round! Keep the bolts quiet! Fire without hesitation! Some say that it's for today!"

The three men could now indeed hear the sound of walking, the sound of a small troop which was approaching them unhurriedly, even slightly hesitant. The white streak that heralded the daybreak had not yet cleared the darkness. The steps were now very near. The sergeant aimed the beam of his pocket lamp in front of him. In its halo, he saw a Dutch gendarme appear, an NCO like him, followed by strange silhouettes that, at first glance, he could not identify. Another gendarme brought up the rear.

"I'm bringing back some prisoners, Sergeant. We nabbed these men in our sector."

"Without weapons?"

"They threw them away. We left them on the ground. There were too many. Rifles, grenades, ammunition, a real pile. They will have to be picked up."

"Deserters", thought the sergeant.

He cast a pale light over the group. The Germans, their heads down, were not impressive. The *feldgrau* side-caps were placed more or less crooked on their heads, the long grey-green greatcoats, with no belts, were longer than calf length. A single prisoner, the smallest one, followed the scene attentively. The sergeant noted that his cold eyes seemed to be looking everywhere at once. His square-jawed face, with jutting out cheekbones, breathed an extraordinary energy that was reminiscent of a bird of prey. He made a strong impression on the sergeant who, taken over by a vague presentiment, headed towards the telephone post which was on his right, to ask for instructions from his leader who, along with the rest of the platoon, was mounting guard at the other end of the bridge.

But he had scarcely taken a step when he was seized around the throat. It was the little prisoner. He had an iron grip. The two soldiers had seen a German rush towards their leader. They opened fire on the others. Naturally, the Dutch gendarmes let the prisoners throw themselves immediately onto the two soldiers and knock them down with a dexterity born of a long training.

"*Und nun, Herr Oberleutnant ?*" [7]

The question was addressed to the little prisoner, who brought back the dishevelled sergeant, his pistol in his ribs.

Lieutenant Wilhelm Walther had himself taken the head of the 1st Platoon of his company, with the mission of seizing the Gennep bridge ten minutes before the beginning of hostilities. He glanced compassionately at the three injured men who were lying on the ground, leaning over *Unteroffizier Zimmer* grimacing with pain. He had a broken tibia, a stroke of bad luck. He was the one who had to accompany him to the other end of the bridge where the bulk of the work remained to be done. But Walther was not the sort to let a stroke of bad luck discourage him. His temperament, like the training he had received, meant he gave a staggering response. Everybody knew their role. Two men were already positioned behind him with their false guard. The other Germans pushed the sergeant and both the captured Dutch soldiers into a hollow in the ground, put the injured away from the embankment and took position, after freeing the submachine-guns and their magazines concealed under their greatcoats.

Lieutenant Walther commanded absolute silence with a quick gesture and listened attentively. He was expecting to see the other Dutchmen turn up with the sound of the reports of fire-arms. But nothing. Nobody seemed to move at the other end of the bridge.

"Five thirty-five!"

"Let's go!" he said laconically.

The small group walked between the rails. The three Germans would rather have been anywhere other than on this damned bridge. The Dutchman felt his gendarme's uniform burning his skin. They were thinking of the thirty rifles that were probably aimed at them. In seconds, they would be riddled with bullets. There was nowhere to seek shelter on the flat, bare roadway.

7 "What now, Sir?"

70

However the soldiers, whose outlines could already be seen at the end of the bridge, did not fire. What were they waiting for? Walther wondered whether a misunderstanding was working in his favour. He remembered that after crossing the border, his men had heard some explosions nearby. One of them had even said: "That's it, the bridge is blown, now we can leave." His keener ear however had identified charges that were a lot less powerful, such as those used for felling trees to make antitank obstacles.

He reassured his soldiers. Had the Dutch assumed that the sound of gunfire was an alarm signal, or a mistake? It was possible as there was no counter-attack. Walther started to hope once again. That was surely the answer. His walk became sure once more. He had almost forgotten that he was acting the part of a prisoner.

The false gendarme was more hesitant. Walther had to push him forward rather brusquely. Faced with an officer of Queen Wilhelmina who asked him in a haughty tone what it all meant, he responded per regulations:

"Three Germans taken prisoner in Dutch territory, Sir."

"Good", replied the lieutenant, "I don't need you any more. I will take responsibility for them."

The young Dutchman, little wanting to fight against his own, was happy to be able to turn around and disappear, without worrying about his German comrades.

Walther swore under his breath, ready to fight hard if the officer tried to search them.

But he did not and designated a corporal and four men to take the prisoners to the company CP, two kilometres away. Just when the corporal ordered the Germans to set off, the Dutch lieutenant noticed, under Walther's open greatcoat, his magnificent Zeiss field binoculars. His eyes shone in ill-concealed greed.

"Not declared to customs. Contraband! I'm confiscating them."

Happy to have escaped so lightly, the German did not bat an eyelid and the group started off.

"Get ready to do like me," he whispered to them.

Their guards followed ten metres behind, so as to be able to use their weapons with no risk. This precautionary measure aided Walther's plan. At that moment the first squadrons of the Luftwaffe passed overhead.

"Get down", he shouted.

The Dutch threw themselves onto their bellies. But they had not followed the *K2-Lager* training!

Once on the ground, Walther turned round in a single movement. He extracted an hand grenade from his pocket, pulled the metal cap and threw it onto the guards. His two companions imitated him, with less than a two second delay.

The Dutch laid dead.

"Follow me!" shouted Walther.

Just when the planes were flying over them, he saw that a path passed under the embankment of the railway line, some 80 metres further on. They ran to seek refuge as much from enemy fire as to be able to readjust their clothing. Three soldiers who reappeared lower down on the embankment with helmets pushed down over their eyes and the submachine-gun at the ready. They were on the attack.

Lieutenant Walther had noticed that there was a hut on the right of the abutment protected by a ring of barbed wire enveloping it up to the roof. There was no doubt in his engineer's eyes that the wires left from there; constant comings and goings through a door left ajar confirmed this. He chose to advance on the left of the embankment, to have a good field of fire towards the right. Private Meyer, whom he had ordered to follow the embankment by the right, had to prevent the enemy from returning fire.

Walther knew that their submachine-guns were not effective at more than a hundred metres. They had to get nearer, exposed to rifles with had an effective range of four hundred metres. The three Germans rushed forward, letting off occasional bursts of fire. Did they realise the heroic nature of their actions? They had one predominant objective: either they rout the enemy and preserve the bridge, or the bridge blows up and they are knocked down like flies.

At thirty metres, submachine-gun fire was fully effective. Badly commanded and even more badly trained, the Dutch had not set up any tactic and reacted individually. The three Germans stormed the position by emptying their magazines. The Dutch fled in every direction. Their officer remained alone, upright, haggard, his pistol in his hand. He fell.

Lieutenant Walther rushed towards the hut, preceded by a potato masher grenade. He entered, choking on the pungent odour of the explosive. In one corner, the blasting machine was ripped open. To be even more certain, the officer ripped out the wires which seemed to him to be still intact. It was over. He left and went to find his two men, stepping over bodies on his way.

"We are out of magazines, *Herr Oberleutnant!*"

"What about all that?" replied the officer pointing to all the Mannlicher rifles and the ammunition pouches strewn on the ground.

The two soldiers laughed and took aim at the retreating troops as if they were at the rifle range.

However, a line of Dutch light infantry was already outlined on the horizon. On the bank of the river, the casemates were at last awake and directed heavy fire towards the bridge. At the same time, a rumbling of tank tracks announced the arrival of the Panzers. Walther saw the first armoured fighting vehicle coming towards him on the roadway. Mad with joy, he waved the agreed recognition sign, a green handkerchief, in front of him. As it was already broad daylight, a mistake would be impossible. But, too impatient to cross swords, the Panzer gunner let forth a burst of machine-gun fire. Lieutenant Walther, miraculously spared from the enemy bullets, fell under those of the Germans. A projectile went clean through his helmet and glanced off his skull. He collapsed, his face covered with blood, and the tanks of Major-General von Hubicki's 9th Panzerdivision passed by him, just missing his legs.

The two Brandenburgers picked their commander up and applied a field dressing to stop the haemorrhaging, while bullets whipped over their bent down heads. The German motorised Rifles were now progressing on the bridge by crawling. And yet Wilhelm Walther felt good. His pain was eclipsed by the joy that was washing over him. His mission was completed. He had taken the bridge, 'his' bridge. He wanted to feel it beneath his feet and pushed his two soldiers back, got up and tottered. Everybody was lying down. He was alone, upright, very tall now. He walked, his arms slightly raised to keep his balance. The ringing bullets ricocheted on the iron girders and fell in a deathly rain, Walther advanced, a smile on his lips, his face smeared with blood. He reached the other end, untouched except for a ripped field blouse.

He was greeted by the four men that he had left there, still conscious enough to hear them say they had supported his progression to the hut with their fire. He was happy to learn that the Dutch had fled, not because they were afraid, but because they had been taken in the rear.

"Thank you, men!" he said, before losing consciousness again.

The tanks had pushed through the lines and silenced the pillboxes. Engineers ventured under the roadway of the bridge to remove the explosives from their chambers and throw them into the Meuse. Two motorised divisions were to come through in twenty-four hours, and pour out their formidable power into the low plains which spread out to the Boulonnais hills.

An ambulance arrived to transport the injured. The doctor took particular care of the little lieutenant:

"Was it you who took the bridge?"

"Yes, it's my team", replied Walther, without opening his eyes.

"There's not much left of your company."

At that, he opened his eyes:

"Company? There were nine of us, including me. Four injured and not one killed."

"But that's impossible!"

"We are the Brandenburgers."

And he closed his eyes.

The Maaseyck bridge, which joined the Dutch side of the Meuse to the Belgian side was, because of that very fact, doubly guarded, by the Dutch on one side and the Belgians on the other. Surprise could be obtained against the first, but would leave the second the time to get into a combat position. The Dutch had been on alert several times against an imminent German attack. Thus, when on the 9th of May, the border troops learnt that the attack was to take place the following morning, the majority of them disbelieved it and took no special precautions. This was not the case with Walther's 2nd Platoon, operating under lieutenant Grabert. With just reason, for this time the intelligence came from a sure source: the Dutch military attaché in Berlin, to which, despite the warnings of Admiral Canaris, the head of the Central Department of the Abwehr, Colonel Oster, had communicated X-Day and X-Hour.

The small team commanded by Grabert, even though they were dressed in the Dutch grey-green cloth, was greeted in front of Maaseyck by a shower of bullets. The officer acted quickly, bringing all his ingenuity into play, but was unable to knock out the two bunkers which prevented him from gaining access to the ignition wires. The bridge collapsed into the Meuse in before his very eyes.

A touch of daring allowed Unteroffizier Hegel's team to avoid a similar failure, even though the affair started badly. This mission was to take another bridge further north, on the Juliana Canal: the surprise he had hoped for never materialized. The Dutch were expecting him: imperiled by surrounding fire, he had to give himself up to avoid being wiped out. After a brief search, his group was directed towards the bridge then towards the rear.

It was at that point that Corporal Berger, who had hidden a stick hand grenade between his legs, remembered opportunely of an exercise that he had rehearsed several times. He took the grenade, pulled the porcelain bead and threw it shouting *"Volle Deckung !"* [8] Dutch and Germans threw themselves to the ground. The grenade exploded without injuring anyone, leaving the Germans the time to jump further down the roadway, from the opposite side, after retrieving their weapons left in a pile on the ground. A hand to hand combat ensued, and the ill-trained Dutch were quickly subdued. The Germans progressed rapidly towards their objective and managed to cut the wires before an enemy engineer could blow the bridge. At the first exchange of grenades, Corporal Hegel was seriously injured. He was evacuated as soon as the first armoured column of the Wehrmacht

8. "Get down!"

arrived, who relieved the group which had run out of their ammunition.

The northernmost target of the Brandenburgers was the bridge at Arnhem, which was to become famous in September 1944. The operation had been launched directly by the Battalion Staff.

With insufficient information and perhaps deceived by the Dutch who they had not sufficiently tested, the Brandenburgers fell into a trap. Despite stubborn resistance, they were overpowered by numbers and forced to surrender. The Germans were put into a bus seated facing the front, their two guards armed with pistols had received the order to shoot whoever turned his head. The vehicle took them inland. After several kilometres, it was blocked by a traffic jam of civilian vehicles and military field waggons, refugees and columns of soldiers. The Luftwaffe passing overhead made the prisoners, and above all their guards, yet more nervous. It seemed impossible to them that the German armoured vehicles could catch them up and release them as the bridge had been destroyed behind them.

Suddenly, the crowd blocking the road was seized by a wave of panic, as the grinding of tank tracks could be heard, very near on the roadway, accompanied by the characteristic reports from Panzer III 37-mm guns which could only belong to the *Panzerregiment 33*. [9] "Our liberators!" thought the prisoners immediately. "And they must be very near!" Corporal Wurst could not master his impatience. He quickly glanced behind him. The guards opened fire immediately. The NCO fell, dead. A second later, a tank with a black cross arrived level with the bus. The two guards stood up thinking that their last hour had come. They dropped their pistols and raised their hands.

The team of Grabert's platoon in charge of taking the road bridge at Roermond intact, fifty kilometres further down as the crow flies, also lived through some dramatic moments. *Feldwebel* Weber and his nine men, reinforced with a Dutch *V-Mann* disguised as a lieutenant, had concealed their uniforms under a greatcoat and a Dutch steel helmet,

9. The 9th *Panzerdivision's* tank regiment.

while keeping on to their German weapons, with the hope of carrying out their mission before the daylight would betray their identities.

At 2 in the morning on the 10th of May, they set off on their way. A German was waiting for them at the border to guide them over into Dutch territory between two patrols. Soon they saw the little town of Roermond brilliantly lit up. They entered it while the sky was still as black as ink and were amazed to see so many people in the streets. Two of them, who spoke Dutch, exchanged words gaily with the young girls at the windows, who in turn replied in the same way. The Germans, having just left a country that was deeply asleep, were much perturbed by this unreal scene and found the crossing of this town of thirty thousand inhabitants very long indeed.

At last they arrived at a closed level crossing. The *Feldwebel* wanted to avoid passers-by and turned off to the left, taking the path along the track, that he knew could be crossed a little further up. A civilian followed them from a certain distance. He stopped when they stopped and started off at the same time as them. Suddenly, a Dutch patrol blocked the road.

"Where are you going? Have you got a pass?"

The false Dutch lieutenant presented his compatriot with the document made by the Abwehr at Munster. Weber felt that something would go wrong, for their Dutch companion appeared nervous. The patrol leader cast him a suspicious look.

"Who drew up this paper? And where do you come from? We've never seen you here before!"

A Brandenburger is prepared for any situation. The *Feldwebel* shouted:

"You others, hands up!"

This time the enemy proved itself to have good reflexes and the patrol disappeared in several seconds.

"*Los! Los!*"

Weber rushed in the direction of the road bridge, followed by his men. The Dutch had not fired, because, in the jostling and the darkness, it was impossible to make out friend from foe. Having seen a small garden, Weber pushed his soldiers into it, who then took off their greatcoats and their Dutch helmets and put on their field-grey *Feldmützen*. They had scarcely started on their way when, in front of them, the sky was lit up with a huge red light, followed by a rumbling of powerful explosions which broke the windows all around.

The Germans stopped, disconcerted, then let their anger burst forth, making the walls of a tiny anonymous street in Roermond echo with every imaginable swear word. Then they surged back in the direction of the suburbs, in the hope of reaching the countryside where they could not be captured. It would indeed be stupid, for in a few minutes, the German army would cross the border very nearby. A group of men coming in the opposite direction were coming toward them. The Germans surrounded them and aiming their weapons made them subdued them. They turned out to be Dutch soldiers! The oldest was a major. When questioned he admitted being the community commander. Weber informed him he was a prisoner, took away his weapon and told him to walk next to him.

While they walked along, he asked some questions. The major was not angry, because he was very curious to know who these Germans were and what part of the sky they had fallen from. The *Feldwebel* explained briefly, then sought himself to elucidate a mystery:

"Then why did the patrol tell us that it did not recognise us?"

"For a very obvious reason," replied the old Dutchman with a smile. "Here, everybody knows everybody else. The same company has been in the town garrison for the last two years!"

"But how was it that the bridge guard had guessed our presence, before the patrol had the time to raise the alarm?"

"They never knew they simply obeyed the order to blow up the bridge twenty minutes before H-Hour."

"But how did you know that?"

"There are traitors in every camp," said the major dryly, casting a hard stare at the false Dutch lieutenant who was walking at the head of the troop.

But there were yet more bloody failures. The team of the 4th Company in charge of the Buggenum railway bridge, downstream from Roermond, who disguised themselves as metal workers, were unmasked just when they were going into action. The bridge was ripped from its piers with a deafening crash under the feet of the first Brandenburgers, who lost three men and three seriously injured.

The success otherwise obtained by the 4th Company won Lieutenant Walther a letter of congratulation from General Wodrig, commander of the XXVI Army Corps, and the awarding, on the 24th of June 1940, of the very first Knight's Cross of the Iron Cross accorded to a Brandenburger.

This Rittekreuz proved publicly that the volunteers of the *Bau-Lehr-Bataillon zbV 800* performed authentic acts of war, and were officially rewarded as such.

Chapter V

From the Netherlands to Luxemburg

The seizure of other bridges that were also situated in Dutch territory had been entrusted to a platoon commanded by the very recently promoted Second lieutenant Hermann Kürschner, an officer of the HQ Company at Brandenburg. To this end he began setting up a *Stosstrupp* from the month of January 1940, which finally became the *Bau-Lehr-Zug zbV* but was more familiarly called the *Westzug* (West Platoon).

The treaties had left the Netherlands a belt of land situated between Belgium and Germany, opening out at one end at the town of Maastricht, by Aachen, immediately north of Liège. The Meuse, particularly meandering at this point separating Belgium and the Netherlands, had been replaced on the east, in Dutch territory, by a waterway making a deep trench, the Juliana Canal, more easily defendable than the river as long as the four bridges which crossed it were destroyed in the time required. That was what the Abwehr had decided to prevent.

At nightfall on the 9th of May, *Leutnant* Kürschner was preparing to leave the camp at Erkelenz. Von Hippel had decided to do things in a big way and the operation would be carried out using the *Volltarnung* or full clothing camouflage: the men wore full Dutch uniforms.

The signal for departure was given at 0.30 a.m. It was only several hundred metres from the chosen crossing point, near the village of Mitten, that the Brandenburgers, transported in carefully covered lorries, put their feet on the ground. They were all equipped with a high Dutch, bicycle painted black. At the planned time, they crossed the border in a column, in absolute silence. Their guide, a seasoned smuggler, led them across fields along paths that did not appear on any map. To cross the marshy brook at Geleen, 1.5 metres deep at its centre, the head of the column was supplied with a floating footbridge. They continued their progression in silence. They reached a large orchard, encircled with walls, the planned point for proceeding to split up into four squads, each one with the task of securing one bridge over the Juliana Canal, at Berg, Obbicht, Stein and Urmond. They started off at ten-minute intervals.

The officer reserved the first objective, the bridge at Berg, for himself. Ready for action, in the early morning mist, he saw that two huge cylinders mounted on wheels and filled with cement were blocking the roadway. The intelligence service had not told them of this new type of antitank device.

Kürschner made the decision to move forward between the two cylinders, which at least had the advantage of protecting him. Several Dutch soldiers were seated in the middle of the bridge. They doubtless found the group that was advancing towards them very strange, as they moved away hastily.

Kürschner, who spoke Dutch very well, called them back:

"Halt! Where is your commanding officer?"

Hesitating, they stopped and let the Germans approach them. When they were just in front of them the lieutenant challenged them brusquely:

"Jongens, legt de wapens neer!" [1]

Before they could react, they were vigorously grabbed hold of and disarmed. A little further on, a Dutch NCO had witnessed the scene and leapt towards the parapet, he did not have the time to scale down

1. "Young men, put down your weapons!"

the bridge as Corporal Bergner fired several bullets into his legs. The *Unteroffizier* had not disobeyed, as his watch showed 4.45 a.m. precisely. The Dutchman fell on the ground. Further along the bridge, others gave up quickly:

"Don't shoot! Don't shoot!"

Without paying them any attention, Kürschner ran towards the bridge where the two ignition wires passed under the roadway and cut it clean through with his wirecutters.

He couldn't help shouting: "That's it! We've got it!"

Just then, bursts of fire rang out at the entrance to the bridge. They had to shelter. He tried to risk his all:

"Don't do anything stupid, men, or you are done for!"

Convinced they were surrounded and outnumbered, the Dutch gave themselves up. But some others, who had dispersed into the surrounding area at the beginning of the event, fired from afar. The German lieutenant had a bullet through both thighs and had to be evacuated.

At the Obbicht bridge, Corporal Landvogt's squad was pinned down by machine-gun fire. However, the NCO had spotted the explosive charges firing point and had stopped access to it with bursts from his submachine-gun. At 7 a.m., the first German troops from a reconnaissance battalion arrived and silenced the blockhouse with blasts of 37-mm antitank shells. Landvogt rushed onto the bridge with his men and defused the charges.

The bridges at Stein and Urmond were taken by surprise by the squads of Corporals Klein and Klausmeier. There was an exchange of fire with detachments of the border guards who were withdrawing towards the canal and found themselves caught between the bullets.

The mission of Kürschner's platoon was therefore on the whole a success. Along a length of 30 kilometres, the bridges of the Juliana Canal fell intact into the hands of the attackers. The casualty list was more than satisfying: two seriously injured, twelve slightly injured, not one killed. In addition, the Brandenburgers had captured 175 prisoners, including five officers.

Throughout the entire day of the 10th of May, the columns of the 7th Infantry Division, the same one that had been at the Jablunka Pass on the 1st of September 1939, crossed over the four intact bridges without stopping. The Brandenburgers met up again that night at their camp at Erkelenz and celebrated their quadruple success with tankards of beer late into the night.

The breakthrough and rapid crossing of the Ardennes massif constituted the essential phase of the plan of operations of May 1940. It was along this corridor that the motorised army corps had to sweep in and it was, for the enemy, the easiest sector to defend as the entire Belgian Army could concentrate its fire power along a front of 60 kilometres. Nevertheless, the OKW plan was particularly complex, attaching much importance to the disrupting of communications as to the crossing of border obstacles.

Two points appeared more important than others in this regard: the Neufchâteau road network and the centre of military communications at Stavelot. The first had to be cleared for the arrival of the tanks of Guderian's XIX Motorised Corps. The Luftwaffe were to transport four hundred men from the Grossdeutschland Infantry Regiment there in a hundred or so Fieseler Storch monoplanes, with the mission of holding down the *chasseurs ardennais*.

The Stavelot operation was carried out in a very different way.

Twelve Brandenburgers were chosen who possessed some knowledge of electricity. They were sent to Quenzgut under the command of Corporal Röhricht to undergo physical training alternated with lessons relating to improvements in telecommunications. One day, they had the surprise of being introduced to eight young women, all *Führerinnen* [2] from the *BDM* [3] or the *RADwJ*. [4] The instructor, having assembled them, was not very clear.

2. Feminine of Führer, leader.
3. Bund deutscher Mädel, League of German Girls, female branch of the Hitler Youth.
4. Reichsarbeitsdienst der weibliche Jugend , Women's section of the National Labour Service.

"From now on you are students using the services of a travel agency. You will be given your tickets at the required time. This evening, we will choose the names that you will have, the town where you live and the studies you are doing. You do not need to know any more for the moment. I can only tell you that this voyage will take place in Luxemburg and that it covers an operation set up in the interests of Germany."

It was a happy band of young men and women, who seemed to have known each other for a long time, that got out of the train three days before X-Hour in the capital of the Grand Duchy. Amongst all the other tourists, they passed completely unnoticed. To facilitate the following phase of the operation, the girls put up at one hotel and the boys at another. They were not to see each other again.

The following morning, a Dutch *V-Mann*, a supporter of Mussert, acting as a guide, took the young women to visit the town and its surroundings, while the young men, in small groups of two or three, took the train for Belgium, in one direction or another, to meet up at Stavelot on the morning of the 9th of May.

At midday, everybody was there and the contacts made. In the evening, in the rooms that they had rented for the night, the Brandenburgers listened to the German radio anxiously. At 10 p.m., when they heard the fateful key word 'Morgenröte' (dawn), they knew that the attack would be launched in six hours and forty-five minutes. They meted out the tasks, the local *V-Mann* having supplied them with indispensable information during the day.

At 3 a.m. two men cut the main cable linking the communications centre with the town post office, and two others were to skilfully sabotage an essential relay station. Liège was alerted for the repair of the cable. As for the relay, since no major destruction of equipment was visible, the head of the centre telephoned the local electrician, qualified to carry out routine repairs. Three Brandenburgers who got out of his car and presented themselves as assistants to the electrician who was stuck in bed with flu. He was indeed in bed, but tied up and under the guard of other Brandenburgers.

Thanks to the wireless, an important piece of news meanwhile reached the main post office centre: the Germans had violated Belgian neutrality. The head of the centre gave the order to his night shift employees to destroy the installations. At the same moment, the nine remaining 'tourists' made their appearance, holding a 9-mm automatic pistol. They herded the personnel together in a room and barricaded the building, in order to be able to hold out there until the arrival of German forces and hand over the communications centre intact. The three Brandenburgers responsible for the relays put the devices that they had cleverly neutralised several hours beforehand back into operation; because of this operation, the orders from the HQ at Brussels did not reach the front, and information concerning the German advance did not reach Brussels. The objective of the mission had been achieved.

On the border proper, the Brandenburgers encountered no insurmountable obstacles. Between Maastricht and the northern point of Luxemburg, the Belgian-German border spread along a length of sixty kilometres as the crow flies, across wooded country otherwise deprived of natural defences. Along this border were the two districts of Eupen and Malmédy - Saint-Vith, separated from the province of Rhineland in 1919, whose population had remained, for the most part, wholeheartedly German.

To stop aggressors, the Belgian High Command was relying principally on natural obstacles more at the rear, in the north by the Albert Canal and in the south by the Ardennes massif. It had nonetheless blocked the paths of entry with antitank obstacles and minefields, and had prepared for destruction of bridges and crossroads.

Captain Rudloff, commander of the 3rd Company, was in charge of neutralizing these obstacles. His unit had been created on the 15th of December 1939 from a recently formed group at Münstereifel for action on the Western Front. It was historically the first Brandenburg company set up specifically for participation in the campaign of May 1940.

The first difficulty was to get a relatively high number of armed soldiers over a closely watched border without arousing the attention of the Belgian units positioned in the region. None of the small groups assigned to each target had sufficient firepower at their disposal to force their way if the effect of surprise was lacking.

The times when the rounds took place had been carefully noted, different groups worked their way cautiously into Belgium, their uniforms concealed by civilian coats.

In the north, everything was going off as planned. The group chosen to occupy the railway station at Saint-Vith reached it just when a unit of *chasseurs ardennais* was boarding a train heading west. They opened fire with such ardour that the locomotive driver took fright and set the train on its way. It went onto a bridge that had just been occupied by another group of Brandenburgers, who, as the train was crossing, directed heavy fire onto it.

The sound of the gunfire alerted the neighbouring road bridge guard post. It blew the bridge immediately, to the great displeasure of those who had to take it intact. All the other objectives around Saint-Vith were taken by surprise and detachments of Belgian engineers taken prisoner before being able to spring the charges.

The gendarmerie however was to offer an unexpected resistance and the group of Brandenburgers would not have been up to the job, without the unhoped-for support of local civilians, armed with peashooters of every possible origin. After a half an hour of gunfighting, the Belgian gendarmes brandished a white handkerchief.

Several other groups could not reach their targets in time. They were caught up and overtaken by motorised units of the Wehrmacht.

Luxemburg itself offered no serious obstacle to the German advance. It posed a different problem. The OKW knew that a secret agreement between the Luxemburg and French Governments authorised French forces to occupy Luxemburg territory to defend it in the event of a conflict. The German Army therefore had to reach the French-Luxemburg border before the French. If it didn't the French Army would threaten the flank of the German columns pointing towards the Sambre across the Ardennes.

A German reserve officer, Lieutenant Schöller, a land-agent in Luxemburg, knew the terrain intimately. He was put in charge of setting up and preparing groups brought to operate in this zone.

Fortunately, the border between the Reich and the Grand Duchy was mostly open. It followed the Mosel River up as far as Trier, then its tributary the Sûre and finally the Our. The gendarmerie and the Luxemburg Militia were in place less to put up an armed resistance to a possible German attack, than to survey the opposite bank night and day, in order to give the alarm in the event of an attack.

On their side the Brandenburgers had set up an equally minute surveillance system that involved noting the times when the patrols passed, espacially at the points that were the most hidden from view, because of the bends in the river.

Schöller assumed that once in Luxemburg territory, his task would be made easier by the collaboration of local elements. In the same manner as in other ancient march-lands of Germany, the Grand Duchy was pulled between two opposite poles. While the middle classes were largely gallicized, the lower classes had remained mostly German speaking. German intelligence recruited heavily from that class.

Schöller adopted the formula of semi-camouflage for his group, which consisted of concealing German uniforms under an easily removable civilian coat and hat. They crossed the Mosel, the Our and the Sûre without being identified. The main detachment, led by the lieutenant himself, had to meet up with a group of local *V-Leute*. The rendezvous point, a mill which was highly visible from the main road, was not chosen with much enthusiasm.

On the evening of the 9th, with the night already drawing in, a car transporting half a dozen young people got lost in the region. They asked one passerby, then another, where the *Felsmühle* was. Shortly, a second car did the same thing, then a third. The gendarmerie was alerted and sent over an armed detachment.

When Schöller's group arrived, there was already gunfire taking place between the occupants of the mill and the gendarmes. However, the arriving of the Brandenburgers who were not immediately recognized for what they were, adding to the confusion and the Luxemburg police hesitated, not knowing what to do. At that moment, an Upper Silesian among the Brandenburgers, not yet fully conversant with the situation in the western march-lands asked in a powerful voice:

"Herr Oberleutnant, dürfen wir schiessen?" [5]

The gendarmes had no more doubts as to the identity of the newcomers. They asked for and obtained reinforcements. Schöller could have scattered them easily, even though there were already several injured amongst the Luxemburg *V-Leute* and in his own group. However, he had strict orders from the Abwehr not to open fire before 4.45 a.m. He could only give the order to take cover shelter without returning fire. When daylight came, the German tanks of the 1st *Panzerdivision* filed along the main road and the Brandenburgers could get back to their starting point.

Everywhere else in the Grand Duchy, teams of three to six men, made of civilians and soldiers, overran posts of the gendarmerie, took possession of the larger post offices, withdrew antitank obstacles from the roads, protected bridges and if necessary, cut telegraph and telephone wires.

On the 11th of May, Captain von Hippel's assessment of the first day of the Western Campaign showed a balance of 42 out 61 targets assigned to the Brandenburgers, handed over intact to invading forces. In addition to the *Rittekreuz* of Lieutenant Walther, his men were to receive 120 Iron Crosses 1st and 2nd Class.

This success bolstered his request to form a genuine regiment, having its own rules of engagement and complete autonomy within the Wehrmacht.

5 "Sir, may we open fire?"

Chapter VI

The locks at Nieuport

The OKW did not wait for the end of operations in the West to respond to Captain von Hippel. On the 15th of May, the Brandenburg Battalion officially became a regiment of three battalions of four companies, each company split into 'half-companies' replacing the usual platoons. The Regiment's Staff, the Operations Staff already in existence and the Liaison Staff with the Abwehr were established in Berlin.

I Battalion remained at Brandenburg and acted as a processing unit for recruits and as a pool of talent for the *Abwehr II* which would continue to draw from the regiment as long as it remained under the control of Canaris. II Battalion moved to Baden-Unterwaltersdorf, near Vienna, and began assembling volunteers for Eastern Europe and the Balkans. III Battalion was barracked at Aachen and was made up of units destined for other theatres of operations.

The command of the regiment went to Major Kewisch, not to Captain von Hippel, who took I Battalion.

In practice, this transformation was carried out over several months. Several new companies had been created in the home bases before the 15th of May, but it was not before the end of the year that the *Lehr-Regiment Brandenburg zbV 800* acquired any cohesion. Throughout the Spring of 1940, units were continually shifted.

In any case, the French campaign had not finished for the Brandenburgers.

91

When the German forces reached Ostend in the north and Calais in the south, they trapped the British Expeditionary Force and the French No. 1 Army Group under General Blanchard in a pocket that they sought immediately to pierce.

But even though they were carried on the wings of victory, they found themselves confronted with a risk. At 17 kilometres to the west of Ostend, in the zone still believed to be held by the British, was Nieuport, on the mouth of the Yser, blocked by powerful locks. These locks controlled the flooding of the entire neighbouring region, situated below sea level. In 1914, the Belgians had blown them up, which had given Dixmude an impregnable flank and allowed a definitive halt to be brought to the German offensive. It was now supremely important to prevent the same misadventure from being repeated.

To throw the infantry immediately in advance to occupy Nieuport was not an option. It was certain that the locks were mined. Although their destruction had been delayed so as not to hamper the Allies, there would be no further hesitation if German advanced guards appeared on the scene. The only conceivable action was a Brandenburger type mission.

Following operations in the Netherlands, Lieutenant Grabert's platoon was sent on leave. A telegram from Captain von Hippel recalled them immediately. Lieutenant Grabert and Corporal Janowski thus found themselves in the company office of the very barracks that had witnessed the birth of the unit.

The *Kommandeur* was brief: "I have been asked to put a group en route for Belgium immediately. Your name, Grabert, was mentioned. I don't know what it's about. But it is without any doubt in your line of work. Select your men. You will be given our best equipment. Good bye, men. *Hals-und Beinbruch!*"

The two men came to attention while their leader left the room. Grabert turned towards his corporal.

"Are you still here, Jano? Rake up the best of what you can find for me in the clothing magazine and the armoury. I'll take care of the paperwork. Assembly for departure in two hours. *Verstanden?*"

Two hours later, the thirty-two armed men of the platoon were assembled in the barracks square. They travelled towards Cologne in reserved compartments with the curtains lowered. A useless precaution in the middle of Germany? Perhaps, but they had to get used to living in total secrecy. To pass the time they practised stripping and reassembling their new MP 38 machine pistols that had just been delivered, still a very rare weapon in the Wehrmacht.

At Destelbergen, near Ghent, they were informed of their mission. They learnt that they would be facing the entire British Expeditionary Force. Were they concerned? Several training lessons ended in ensuring the homogeneity of the small force.

"Who has not yet had the opportunity of using live grenades?"

Three men raised their hands, including a former student named Burrer, a very new soldier. He could salute only with great difficulty. He knew nothing of the military science that had been the glory of Prussia. Lieutenant Grabert made him leave the ranks and placed him in front of the platoon and explained clearly to him the way a Model 1924 stick grenade should be handled:

"In front of you, there is an ornamental lake. In the middle a little island. Can you see the white bench under the beech tree?"

"*Jawohl, Herr Leutnant!*"

"Distance, approximately 50 metres. That's your target. Do it well or you are *kaputt.*"

He turned towards his platoon:

"Thirty metres backwards, march!"

He distanced himself as well.

"*Sammeln! Feuer!*"

Burrer unscrewed the metal cap of the stick, pulled the length of cord which had a porcelain bead on the end of it, counted and launched the grenade with all his might before throwing himself to the ground. He looked under the visor of his helmet.

A cloud of dust, an explosion... The bench went up.

"Excellent", shouted the second lieutenant, who was surprised. "Tomorrow, we will take care of Nieuport. You will accompany me as a grenadier."

To allow Grabert's platoon to arrive discreetly on site with its equipment, he was allocated a small country bus which still bore the name of a local hotel on its sides.

The men got on board, laughing:

"We're going to the seaside, folks. Don't forget your shrimp net!"

They drove along the road leading from Ostend to Nieuport. Belgian military personal outfits in khaki canvas were strewn along the road side. Nieuport seemed deserted. They crossed the town and arrived within sight of the locks. At the same moment, the little bus came under light machine-gun fire and its windows crashed down with a thin noise. The vehicle was empty almost immediately: the excellent training received made itself felt once again.

They could make out a hollow near the canal and assembled there. It was only 7 p.m. and they realised that they had arrived too early. But how could they recognise the objective in the darkness?

Although they fired at anything that moved, the British however had certainly not guessed the real purpose of the occupants of this unexpected bus. Grabert, from the hole where he was hiding, swept his binoculars over the landscape.

He saw written on a large stone by a road the inscription: *"The German Army was stopped here in 1915."* And he thought: *"The German Army will not be stopped here in 1940."*

He could make out enemy soldiers, who were not even hiding, less than a kilometre away. It was unthinkable that the locks were abandoned. They must therefore be near a detachment of engineers with the task of firing the charges.

Above all they must not expose themselves and wait for nightfall before going into action.

His assistant platoon leader wanted to determine the blind spot of their position. He perched his steel helmet on a long pair of wirecutters and slowly lifted it up above the parapet. The enemy machine-gun rattled out. Hit by the projectiles, the helmet spun on its support like a top. The *Unteroffizier* understood and brought it back down, as another bullet whipped through it from one side to another.

94

Night fell at last. Grabert's men took advantage of the last light of the sunset to check that the fighting packs were well strapped, the weapons ready for use and the magazines loaded. Then, on a signal from the leader, they left their hole, one by one, crawling on their elbows.

Every three or four minutes, the British fired a flare above the canal bridge. Between each one, the men covered, metre by metre, the five hundred which separated them from their objective.

Hampered by his stout build, the NCO started to get tired. He held his large wirecutters in his right hand and his submachine-gun in his left, putting them down during the periods of light to feel around for a wire nearby, while his eyes searched the terrain. He had the satisfaction of seeing that his lieutenant was no farther ahead of him, ten or so metres on his left. Between them lay the body of an NCO, who had fallen by his bicycle; his aluminium collar stripes and shoulder straps shone every time a flare went up.

At last, the bridge. Two men acted as scouts, still crawling. Grabert followed them along the left hand guard-rail and the *Unteroffizier* along the right hand one. Behind them Johannes and the last three men fanned out to cover the progress.

The NCO at last held a wire in his hands, laid below the footbridge. He cut it with the cutters.

At the same time he heard the lieutenant whisper: "I've got it!" He replied softly: "Me too!"

But where did these wires end up? Probably under the abutment. There must of course be others. But where? They were crawling now in the direction of the other bank of the canal. The NCO was trembling with fear and thought that his leader was probably trembling as well. They had, between their clenched teeth, a one-way ticket to heaven. The bridge could go up at any second. But they had learnt to live with fear.

Grabert's assistant platoon leader wiped away the sweat that was obscuring his vision. He reached the end of the bridge and let himself roll down the slope to the towpath. There, he could stand up. Two magnificent wires disappeared into the shadow of the roadway. Just when the severed end fell on to the ground, a burst of blue flames spurted out.

"*Donnerwetter!*"

The NCO had turned pale. Grabert approached.

"Have you cut it?"

"Yes, *Herr Leutnant,* but the safety fuse burned out in front of my eyes."

"We are very lucky. But we could still go to heaven if they are set up for electric firing. We have to find it."

They looked everywhere, and found it hooked to the telegraph poles.

"Let's say thank you to the British," whispered Grabert, "they left us the time to work."

The NCO and one man were left in a rear guard position, half way between the two bridges. The six others stealthily drew nearer to the lock and reached a house, or rather a café, from where the wires seemed to come out and go towards the railway bridge and the lock. A dreadful noise troubled the deep silence of the night. The delivery hatch for the beer barrels had opened when Burrer stepped on it, he was now in the cellar sitting on a mound of broken bottles, seemingly unharmed. His comrades, who had stayed outside, were expecting a reaction from the enemy at any moment. They had their fingers on their triggers. The officer did not wait for the racket to end before diving onto the wires and cutting them.

Now, the six men were looking at each other, amazed that nothing was happening.

"These fellows need to go for a tour at Quenzsee," observed a Brandenburger in a low voice.

A quiet whistle and the rear guard rejoined them. To go back, the group took the lock bridge, so as to keep out of the line of enemy machine-gun fire.

The country bus was shattered. They had a four-hour walk in front of them. But, once again, they were lucky. While they were crossing the ruins of Nieuport, they found an abandoned British car with the keys on the dashboard. The driver had left it with a body on the seat. They put it on the ground and got in.

On the road they met the head of the infantry and advised them to secure the bridge immediately.

At Ostend, a general received them in a royal fashion. Flanders will not be flooded.

The NCO received the Iron Cross 1st Class and Lieutenant Grabert...a good dressing down. The following day the Army Staff had visited the locks and realised that he and his men had left the scene without emptying the mine chambers! As stray shell could have caused a disaster. He was nevertheless promoted to *Oberleutnant*. His platoon was to make up the core of the new 8th Company re-formed at the end of the Summer in Baden.

Chapter VII

England will not be destroyed (Operations 'Seelöwe' & 'Felix')

With German forces lining the Channel following victory in France in June 1940, Hitler realised that England was a gigantic aircraft carrier that would strike him in the back while he attacked Russia and he decided to finish her off.

When an offensive was prepared, it was now customary to call upon the services of Brandenburgers. From the month of July, I Battalion under von Hippel and III Battalion under Captain Rudloff were put on alert. Only several troops of I Battalion, which still only comprised two companies, were sent with the 10th Company of III Battalions to train on the Helgoland rock in the North Sea.

I Battalion was then transported from Brandenburg/Havel in France. It was to be spread out from Normandy as far as Flanders, at the disposal of the 16th Army, whereas III Battalion had to cover from the Seine to Cherbourg, subordinated to the 6th Army whose HQ was to the north of Caen.

In mid-July, the Lieutenant Schöller's 11th Company left Aachen for Normandy. Training started straight away, while the planes of *Reichsmarschall* Göring attempted to destroy the Royal Air Force.

Many were the men who saw the sea for the first time. Their clumsy efforts to get on board, to sheer off, to scull, made French sailors who watched them smile. They were seen mooring the jolly-boats too short at high tide, only to find them, six hours later, hanging at the end of their moorings. In all the Channel ports there was a mass of floating hulls of all types and ages, very few of which seemed to have the personnel capable of manoeuvring them.

The 11th Company left Dieppe at the beginning of August. The 10th, arriving from Helgoland, set up near Bayeux. At the end of the month, a new 11th Company, in fact the 8th rebaptized, arrived in Upper Normandy. It was quartered at the chateau of La Chapelle, near Dieppe, and was training to land at the foot of the cliffs at Eastbourne. Officers were familiarising themselves with their objectives from air photographs marked with a circle, but were unable to determine whether it was a machine-gun position, a gun under cover or an observation post or radar station. Finally, the officers and NCOs assembled at Aachen to form the 12th Company were sent to Büsum, in Schleswig, to practise scaling the chalky cliffs, very similar to those in Kent. On their return they would train the others, just as their comrades sent to Helgoland would.

The Brandenburgers sometimes had difficulty in taking seriously the improvisations that had no merit other than wanting to give the illusion of a serious preparation. It was assumed that the lead detachment would land by surprise. It could however be in a position of having to ask its way or to reply to challenges given by sentries or patrols. The men had to be prepared for these possibilities.

Lance-corporal Manfred Oberländer, a university professor in civilian life, was in charge of giving English lessons to the Brandenburgers every day after exercises. There were many Germans from the Baltic, Silesia, Sudetenland, from Rumania and Hungary who had never heard a single word of English. Seated in a semi-circle on the lawn, in front of the professor, they repeated in a chorus: "Where is the nearest way to London?" or "Are there any mines?"

And if a sentry were to ask anything: "Shut up you bloody bastard, I'm Captain Roberts!" Hearing the croaks of his classmates attempting to repeat after the professor, a former machine-gunner lance-corporal of the Brandenburg Battalion's 2nd Company, could not contain his hilarity.

Dr. Oberländer took offence: "Röseke", he shouted, "You may think it's funny, but I don't!"

As for von Hippel, in this early September, laughter was very far from his mind. He had however just been promoted to *Major* and at last had three companies at his disposal. The 3rd under Lieutenant Weinert had just been formed.

Since his arrival at the Channel coast, he had been shaping and forming his men like the blacksmith beats the iron on the anvil. He demanded from the ordinary soldier intelligence, initiative and the sense of responsibility that is expected of NCOs in an ordinary unit. He subjected his half-companies to endurance and pain threshold tests that appeared comparable to punishment for those unaware of the level of pride maintained by the combatants that old battalion commander commanded.

Lieutenant-General Model, chief of staff of the 16th Army, came to realise the state of preparation of his forces and came across, rather by chance, the Brandenburgers.

"What is your task, *Major*?"

"On X-Day, we have to occupy the port of Dover by surprise and hold it until the arrival of the invasion forces, *Herr General*. Our other battalion will embark at Cherbourg and take Weymouth."

"It's a suicide mission, but it is suitable for battalions such as yours. No troop would stand the tough training that you subject your rogues to."

Von Hippel raised his head at the comment. The little general continued:

"Is it a penal unit that you command? The 540 Battalion? The 500?"

"*Herr General*, these men are not out of prison. They are the Brandenburgers, not cannon fodder. If their mission is indeed suicidal, they have nonetheless all volunteered to carry it out."

"I am happy to learn that," replied general Model, "and I regret any misunderstanding. However, the fact remains that your soldiers from the Abwehr sometimes take it a bit too easy, like those two chaps who are to come up before a court-martial for cowardice faced with the enemy."

Von Hippel discovered that the special role of his unit was even less understood by the military judges than by the military personnel with a traditional training.

The two the General referred to were volunteers from South Africa, who spoke English well and had agreed to be parachuted into Ireland. The Abwehr wanted observation posts which would indicate movements of ships sailing under convoy and would send weather reports.

Over a period of two weeks, the young men had undergone intensive training, received technical instruction for wireless operators and intelligence agents and carried out almost daily flights over the Channel, including many parachute jumps over the sea. At the last minute they decided to give up the mission.

Von Hippel had gone immediately to the 16th Army HQ, at Nieuport, to meet the armed forces official responsible for the investigation of the case.

"These two NCOs justified their actions," explained the official, "by claiming that you had said it was their duty to give up if they had any doubt."

"Quite true! We can expect nothing from men who lack confidence in themselves once they are let loose on their own. I admit that they went about it a little late and that justifies serious action. However, they obeyed my orders. I am the only person responsible."

"Well, *Herr Major*. I don't know what gives you the authority to modify the Army Act just because you command a special unit. If others were to follow your example, discipline would disintegrate and there would be no more army."

"If they are not in command of the Brandenburgers then they are not meant to follow my example. It seems natural to me that the Army Act does not apply strictly to men whose tasks do not fall within a strict military framework."

The two men separated with a rather cold handshake.

The matter went as far as Colonel-General Ernst Busch, commander of the 16th Army. On the intervention of General Model, who had the reputation of being a very severe but intelligent officer, the two defendants were released and sent back to their barracks. Both of them were to earn the Iron Cross the following year.

When he left for Belgium, von Hippel left Brandenburg to his adjutant, Lieutenant Johannes, with instructions to inform him of any unpleasant surprises. Thus he learnt that an order from the High Command was to be sent to him, requiring him to make his men engage under oath to carry out any mission that they were ordered to do by the OKW. This order was in direct contradiction with the principal of voluntary acceptance, which according to Hippel made up the foundation of the military ethics of the Brandenburgers. He made up his mind to oppose this as resolutely as he could.

The meetings of unit commanders of the Army Group D, held at the end of September in Saint-Germain-en-Laye, were to provide him with the opportunity he was waiting for. He was present at the *Ic* [1] cell meeting. Colonel Stolze and Major Kewisch commanding the *Lehr-Regiment Brandenburg zbV 800* represented the *Abwehr*, bearing the order of Admiral Canaris to all Brandenburgers that they take the new oath. Von Hippel exploded. For as long as he was *Kommandeur* of I Battalion, he would refuse such an order. Colonel Stolze pointed out to him that this measure was the express wish of the Führer.

"In that case," replied Hippel "the Führer has been badly informed!"

The officers stiffened. They looked with a mixture of astonishment and admiration at this strange officer who dared to challenge the disciplinary tradition upheld by Potsdam.

Aware of the gravity of his insubordination, von Hippel requested curtly that a preliminary investigation be opened against him and that he be replaced at the conclusion of the current operation, in this case, 'Seelöwe'. Then he gestured to the two officers who had accompanied him and left by car without taking part in the dinner that evening.

Shortly after, on the 12th of October, operation 'Seelöwe' was postponed, and von Hippel summoned to appear before his superiors, at the seat of Abwehr, Tirpitzufer in Berlin.

1. Equivalent of the 'Intelligence cell' in a German formation's staff.

His case was to be examined at 3 p.m. in his presence. He waited in a corridor, on a bench, like an accused person. An orderly led him in at the appointed hour. Von Hippel relaxed when he saw the admiral approach him smiling, his hand outstretched. Behind him, Oster and von Lahousen seemed more reserved. Stolze and Kewisch were also present.

"My dear Hippel, nobody knows better than I what you have done for the Abwehr until now. But there is one thing that you are not yet aware of, that orders are made to be obeyed!"

Von Hippel decided to hide nothing.

"*Herr Admiral,* I request permission to explain myself frankly."

Canaris approved with a nod.

"In venturing behind enemy lines half-disguised, our men are already in an extremely delicate situation. But, well, they have the chance of escaping an ignominious death if they are captured. It is not the same for those that we have to use in complete enemy uniform or civilian clothing. If they fall into the hands of the enemy, they can expect no mercy. It is clear that we do not have the right to give an order to a man to violate the rules of war, that Germany, in other times was committed to respecting. In this case what we are asking him to do is to accept to sacrifice himself voluntarily for his country. He has the perfect right to refuse. An order of the Führer need be no obstacle."

"That is why," interrupted Major Kewisch, "I cannot go along with you on that. I find it difficult to admit that we make our men run such risks with full knowledge of the facts. Our tasks are special, but they must be carried out by respecting military practices as much as possible, to prepare them meticulously enough so that this type of problem not arise again."

"It *is* happening," replied Hippel. "There is no reason to set up a unit like ours if we cannot resort to war ruses. We send small groups of men to the enemy. What can ten, twenty or even a hundred men with only light weapons do against an enemy army? Without the camouflage which enables them to reach their objective unidentified they would be unmasked and killed without fail. But there is another aspect of this question of the new oath which I would like to draw the attention of *Herr Admiral*. It was specified in our attack plan for occupying Dover that the first parachute detachments would wear British uniform, speak English and would be provided with British weapons. Suppose that several among them were taken prisoner after having taken this oath? There would be one ready to confess that he was a soldier acting under orders, to escape hanging. And the British would exhibit him in front of journalists and photographers and interview him on the wireless, to show the whole world the treachery of the Germans."

Without saying a single word, Canaris gestured to von Hippel to leave the room.

When the door was closed, he turned towards his collaborators: "Gentlemen, von Hippel is right. He will be punished because I can't do otherwise, but perhaps, because of his courage, the matter can rest there."

The *Major* was shown back into the room no more than three minutes later.

"*Major* von Hippel," began Canaris in a voice he tried to make as 'formal' as possible. "In accordance with you frequently expressed desire, you will be transferred to Africa. I must pass on the thanks of the head of the OKW, Marshal Keitel himself, for the services you have rendered." Then turning to Kewisch, commander of the Brandenburg Regiment:

"Use this transfer to draw up a suitable order of the day."

Coming to attention, von Hippel requested:

"May I respectfully ask what action is taken concerning my request for prosecution for refusing to obey?"

The *Admiral* smiled.

"Don't be silly!"

So Hippel lost his command. Major Kewisch, without it being known precisely why, was also put in the same boat. The officers who replaced them did not renounce their lessons. *Major der Reserve* Hubertus von Aulock took over the regiment temporarily, to entrust it to Lieutenant-Colonel Paul Haehling von Lanzenhauer on the 28th of November. I Battalion passed quite naturally to Lieutenant Wilhelm Walther, the prestigious CO of the former 4th Company.

Canaris, however, was not to get himself out of the situation so easily. Several months later, Marshal Keitel sent him a sharp note to ask him what the situation was concerning the oath of obedience under the Führer's orders. Colonel Piekenbrock, head of Abwehr I, expressed once more what everybody more or less thought at the Abwehr: "*Let's say once and for all to Mr. Keitel that the military intelligence service is not an organisation of criminals, unlike the SS or the SD.*"

The Admiral turned a deaf ear. He had nothing to gain in creating a stir which would provoke a split with predictable consequences. He merely replied: "*In response to your request, I refer to my position and the fact that you accepted it, during the Weygrand case, in 1940.*"

In the month of December 1940, an order from Marshal Keitel had been handed to the head of the Abwehr, asking him quite simply to have General Weygrand assassinated in North Africa where he was suspected, rightly so, of organising a military force destined one day to join the British.

Colonel Lahousen Edler von Vivremont, head of *Abwehr II*, specialist in subversive actions abroad, had inherited this dubious mission. His response remains engraved in the collective memory:

"This order is null and void. My department and my officers are fighters not murderers."

"You are right", concluded his superior. "Let's refer back to Article 14 of the German Army Act which says, and I quote: '*It is a crime to carry out a criminal order.*' I will say nothing more to Keitel."

And this time, nothing more was heard on the matter.

By Autumn of 1940, the battle of Britain was over. The Luftwaffe had lost 1,636 aircraft of all types. Despite the loss of 1,172 planes, the RAF was still able to draw up more than a thousand Hurricane and Spitfire fighters, the latter being easily as good as the Messerschmitt Bf 109 at low and high altitude. Göring was beside himself and Hitler was disgust. Throughout October, the Brandenburgers, bored with their extended vacation, had rejoined their barracks at Brandenburg, Baden and Düren where II Battalion now had its home station. In Berlin, the Regiment's Staff and the Operations Staff had just finished settling in.

Meanwhile, another large-scale operation had been conceived which, even though it meant mobilising fewer forces, represented insurmountable difficulties of a different order: capturing the rock of Gibraltar. If they could do that, the Germans would control the straits with their heavy artillery, stop the supply of Malta and force sea convoys, which would normally use the Suez Canal, to go round Africa.

But the Reich could not have its forces cross Spanish territory without the consent of the Government of General Franco. The diplomatic preparation of Operation 'Felix' raised the enormous problem of resupplying Spain. If she sided with the Axis Powers, the British would also immediately set up a blockade. In 1940, ruined by civil war, the Spanish people lived in misery and could offer no help in the war. Admiral Canaris, who had the ear of Franco, was given the responsibility of diplomatic representation to the Führer.

Meanwhile the military operation was put into shape. Gibraltar was a gigantic natural bunker sheltering a large, well protected harbour. It had been British since 1713, and Spain considered it a thorn in its side. It had attempted several times, in vain, to reconquer the territory. It was a hard nut to crack. The rock was honeycombed with caves and the majority of vital installations were sheltered from bombs. However the town and the whole defence layout off the rock were vulnerable.

Operation 'Felix' could only be prepared following covert visits by officers of the *Abwehr II* and unit commanders from the Brandenburg Regiment designated to carry it out. It had to take place under the XXXXIX Mountain Army Corps who felt that they too ought to send troops it fight in Spain [2]. It was on this occasion that a gross error was committed. On the 22nd of July, Captain.Rudloff, the titular head of III Battalion, took off for Madrid to meet up with the Admiral, Colonel Piekenbrock and the commander of the 51st Engineer Battalion.

2. A reference to German military participation in the Spanish civil war.

The officers put up at the Plaza, the smartest hotel in Madrid, where the secret services of all countries conducted meetings. Generally speaking, persons worth spying on stayed there.

There was no mistaking this group of men with shaved temples, cigars at their lips and speaking German sotto voce. Their civilian suits, which still bore heavy creases from the uniform cases betrayed their military connection at a hundred paces. Two of them were reckless enough to go and visit Algeciras, opposite the rock. All that lacked a great deal of discretion.

Any attack naturally had to take place by surprise, preceded by violent bombings and shellings. While bombs from the planes could destroy the exterior installations and the ships at anchor, only high calibre guns could strike the cliffs with a direct hit. Taking off from France fully loaded, the bombers would land on Spanish airfields, refuel and return to France. The installation of heavy batteries at Tarifa on the Spanish coast on the other hand posed a very difficult problem. Theoretically the simplest solution would be to bring them by sea. There remained the road or railway. In both cases, their passage across Spain and above all their bringing into action in the sight of British observation posts would compromise secrecy many weeks before an attack. Even if they were brought, they would be rapidly silenced through lack of concrete protection.

Colonel von Lahousen laid down the task of the Brandenburgers with his usual competence and meticulousness. Lieutenant Count Thun was in charge of choosing two officers and one hundred men with the requisite experience and assembling them near Biarritz. He had to train them, without of course informing them, until the very last minute, what their objective was.

In the forty-eight hours preceding X-Hour, the agents would have to enter the British zone one by one to sabotage the fuel dump at Coaling Island, the coal dump at Admiralty Mole, the oil tanks at Sandy Bay, the airfield at Rennbehn, the seaplane station, the electric power station and the sea water distillery system. Putting only half of these installations out of service would paralyse the resistance of the fortress.

At X-Hour, Thun's company had to go into action. It was up to him to cut or blow up the ring of barbed wire separating the British zone from the neutral zone, to prevent the destruction of the roadway situated to the west of the wet dock, at the north-western limit of the rock, and the tunnel built from east to west to the north of the rock. The occupation of the objectives situated more forward in the peninsular depended on the progress of the attack by the engineers of the 51st Engineer Battalion who had to follow the Brandenburgers, and subsequently take over the lead.

It was no accident that the taking of the grand bunker had been entrusted to Lieutenant-Colonel Hans Mikosch, commander of the famous 51st Engineer Battalion, a GHQ unit of the army. It was he who, with parachutists from the Koch assault group, took possession of the fort at Eben-Emael, reputed to be impregnable, in May 1940. Its capture opened Belgium to the Wehrmacht. Now Mikosch had to repeat his exploit under even more difficult conditions.

Colonel von Lahousen wanted to avoid arousing the suspicion of the British with the arrival of the Brandenburg detachment several days before the passage of forces of the XXXXIX Mountain Corps over the French-Spanish border. He specified at the end of his order that the transport of units over British territory could be partially carried out by speed boats and the use of civilian clothing or British uniforms was to be provided for depending on the circumstances.

One month later however, on the 6th of December 1940, an order from the OKW, which had overall responsibility for the whole operation, revealed imprecision in the plan of attack. The Brandenburgers were now to *"assist the Spanish division situated opposite Gibraltar"*, to prevent the British from occupying the neutral zone separating the two territories and consequently to seize positions planned for the artillery. These instructions highlighted for the first time the fundamental differences between the *Oberkommando der Wehrmacht* and the *Abwehr* on the subject of the employment of the zbV 800 units, a problem which would only get worse over time.

The *Abwehr* intended them to be used exclusively for special missions making them very similar to secret agents in uniform. OKW former was still attempting to use them as a simple shock unit.

On the 9th of December, Colonel von Lahousen seemed to warm to OKW point of view and specified that, so as not to attract attention, Lieutenant Thun's men were to reach their assembly areas by sea. The hundred Brandenburgers, dressed as merchant seamen, passed themselves off as sailors shipwrecked by a recent torpedoing. The guns had to arrive by the same route.

This was all rather unrealistic, because the British held the sea. Moreover a long interval of time was planned between the air attack of the Luftwaffe and of land forces, operations with a very little support by the railways. How could they talk of surprise under such conditions?

Operation 'Felix' contained too many question marks to carry any conviction. The Spanish Government was to give it the *coup de grâce*.

As long as he believed in the imminent invasion of Great Britain, General Franco let it be known that he was disposed to join the operation. But when it turned out, in October, that Hitler had abandoned the project, he was forced to consider what the economic situation of a Spain brusquely deprived of its overseas imports would be. He made it known to the Government of the Reich that only the delivery of a million tonnes of wheat, 500,000 tonnes of meat and 180,000 tonnes of sugar would allow Spain to overcome the blockade that it would suffer. This did not include fuel needs: five hundred waggon loads of coal crossing France every day to bring coal from the Ruhr replacing the coal from Cardiff was a minimum.

It goes without saying that the foodstuffs, fuel and waggons immediately available did not reach a tenth of these quantities! As for the question of transport across Spain, it was insoluble. The railway lines, too few and often single track, had only been used up until then for home traffic, almost the entirety of Spanish imports and their distribution being carried out by sea.

Spain was condemned to neutrality and the Brandenburgers were deprived of a new exploit. Subsequent attempts to reactivate operation 'Felix' did not have much success.

PART TWO

THE BRANDENBURG REGIMENT (1940-1942)

Chapter VIII
From the Balkans to Asia
(1940-1941)

The abandonment of the plan to invade Great Britain enabled Hitler to transfer all his attention back towards the East. The immediate priority was to secure continued delivery of Rumanian petroleum, which enemies of the Reich planned to prevent.

Admittedly, Germany had assured itself of large supplies of fuel by its agreement of the 23rd of August with the USSR. But the hydrocarbons from Rumania — the oil field at Ploesti, north of Bucharest — continued to be the surest source of its imports, transported either by the railway or the Danube.

The Allies were strongly settled in Rumania, especially the British who controlled both the financial and technical aspects of many oil companies. Their owners formed a sort of private State at the heart of the Rumanian State, and therein lay the danger.

However, under German pressure, the Rumanian Government had imposed excessively severe contracts on foreign companies which forced them to maintain production levels and to deliver 90% to the Reich. In 1940, there was only one way of putting an end to these deliveries, and that was to directly sabotage their own installations.

That is why the advanced party of the Brandenburgers arrived at Bucharest on Christmas Sunday 1939. They were three NCOs,

115

Feldwebel Gustl Süss, Corporals Kriegisch and Stöhr, dressed like impeccable gentlemen. They put up at the best hotel in the capital, their pockets full of lei and dollars. A Swiss banker had transferred two million francs to the account of a highly placed Bucharest personality who had received an identical amount in Reichsmarks from unkown sources.

At night, the three gentlemen frequently went to Ploesti, situated 60 kilometres to the north. They were not seen in the gleaming bars of Campina or the brothels, despite their allure. The men spent hours scaling and walking along walls, nosing around inside pumping stations and refineries, to surprise any suspect comings and goings, initial signs of acts of sabotage that it was their mission to prevent. They took notes on the numbers and activities of the watchmen and drew sketches.

At dawn they left by the entrance door. In general, nothing was asked of somebody who was leaving premises that were being watched. If they were stopped and questioned by the police, they showed Czech engineers' papers which were perfectly in order, and which justified their lack of knowledge of Rumanian. If the need arose, they would show proof of a German mother, which would explain their perfect knowledge of the German language.

One night their commander, *Feldwebel* Süss, entered the guard dormitory of a British refinery, in order to get the height of the ceiling, making his superiors whistle with admiration.

An agreement between the German and Rumanian secret services was concluded by Dr. Drögsler who came, in January 1940, with a commission of second lieutenant in the Brandenburgers, accompanied by twelve men. Surveillance teams were formed, made up of one Brandenburger and one young inspector from the *Siguranza* [1] who split up in the oil field. At the beginning they carried out small acts of sabotage carried out by British agents. The Brandenburgers, as a result of previous reconnaissance were routinely able to discover the culprit. It was generally a Rumanian, who would be arrested and punished.

1 Rumanian security police.

However, the acts of sabotage rapidly increased and production dropped. In the space of a few weeks, the enterprises had required of Great Britain several hundred redundant technicians, whose outline betrayed their membership of the British Army. By intensifying the interrogations and promising immunity to Rumanians caught red-handed, it was easy to obtain the information desired. Swiftly unmasked, the British agents were expelled in great numbers, production was restored and, every day, long trains of tank waggons left for Germany.

But soon, the flow of trains slowed up in a rather worrying way following a rash of incidents: it was discovered that sand had been poured into the axle lubricating boxes.

Each train was composed of 35 tank waggons, four of which had a surveillance cabin, where a Brandenburger dressed as a railwayman was posted. At each stop, and there were a hundred or so before Vienna, the Brandenburger jumped out to inspect the grease-boxes.

In addition, not having the same mistrust of Jews as prevailed in official circles, the Abwehr was to soon have each Brandenburger accompanied by a second Jewish false railwayman who remained hidden in the cabin. By Vienna, these covert agents were led with excellent forged papers to Trieste, from where they left for Palestine. Overcome with gratitude, they were happy to contribute to watching over the trains.

Dr. Drögsler had many strings to his bow. A jewish businessman, with good relations informed him of indiscreet conversations that he had overheard in Bucharest high society where all the threads of intrigue, from the Balkans and the Middle East, ended up. As the information that Drögsler transmitted was regularly confirmed by events, the Abwehr wanted to know the source. To reveal it would have been imprudent on the part of Drögsler, as it was hardly recommended for members of the Wehrmacht to establish relations of this nature. He procrastinated as long as possible. Eventually the order arrived from Berlin for him to come and explain himself. He went, not without anxiety. Reassured by the frank and friendly welcome of Colonel Stolze, he requested a private conversation.

Acquainted with the facts which did not oblige him to keep his superiors informed of the information obtained, the colonel approved the conduct of his subordinate and decided to cover him.

Having received carte blanche, Dr. Drögsler searched nonetheless for another source of information, less risky and more pleasant. He discovered, among the prostitutes who populated the elegant bars of the capital, an intelligent girl who spoke good English, and placed her in a brothel which was much frequented by rich British men, seemingly vested with great responsibility. The woman performed admirably and, helped by flowing champagne, became sufficiently attached to any passing lover for him to pour out his feelings to her. Each bit of information gained was fragmentary, but contributed, once put with all the others, to establish with enough clarity the plans of the enemy.

When the girl had gotten everything useful from the clientele of one house, her new protector would place her in another.

Thus the Brandenburgers could draw up a detailed card-index of more than a thousand suspects, agents or declared enemies, spread between the capital and the oil field.

During the Summer of 1940, more and more waggons, some filled with gravel and others with sand, stopped along the arrival platforms of British enterprises. There soon followed waggons of quick-setting cement. Then containers of steel balls were unloaded on the platforms of Astra Romana, the biggest oil company in Rumania, attached to the Shell group. A girl in the pay of the Germans feigning a deep-rooted hatred of the 'Huns' made one of the British guards talk about a plan of pouring concrete mixed with steel balls into the oil wells. There was no machine capable of emptying such a mixture.

Rapid action was necessary, for the materials were ready; 375 waggons of gravel and 750 of sand.

The Brandenburgers consulted each other. What weird plot could be hatched to compel the Rumanian authorities to take proceedings against the British to stop the Intelligence Service plan? An affair that the Rumanian press would exploit had to be set up! Four of the

Brandenburgers made Dr. Drögsler a proposition that left him dumbfounded. When he had recovered from his astonishment he exclaimed:

"I will never go along with this prank. I was in the First World War. You are young, it's up to you to do the Second."

The outburst of temper by the grey-templed Viennese chemist was not without reason. The plan was to murder him in his bed! Naturally, he would be moved away from it at the precise moment the bullets were to pierce through the blankets.

The four Brandenburgers, knowing that the indignation of their leader was more affected than real, were insistent. They reminded him of the gallant officer that he had been, who did not lack the self control necessary for the success of the operation. He ended up being convinced.

One evening in the month of August, the assassins stopped at 9.30 p.m. exactly in front of the house with its small garden, where *Leutnant* Drögsler who had become, for the purpose in hand, the Rumanian Dr. Luptar, had taken up residence. Two of the men took a path which led them round the back of the house, where his bedroom was situated. The third stayed at the wheel of the car which bore a false registration number, the engine ticking over, while the fourth mounted guard at the end of the street.

The doctor had, as was the custom, dined with his landlady and retired to his room at 9 p.m. He came out again at 9.20 p.m. to ask for a glass of water and then went to the toilets. All that so that it could be claimed that he was in his bed before the arrival of the assassins and that he would have escaped their bullets only by pure chance.

The Brandenburgers had studied the plan of the premises and knew exactly in which direction and at what angle they had to fire blind through the windows and the curtains. At 9.33 p.m., a hail of pistol bullets riddled the bed and the pillow of the doctor. On hearing the noise, the landlady opened her window at the front of the house, just in time to see two fleeing assassins, whose British style raincoats she could clearly distinguish in the clear moonlight, pass in front of her.

The day before, the two men had broken into the lodgings of two

British technicians when they were at work. They stole a sports shoe, to print the sole firmly in the flower beds of Dr. Luptar's garden. They were dressed in very light Burberry raincoats similar to those usually worn by the two British.

The police immediately made the connection and showed the photo of the two suspects to the landlady who naturally recognised them. The left shoe discovered in their home corresponded perfectly to the plaster mould taken from the print of the right shoe. As the search led to the discovery of prohibited weapons and ammunition, nothing could prevent the arrest of the two British men. Keen to avoid the scandal of a trial, the Rumanians followed the suggestion of the Germans and were satisfied with deporting them.

As predicted, the Rumanian press protested at the top of its voice against the impudence of these foreigners who took Rumania for a battle area where they could settle their differences.

Now they had to pass on to the next phase.

Among all the information gleaned by female informers in this month of August, two took on major importance: first, British companies send detailed plans of their installations to Egypt; second, all the directors of the oil companies had been summoned to a very secret meeting in the summer residence of Astra Romana, on Lake Snagov. These two pieces of information could not fail to strongly interest the Siguranza. Certain of their collaboration, the Germans brought them into the plan that Colonel von Lahousen, head of the *Abwehr II*, had prepared in Berlin with remarkable foresight of up coming events.

The Brandenburgers were divided into small groups and supplied with explosive cartridges and slabs of British origin. Wearing different disguises, they made their way to the nerve centres of the oil field and Lake Snagov.

British businessmen and their technical managers arrived one after the other. They were surprised to be welcomed by a group of officers in civilian clothing, some of whom, having arrived directly from London that same morning, appeared to have made themselves at home in the Astra residence.

Introductions were made, with a glass of port in hand. The man who seemed to be the commander spoke:

"Gentlemen, I am the one who summoned you. I am Colonel... shall we say Smith, on a special mission and I am fully empowered to act. Several of the officers who have been given to me as assistants are already known to you. Briefly, this is what it's about. The Germans, on pretext of the danger from the Russians, have obtained from the Rumanian government that 90 % of oil production will be reserved for them. Consequently, all of you here are currently working for the defeat of Great Britain. Our Government has decided to put an end to this intolerable situation. You know our plan, because you have already prepared to put it into operation.

"You now have at your disposal all experienced personnel necessary to block up the wells. We have calculated that three days and three nights will be required for the concrete to set. You must avoid being discovered before this time and especially before the operation begins. To this end, the enemy's attention must be diverted and their mistrust dispelled by notably increasing our production in the coming two weeks. You will be forewarned of H-Hour when the time is right. Everything is already timed down to the last second and the countdown begins today. My men will be positioned everywhere to prevent any exterior interference. Any objections?"

None were given. But the faces were pale, despite the heat which dominated the large room with its lowered curtains. For these hard-working men, these pioneers who had made this amazing industrial complex spring up out of the virgin soil, the moment was very moving. When Miller, the general manager of Astra spoke, his lower lip quivered:

"Give your orders, Sir. We will obey."

"I want to reassure you on one point," continued colonel 'Smith'. "The boats which are to repatriate you and your families are, or soon will be, alongside the quay in Constantsa. No departure must take place before the wells are blocked. That would alert the enemy and jeopardise the operation."

Robertson, the personnel manager, had a question to ask: "As far as our British employees are concerned, there are no special precautions to take. But what about the others? We have got rid of our Germans from Rumania. What do we do with the Rumanians?"

"The Rumanians, my dear fellow, will have to be kept away from the wells. From Monday start transferring posts. You will make them believe..."

At that moment one of the sentries came in hurriedly:

"The Rumanian police!"

Behind him, violating the extraterritoriality that Astra Romana had profited from until that point, six armed Rumanian officers came in preceded by Captain Stefanescu, who saluted and declared:

"I apologise for this intrusion, gentlemen. But Colonel Morusov handed me a search warrant and I am responsible for carrying it out."

Miller, holding back his anger, came forward with an affected air of calm.

"Have I the right, as manager, to know the reason for this surprising decision?"

"Certainly: smuggling of weapons, ammunition and explosives."

The British, relieved, burst out laughing:

"Go ahead, Gentlemen, feel free. Here you are in a house of glass."

The search began in the cellar. The owners were amazed to see the Rumanian police come back up with their arms loaded with revolvers, submachine-guns, explosive slabs all 'Made in England'. The search continued in the bedrooms. The Rumanians brought back yet more arms and ammunition.

"Idiots, I told them it was forbidden," muttered the manager.

Then he turned to the colonel:

"I cannot explain this discovery in the cellar. I can assure you that all this arsenal was not there before."

"What visits have you had these last few days?"

The manager went to find out from the personnel, while the Rumanians drew up the seizure report. He came back a short while later and took the colonel to one side.

"Yesterday, two countrymen in local dress came offering cakes and eggs. One of them spoke such funny English that the personnel drew rings around him in the kitchen. They let him taste some whisky, then the bottle had to be snatched out of his hands."

"Men from the Abwehr! It's written all over! While two of them were amusing your servants, the others brought weapons into the cellar by a basement window. Easily done!"

Another serious affair induced the Rumanian Government to act swiftly: Giurgiu.

The river traffic on the Danube ended at the port of Sulina, on the Black Sea. Several days after the failed assassination of Dr. Drögsler alias Luptar, the British tow-boats *Lord Byron* and *Princess Elizabeth*, followed by the French tow-boats *Ixermonde* and *Bruxelles*, as well as the British tankers *King George* and *Scotland*, made a conspicuous entry into the port.

Shortly after, a new British vessel, the cargo ship *Mardinian*, showed up at the quay side. It immediately attracted the attention of the idle yet well-fed sailors, with their shorn hair, who hung around on the quay and in the bars. The *Mardinian* was of a very average tonnage. Trained eyes had very quickly evaluated the disproportionate number of sailors who were swarming about on board. The surprise of the Rumanian employees at the customs was all the greater when the chief officer of the steamship handed him a crew list of 80 men and demanded that its cargo, made up of provisions and spare parts for cars destined for Budapest, be transferred on board canal-boats by his crew alone. He requested in addition, with a great deal of insistence, that his boat should not appear on the list of entries.

Even though the Rumanian officials had received the order not to create any difficulties for the British subjects, they refused. The chief officer offered to accompany them on board to discuss with the captain. They did this and spent several hours in the wardroom, where the steward came in with full bottles and came out with empty ones. At the end, the Rumanians left, staggering, with packets under their arms, having agreed to everything.

Immediately, tow-boats and canal-boats drew alongside the

Mardinian and the transshipment began. It was interrupted for the night and continued the following day, not without difficulty. The majority of deck sailors on the French and British boats were foreigners, from the Levant in general, and set off a sudden strike to obtain an increase in wages and better work conditions. The commanders had no time to lose and put the more querulous among them back on shore, with little hesitation, as they had receved job requests from unemployed European sailors in Sulina. They filled the vacancies and the transshipment was fortunately carried out properly before nightfall.

The flotilla did not leave before the following morning, as it was forbidden to sail on the Danube at night. She stopped at Braila without incident and twenty-four hours later at Giurgiu to spend the night. Both the British tow-boats, the canal-boats and their tankers carried out the anchoring with double anchors, as the powerful river was rising and brought pressure to bear on the hulls. The watchmen had scarcely arrived at their post when they raised the alarm. An unknown tow-boat, coming from its anchorage upriver, dragged on its anchors and, being pulled relentlessly by the current, was heading for them. On board its crew was struggling. The distress anchor was dropped, its chain broke. The inevitable collision occurred, luckily cushioned by a last-minute manoeuvre.

The commander of the *Lord Byron* identified the colliders. "Damned Germans!" But he had no choice. To avoid damaging other boats anchored down-river, he strove to put the two tow-boats side by side, the German one having been the first to fasten a cable on the British anchor chain. The crews exchanged insults, but the two ships remained stuck side by side until daylight.

The alarm and confusion which ensued enabled the crew members recruited at Sulina to have several packs passed on board the German tow-boat. Shortly after, a small motor boat was set loose and sailed to the customs quay, transporting Lieutenant Robert König, a Brandenburger, and four men from his regiment. They were part of the first troops trained by Lieutenant Kniesche who had left Bad-Vöslau at the beginning of the month of September. Once ashore they hurried towards a telephone call box. Warned in advance, the embassy of the Reich immediately transmitted the information to the Rumanian High Command who, in turn, put the authorities at Giurgiu on a state of alert.

Lieutenant König opened the packs that he had brought with him in front of the harbour master, the head of the customs and the commander of the waterways police, all three hurriedly roused from their beds.

"Gentlemen, here is what the men that we had placed on board the French and British ships extracted from the cases that the customs omitted to check at Sulina. Some revolvers, a disassembled submachine-gun, packing boxes of cartridges, one pound, a kilo, two kilos slabs, all labelled in English, an exploder... that's what we had the time to seize. I think that a formal search would give you more."

The Rumanians were dismayed, but had to carry it out. They were bound by an agreement between their Government and that of the Reich by virtue of which any foreigner, of any nationality and above all if he belonged to the diplomatic corps, would be immediately deported if he threatened the security of the State. Until then, the Rumanian authorities had sheltered behind the lack of proof. This time the Germans had brought irrefutable proof with them.

A Rumanian patrol-boat came alongside the tow-boat of the British commander of the flotilla. He was ordered open his hold hatches. All protests were useless. Armed officials occupied the gangway ladder. The cases hoisted on to the bridges were smashed open without care or attention. A complete arsenal was extracted. Now the Germans were astonished: what was such a well-stocked weapon supply to be used for?

They would never know. But it didn't matter. They had found a way of getting rid of their enemies. The reaction of the Rumanian Government was stunning. All British citizens had forty-eight hours to leave the country.

The protestations and even the threats from the British ambassador had no effect. The Red Army, on the northern border, and the Wehrmacht with its eye on the western border, spoke a more eloquent language. One thousand three hundred British subjects abandoned

Rumanian soil, to the indescribable rage of the Intelligence Service, which had planned many things, but not that the Brandenburgers would teach them a lesson. The oil supply was definitely secured. The companies remained legally British, but the British were no longer masters of the production.

The strictly military operations gave rise to the use of the Brandenburgers, naturally greater in number, in the Balkans.

From the month of March 1941, a team was sent to Bulgaria and worked in secret with the Bulgarian High Command. For military operations against Yugoslavia and Greece, only the Brandenburg Regiment's II Battalion was available, although it was short of several units that were still retained in Rumania to protect the oil fields at Ploesti and the shipping on the Danube. I and III Battalions were already preparing for the attack of the USSR.

Assembled at Bad-Vöslau, II Battalion had, without waiting, sent Siegfried Grabert's new company to the southern Carpathians to train. From there, it made its way to Bulgaria. Dressed in Bulgarian uniforms or civilian clothing, the Brandenburgers of the 8th Company hunted down the British saboteurs, like their comrades had done in Rumania.

The 6th of April, X-Day of the attack, a composite battle group commanded by Colonel Bazing and made up of engineers from the army, units from the Luftwaffe and Brandenburgers of the 5th and 7th Companies, crossed the Danube near Orsova, on the Yugoslavian border, by main force. They overran the Serbian blockhouse and command post situated on the enemy bank and prevented cargo-boats filled with cement from being sunk and blocking the Danube.

Another group prevented the destruction of the tunnel between Rosenbach in Austria and Jesenice in Yugoslavia, on the line between Villach and Ljubljana. Commanded by Second lieutenant Gebbers, it was comprised of a *Feldwebel*, a corporal and five skilled sappers. The tunnel, eight kilometres long, passed underneath a chain of mountains of an altitude of 1,600 to 1,900 metres. The mission consisted of crossing the mountains at night, emerging by surprise at the guard post at the exit of the tunnel, capturing it and defusing the charges set to blow up the vault of the tunnel.

When, after having encountered great difficulties with steep terrain and darkness, the group reached its target at dawn, captured the guard post without encountering any opposition and penetrated the tunnel, they found the vault had already collapsed and could do nothing but return to their starting point.

A team of the 8th Company, wearing Yugoslavian uniforms, seized the bridge over the Vardar River, near Axioupolis, after a short fight. Lieutenant Grabert was rewarded by the Knight's Cross of the Iron Cross, the second one in the Brandenburg units.

On the 14th of April 1941, German forces and landed Commonwealth troops faced off in Greece for the first time. But, the next day, considering themselves to be outmatched by their opponent, the British High Command ordered a retreat and re-embarkation. It was not a rout but an organised withdrawal, following a tactic used successfully by the British for centuries.

To reach Athens by Salonika, the Germans had only one road at their disposal, which, along with the railway line, went along the coast. Between the Mount Olympus and the shore, the passage was narrow. Some New Zealanders, hoping to renew the exploit of the three hundred Spartans of Leonidas at Thermopylae, 2,421 years previously, had in several days built a defensive position that posed a serious obstacle for the infantry and armor. The mountain division leading the van of the German forces resorted to an encircling movement. It sent a strong battle group into the mountains to skirt round the Mount Olympus by the west and emerge at the rear of the British, just when the main part of the division was to carry out a frontal attack.

An engineer company was designated for the operation. It had to be preceded by a reconnaissance team provided by the 8th Company and wearing a complete camouflage, in other words clothed in British uniforms that prisoners captured the day before had been wearing.

Some shepherds were requisitioned to guide the group along goat tracks. All the men were supplied with mountain boots. They needed them because, so as not to be spotted, the German column had to avoid all fires, shanties, indeed any human presence, in other words possible informers. There were no illusions to be held on this subject: the British paid swiftly and in gold.

The first hitch: the engineers had not undergone the training of the Brandenburgers. A night march in unknown and steep mountain country, with a heavy load on their backs, was a hardship that they found difficult to overcome. At the time the division attacked along the coast, the column was still five kilometres from its objective. Lieutenant Mohler, who was in command of the Brandenburgers, decided to go ahead with his team without waiting. The captain of the engineers followed him with ten of his men chosen from among the least tired. Soon, the moon shone its light on to a position of a bunker made of earth and a barbed wire entanglement, with an open field of fire.

Before attempting to penetrate it, Mohler wanted to know the strength of enemy forces that occupied it. Without losing an inch of his height, heading his men disguised as tommies, he entered a zig-zag crossing that he had discovered in the barbed wire entanglement. For thirty minutes, they covered the length of the British position, not failing to notice that a machine-gun remained pointed at them all the time. Considering themselves informed, Mohler and his men crossed the barbed wire again, then came across an enemy patrol relatively far away. Lance-corporal Siemens, born in Melbourne, felt confident enough to shout out to the New Zealanders in a friendly manner as they passed. The only answer was the patrol opening fire on them. Simultaneously, the machine-gun that had followed their movements spat out. The aim was badly off, the bullets made a caterwauling noise, ricocheting in all directions. The agility of the Brandenburgers, who dispersed and moved away climbing as quickly as lizards, meant they left no-one behind them. The coming of the night helped them.

"You must have certainly made a mistake in English," groaned the lieutenant to the lance-corporal.

He was wrong. The lance-corporal's English was perfect. But the Germans did not know that, warned against the Brandenburgers, the day before the position commander had ordered all detachments positioned beyond the barbed wire to wear a piece of tin-plate to be attached to the pocket of the battle dress blouse and a knotted handkerchief to be worn on the right arm. That's why Mohler's group had not been assailed inside the position but only on the outside.

Still far in advance, the 8th Company hoisted the flag bearing the swastika on the Acropolis.

On the 21st of April, a detachment landed on the island of Euboea, in the Gulf of Volos, to take the British from the rear. It was being used as starting base by the British so as to take a foothold again on the continent and threaten the Thermopylae Pass once again.

In May 1941, all the companies of II Battalion got back to Baden-Unterwaltersdorf.

They were reasons of a strictly military nature which induced Hitler to increase the number of his submarines or to send an expeditionary force to Africa in February 1941. For him it was not a matter of robbing the supremacy of the seas from England, nor to make the Arab world rise up against the British empire, but to have Great Britain beg for mercy by depriving it of its supplies and to prevent his ally Mussolini from suffering a defeat that would ruin the prestige of the Axis Powers.

The German cultured classes considered things differently. They were rich in men wanting to conceive a strategy on a world-wide level. Admiral Canaris was part of it. He decided to introduce agents in the Near East in order to find a way of stirring up rebellion against the British with the least risk, without spreading military operations beyond the limits of possibility. It seemed once more that the Brandenburg Regiment was not only a formation made up of battalions and companies, but also a reservoir of men from which the Abwehr drew at will for its own missions.

On the 21st of May 1941, the ' Leprosy Study Group', made up of Dr. Oberdörfer and Dr. Brandt, a simple lance-corporal who was not a doctor of medicine but an entomologist, left Berlin for Afghanistan.

Their instructions were unwritten and their cover convincing.

Making the most of the last glorious days of the German-Soviet alliance, they took the sleeper for Moscow and, after paying the ritual visit to Red Square, headed for Baku. There they boarded a steam ship which took them to the Iranian port of Pahlavi across the Caspian Sea. A taxi took them to Teheran. Brandt, familiar with the area, went to see some friends in the bazaar who rapidly found him a highly trusted taxi to take them to Kabul. They made a detour by the north to Meched, to avoid the appalling salt desert as big as France which covered the fringes of Persia at the east, and reached the border without any major incident.

Several widely spaced poles, eroded by the wind and the sand, indicated to the traveller that he was in a different country. Passports were checked at the fort which stood in the steppe 15 kilometres further on.

The commander of the fort, discovering that he had German doctors in front of him, thought that he had the whole of Western science at his feet and, keen to make the most of it, immediately found a number of minor ailments. He had his blood pressure taken, his chest sounded, throat, ears and nose looked at and his abdomen examined quite enough for a visa. He was then overwhelmed with medicines. Wild with gratitude, the commander forgot to have the doctors' luggage searched.

On arriving at Herat, the Persian driver refused to venture deeper in a country not known for its hospitality and disappeared after pocketing his dollars. A replacement driver spoke English, to the great relief of Oberdörfer, who had been very irritated by the conversations between Brandt and the previous driver in Persian.

The journey continued by Kandahar and the Germans reached Kabul on the 5th of June, where their reputation as leprosy specialists had preceded them. The Italian chargé d'affaires was waiting for them and had been advised of their desire to meet the Fakir of Ipi, considered an enemy of the British. His wife appeared to say that she had already met him and could assure the two doctors a safe escort.

Oberdörfer, without consulting his companion, accepted the

proposition with enthusiasm, which seemed to Brandt to be a bit too hasty. Also, the entomologist thought it opportune to make a trip to the bazaar where his knowledge of the language inspired confidence. It didn't take him long to learn that the wife of the Italian diplomat, who passed herself off as a White Russian, was in reality a Communist.

Brandt did not like that. And when, the next day, the woman introduced an Indian gentleman to them who claimed to be a colonel of the British Army in India who had deserted a short while before, he liked it even less. His friends in the bazaar informed him that the Indian had never been a colonel. Brandt sensed an agent provocateur but remained silent. What could he do? The officer of *Abwehr II* who had organised the mission, Captain Marwede, entrusted him to the doctor and appointed the entomologist only in the role of interpreter.

It was at this time forbidden for foreigners to leave Kabul, unless they were leaving the country. Showered with attention by the Russian woman and the false colonel, Oberdörfer spent some pleasant days and relied on his new friends for the organisation of his trip. Brandt, on the other hand, felt the urgent need to inform himself more before coming involved in such dubious company.

His knowledge of the bazaar assured him of a warm recommendation for the head of protocol, which he received with kindness. Brandt explained to him that it was impossible to carry out his research on the insects in the city. He needed to be able to circulate freely in the neighbouring mountains. He was immediately granted authorisation, to which was attached an offer of assistance, from the gendarmes, if the need arose. When Oberdörfer learnt the news, he was intensely displeased. He feared that his companion was seeking to trick him and to establish contact with the fakir without him.

The entomologist set up his tent on Koh-i Baba mountain, at an altitude of between 3,000 and 4,000 metres, and made friends with the nomadic shepherds.

He had been notified that a car was waiting for him at the foot of the mountain. The people of the bazaar had kept their word. Brandt tried hard to obtain contact with the Afridis tribe of the Khyber Pass, irreconcilable enemies of the British, from whom he thought he could learn the truth on the subject of the fakir. There was an Afridi waiting in the car next to the driver, whose mission was to take him to his tribe.

He was very well received and as soon as he named the Fakir of Ipi, he was told that the Fakir was owned by the British from whom he accepted presents and money in exchange for maintaining peace among the turbulent populations of the region. This opinion merely confirmed the rumours that he had heard on this subject in Kabul. He had reported them to his superior, without him deigning to pay attention to this ' gossip' that did not corroborate the statements of his privileged informers, the Russian and the Indian. "This time", thought Brandt, "he will have to open his eyes."

On his return to Kabul, he gave an account of what he had learnt to the doctor. The doctor drew himself up:

"The fakir is a very powerful man that the Afridis are jealous of. I forbid you to mix with them in the future."

Evidently, Oberdörfer was no more than a plaything in the hands of the Russo-Indian couple, who were used to wreck the mission entrusted by the Abwehr. It was more than likely that the doctor, who had been totally circumvented, had talked too much. Brandt therefore had to act before there was any irreparable damage. He instructed the liaison agent of the Abwehr at the German legation to send a coded message to Berlin, in which he gave an account both of what he had learnt and Oberdörfer's blunders. In short, he requested authorisation to separate himself from him. If freedom of action was granted to him, and if sufficient funds were put at his disposal, he would arm the border tribes, which is what they wanted, so as to resume combat against the British.

The officer who received the message in Berlin was unfortunately Captain Marwede, the classic example of a Prussian caricatured by Uncle Hansi, [3] with shaved head, steel-rimmed pince-nez, who lacked only a detachable celluloid collar to become a prototype. His appointment to the Abwehr seemed to be a bad joke on the part of the

3. Hansi (1872-1951) was a famous Alsatian writer and caricaturist.

personnel branch. The captain was staggered that a simple lance-corporal dared to contest against the reports of the eminent doctor, the head of the detachment and of international reputation. He put the message in the bin and sent to Brandt the threatening order to put himself at the doctor's disposal without protest, or risk being brought before the court-martial on his return.

In mid-July, the Russian and the Indian assembled the unit which was to accompany the two Germans. Brandt wanted the voyage to be carried out by car. It was not the doctor who replied, but the Indian 'colonel'. He confirmed that all roads leading to the border were surveyed by the gendarmes and they would not let any vehicle past.

"Besides", he added "no foreigner can leave the town, it's forbidden. We'll have to go by foot and walk throughout the night."

"What fairy tale is this you're telling me?" replied Brandt curtly. "I have a permit in my pocket and I can obtain another one tomorrow for our cars, valid to the border town of Khowst, south of Ghazni, which would suit us well."

Oberdörfer, disconcerted, pulled the 'colonel' to one side to speak to him alone. He returned, sure of himself:

"Your suggestion is unrealistic. We will go by foot, as our friend suggested."

After a succession of arduous and unnecessary night marches, the group reached the border near Khowst. Just when they were crossing it, Brandt was ordered to follow the Indian's advice to lay out the camp in open ground, surrounded on all sides by fallen rocks, forming veritable labyrinths. Brandt was a little reassured by the proximity of a fort occupied by the gendarmes. Suddenly, he saw their guide disappear among the rocks. As he was heading towards the doctor to inform him of this strange behaviour, gunfire broke out, dominated by bursts from a machine-gun, and a hail of bullets ricocheted on the rocks, sending off deadly splinters. As he threw himself on the ground, Brandt was hit by a bullet in the thigh and a fragment of rock split his scalp and some small splinters of rock embedded themselves in his face. He managed to climb up and take cover between two rocks. Oberdörfer did not follow him. He stayed on the ground, unconscious and losing blood.

Soon after, some individuals disguised as gendarmes and brandishing weapons suddenly appeared from all sides and stripped the bodies that lay on the ground. They took everything except their shirts. Brandt was covered with blood; they thought he was dead and were going to strip him as well, when a cry rang out. They fled like a flock of birds. The gendarmes, the real ones, had heard gunfire and had come running.

The two wounded Europeans were transported as far as the road. A car took them to Kabul at top speed. One man, possibly an ambulance man, accompanied them. He leant towards Brandt and murmured:

"For you it's not serious. But your friend has bullets through his chest and stomach; he won't make it to the hospital alive."

After one hour of driving and all the jolts and bumps, he leaned forward again over the injured man:

"He's dead."

Brandt was taken to the Turkish hospital and operated on immediately. Thirty-five splinters were taken from his scalp and face.

The two Germans had been taken to Afghanistan got up as a *Major* and a *Hauptmann* and they had been provided with uniforms adorned with the insignia of these two ranks, so if captured by the British, they would have been treated as prisoners and not as spies.

Oberdörfer had his uniform put back on for burial.

In Berlin nobody understood what had happened.

At the same time as this timid attempt, the *Abwehr II* planned some larger operations aimed at both Iraq, whose Government showed itself to be openly pro-German, and Iran, whose population wanted to free themselves from British domination. The obvious course was to organise underground unrest by means of small teams of agents, who would receive weapons delivered by air or sea.

Overall coordination of the operation had to be assured by a special staff commanded by an officer of the Luftwaffe familiar with the theatre of operations, *General der Flieger* Felmy.

On the 3rd of July 1941, a special fighting formation was created, the *Sonderverband 288*, to be sent to go to the Near East via Syria after German forces occupied the Caucasus. The Brandenburg Regiment participated in the preparations by assigning the Lieutenant Fendt's 11th Company, largely composed of Arabic speaking Germans from Palestine, henceforth organically allotted to the *Sonderverband* as 1st Company.

Once again however, nothing went off as planned. The No. 288 Special Formation was to be transported to Greece, prior to going to North Africa where in 1942 it would become an ordinary *Panzergrenadier* regiment.

Chapter IX
Operation Barbarossa
(Summer 1941)

In April 1941, the regimental units of the *Lehr-Regiment Brandenburg* were finally organised. To the twelve companies of the three battalions already in existence was added the 13th 'Special' Company in Brandenburg, the 14th (Replacement) Company, the 16th 'Light' Company at Düren and the 17th Company, also 'special', at Baden. Another unit was created at the Zossen camp and temporarily took the name of its commanding officer, Lieutenant Trommsdorf. Lastly, a training company was set up at the camp at Meseritz near Frankfurt/Oder. In mid-May, the 1st Company of the regiment, which was still acting as a recruit processing unit, was amalgamated with the regimental HQ Company and the *V-Leute* Company of *Abwehr II*.

At the conclusion of the Balkan campaign, each one of the three battalions disposed of only three ready companies out of four. At II Battalion under Major Paul Jacobi, the 5th Company, just back from Rumania, was reorganised at Bad-Vöslau. At III Battalion, commanded by Captain Franz Jacobi, brother of Paul, Lieutenant Fendt's 11th Company was based at Düren. All the other combat companies were ordered to the East where a huge offensive was being prepared in utmost secrecy for the end of the month of June. Hitler had had to delay his entry into war against the Soviets to fly to the aid of

137

his Italian ally in the Balkans. He had just three months of fine weather ahead of him to wipe out the enemy forces. Little time to occupy a territory two or three times more extensive than that of Germany by force and neutralise three hundred divisions. They had to move quickly and seize the lines of communication before the enemy had the time to cut them during its retreat. The Brandenburgers were flown in for this purpose. The two Powers, which had been allied only by the interests of the moment against Poland, did not trust each other. On each side, German and Russian divisions were massed, ready for the offensive.

I Battalion under *Major* Heinz was deployed in Army Group South's operational zone, and II Battalion in Army Group Centre's zone. Each battalion delegated a liaison officer to the corresponding army group.

The 10th Company, III Battalion under Lieutenant Aretz, was transported from Düren, in the Rhineland, to Suwalki, in the north of Poland, just several days before the beginning of Operation 'Barbarossa'. It assembled in the Plaska forest, several kilometres from the German-Russian demarcation line.

Ahead of Suwalki, roads and railway lines met up with the Bobr River, a tributary of the Narew which flowed into the Vistula down-river from Warsaw. There were eight bridges to seize. To this end, the company formed eight combat teams with the remaining troops following in a second echelon.

Unteroffizier Zöller was not part of the operation. He was sickened by this and opened his heart to two men of his half-company, Ottmann and Wagner, who shared the same sentiment.

"There is a small bridge at Siolko", said Ottmann "which is not mentioned in the plan of attack. It's an oversight that needs correcting."

Zöller, who saw where he was leading, restated the question.

"Have you seen Lieutenant Aretz's map? This bridge is not even ten metres long. It's a small bridge above a path. It won't even be guarded. That's why it has been left out."

"But if the Russians destroy this bridge", Wagner intervened, "the supply trains from Augustovo to Grodno will be blocked for at least forty-eight hours. It has to be taken beforehand."

"Without orders?" exclaimed Zöller.

"Not exactly", specified Ottmann. "Our orders are to advance after the combat teams of the company. Our itinerary leads to the bridge at Lipsk. Lieutenant Kriegsheim, the commander of our 1st Half-Company, is in charge of it. Our bridge is very near there, a little to the east. *So, Herr Unteroffizier?*"

Zöller agreed. When the rumbling sound of the guns awoke everyone along the entire front on the 22nd of June at 3.05 a.m., the three men were already up and equipped. They helped themselves to surplus Russian blouses and side-caps from the unit train of the company and made a small package out of them which was carried underarm. One last scruple pushed Zöller to announce to his *Feldwebel* that he was leaving as part of the vanguard. The *Feldwebel,* who could not imagine that an NCO could act without orders, assented.

The three men marched at a good pace and soon reached the road from Skieblevo to Rudovka. Before stepping out on to it, they slipped the Russian blouses over their German uniforms and put on the caps with the red star. In the clear night, their silhouette was credible. They followed the road towards the east, to take the branch road for Lipsk, leaving Rudovka on their left. The light of dawn allowed them to use their binoculars to cast an eye on the outskirts of the village that they had to leave behind them.

"Wonderful!" whispered Zöller. "A car stuck in the mud. Some Russkis are trying to get it out. There are six of them. Come on, it's ours."

The three men approached, half running, half walking. The Russians waved cheerily from afar. They had already got the car back on the road.

"Feuer frei!" ordered Zöller "Aim well above their heads."

More surprised than anything else, the six Russians abondoned the car.

"And now," said the NCO as he got into the car, "we are going to take the bridge at Siolko!"

They drove off, initially unaware that they were a perfect target for their own infantry, who were half an hour behind them. The road now passed through a wood.

"Not too fast", said Wagner, "we'll catch up with the lieutenant!"

On reaching the railway line, they took a left turn on to the road running parallel to the track, which led them directly to their bridge. With pride, they realized that they could be the first Brandenburgers to take a bridge by car. This thought intoxicated them a little. They could already feel the Iron Crosses on their chests. They wanted to sing, shout and hurl insults at the millions of cowards who, at that very moment, were snoring in their beds.

"The bridge!" they cried out in unison.

The little iron bridge which straddled across their path seemed to be less than two hundred metres away. It had not been abandoned; twenty or so Russian soldiers were still hanging around in a disorganised manner. Zöller slowed down. What could they do? He thought he would have to be daring and go right up to them without firing and summon them to give themselves up. Perhaps that's what they were expecting. But, at that moment, his two companions stood up in the car and opened fire on the Russians with their submachine-guns.

It was a stupid act, resulting from their intense excitement, as they were out of range. And none of them had seen an antitank gun, in a firing position, carefully camouflaged in the ditch. The car took a direct hit from a shell. Zöller landed unconscious in a neighbouring wheat field. When he regained his senses, he saw the car smashed up, with pools of blood and the lifeless bodies of his two men. The Russians did not come near. They must have thought they were all dead.

The NCO was surprised to feel no pain. He slowly moved his limbs, trying not to sit up. He wasn't imagining it, he had no injuries. So an animal instinct pushed him to crawl towards the wreck of the car that he could reach from the side opposite the enemy. A ripped door was hanging off. He moved his arm forward, grabbed a rifle stuck between two seats and went back to hide in the field.

At that moment the Russians opened fire. They must have seen him. But how could they find a man in a field of green wheat?

When Zöller reached the edge he could see the bridge less than one hundred metres away. All the Russians had gone onto it to get a view from above, but saw nothing. The German NCO managed to drop five or six men, just as if he was at the rifle range. Between two rifleshots, he changed position and his adversaries only managed to shoot down ears of wheat. Discouraged, they scattered.

Corporal Zöller took proud possession of the bridge.

Meanwhile, Second lieutenant Herbert Kriegsheim, commander of the 1st Half-Company, accomplished his own mission. He set out by car at the same time as the other teams, before daybreak. He was sitting next to his driver, Lance-corporal Fischer. On the back seat, another lance-corporal, Kochs, kept the guide interpreter company, a young Polishman whose heart was in his boots. Their disguise was very rudimentary, just a Russian greatcoat thrown over the shoulders and a side-cap.

The *Pkw* jolted along on the log road that the engineers had built through the sodden undergrowth of the Plaska forest. It was not easy for the suspension of the car to follow the ups and downs of such a roadway.

"My suspension springs!" groaned Fischer.

They stopped, as a large branch of a tree blocked the road. Two officers came out of the thicket.

"Are you from the Brandenburg Regiment?"

"Of course", replied Kriegsheim impatiently.

Then turning to the driver while the two other passengers got out:

"Turn back and get your precious car under cover."

"I wish you good luck, *Herr Leutnant*."

"Come back safe and sound!"

Without further ado the driver offered his hand. Kriegsheim shook it cordially and smiled.

The two officers, shocked with this display of familiarity, wondered:

"Are you an officer?"

"Yes, *Herr Major:* Second lieutenant Kriegsheim, 10th Company."

"Well, I am the *Ia.*[1] Follow me, I will lead you to the zig-zag passage."

1. An officer of the General Staff Corps in charge of operations in a formation staff.

As they walked, the major gave him several injunctions: "Don't forget: do not open fire under any circumstances before 3.05 a.m. By the way, what is your password?"

"Our password? 'Vöklabruck'. Don't you know?"

"What a question! Well, off you go and good luck!"

They crossed the barbed wire entanglement. Behind them the major shook his head.

Kriegsheim was furious.

"Nobody knows our password and everybody is going to take potshots at us like Bolsheviks. To tell the truth, what a word they have chosen: Vöklabruck!"

"Not such a bad choice", replied Fischer. "The Russians will have difficulty pronouncing it, *Herr Leutnant*. But that doesn't tell us what their password is. What do we reply if a sentry asks us?"

"We couldn't find out. The important thing is to say something. That worked once in Germany. You will reply coldly 'Astrakhan' instead of me. My Russian is not very good."

With one gesture, the officer stopped his men. He wanted to check their direction using the compass.

"Slightly more to the left! Forward!"

Two dark silhouettes stood up in front of them:

"*Stoi! Parol!*" (Halt! Password!)

"Astrakhan!"

"*Niet!*"

A stroke of bad luck. They were frontier guards of the NKVD and they had their rifles trained on them. They could have acted, but orders were orders. No firing before 3.05 a.m. They could do nothing other than put their hands on their heads and start marching in the direction indicated.

Kriegsheim thought feverishly. If they were unmasked, they had every chance of getting a bullet in the back of the neck. If they could get rid of their guards before, only a few gunshots would be heard in the night and the enemy would not be able to draw any conclusions. Orders, sometimes, are open to interpretation. The Brandenburgers are not like other soldiers!

At peace with his officer's conscience, the lieutenant waited for the right moment.

He now saw where they were being led: a low isba from under whose door filtered a ray of light. Once inside, they would be searched. So, there was to be no hesitation.

Risking all, the officer plunged a hand under his greatcoat and got out the pistol from the holster that he wore on his belt. In a single movement, he turned round opening his greatcoat with his left hand to show his German field blouse, while he pushed off his Russian cap. Less than two seconds had elapsed between the beginning of his movement and the report of the cartridge which then lodged a 9-mm bullet right in the face of the nearest frontier guard. The second Russian, who had his weapon at his hip, straightaway fired at random. The bullet hit the ground between Kriegsheim's legs who in turn opened fire once again. Hit in the shoulder, the Russian dropped his rifle and opened his mouth to shout out. But, before the slightest sound emerged, a second bullet knocked through his teeth and entered his skull.

Prisoners less than ten seconds ago, now free, the four men looked at one another, dumbfounded. At their feet, lay two dark motionless forms.

A whistle. A flare lit up the sky. With several leaps, the Brandenburgers threw themselves underneath the bushes which bordered a nearby brook. The little Pole moaned.

"The Russians are going to come with their dogs, *Herr Leutnant.* The NKVD always have them. There's no escape."

"*Maul zu!*" (Shut up!), ordered Kriegsheim brutally.

Other flares went up in the sky. A harsh light made the trees, the curve of a field, the jagged edge of a wood, the clear line of a path suddenly leap out from the darkness. Gun-shots cracked, a machine-gun rattled out. Then suddenly, silence.

Lieutenant Kriegsheim was puzzled. The whole sector was alerted.

"Listen, *Kerle.* It is no longer possible to reach our objective without being discovered. We're going to wait for the artillery preparation before setting off again."

And then, suddenly, there was an enormous, powerful rumbling of thousands of guns and howitzers. Instinctively, the four men ducked down, even though the shells were passing very high above them.

The shelling was brief. It stopped suddenly during daylight. The officer gave the signal to depart.

The four men started marching in the direction of Skieblevo, when, on their left, set a little further back, they saw a group of German riflemen emerge.

"It's the vanguard", noted Kriegsheim, without realising that he and his men were wearing Russian uniforms.

But what are these *Schützen* doing? They have brought a light machine-gun into action and they are opening fire.

"Get down!" shouted Kriegsheim.

The order came too late. Fischer and the Pole had already fallen. An officer and several men rushed up, their rifles sighted. Kriegsheim shouted "Vöklabruck!" at the top of his lungs. The soldiers put up their weapons and the officer approached, confusion written all over his face.

"You idiots", cried Kriegsheim. "Do you want to kill us?"

"Are you Brandenburgers? How could we know? When we saw those uniforms, we fired."

The little Polishman groaned. The stretcher-bearers arrived, put him onto a stretcher and carried him off. Kochs leaned over his comrade, who lay motionless on the ground.

"They hit him. It's finished. Remove all the Soviet clothes, otherwise they'll put him in a potter's field with the Russians."

There were only two of them left. The mission remained nonetheless imperative and so they set off. Some isbas from Skieblevo gave off heavy gunfire. The wood was thicker and enabled them to progress rapidly without being seen. They came out onto a road, but did not know if Lipsk was on their right or on their left. Seeing two Soviet soldiers crouching behind a low wall, Kochs went directly over to them and asked them casually where Lipsk was. With indifference, one of them raised his arm to indicate a fork in the road several hundred metres away. Then, seeming to revive himself, the Russian asked anxiously: "Have you seen any Fascists? Are they coming this way?"

144

Kochs shrugged his shoulders and went back to the lieutenant. The road snaked through flowered fields, occasionally with a small house on the edge. Small groups of Russian soldiers surged back, in total disarray. Nobody paid any attention to their German weapons. With sweat on their brow, they suddenly came to a main road, certainly the one between Augustovo and Grodno. It was packed with bigger groups of Russian soldiers, who were also withdrawing towards the east. The two Germans let themselves be dragged along by the human tide, which soon split into two, and one part of the *Frontoviks* forked off to the right. It was the way to Lipsk. The two Brandenburgers followed them. They reached the large wooden bridge straddling the Bobr, still absolutely intact, where there were disordered columns of crowded withdrawing troops. Without having to consult each other, each one followed a guardrail, from which they could lean over to try and locate the destruction device. But the human tide pushed them forward. At the exit of the bridge, they sat down on the dusty grass verge. Without turning his head, Kriegsheim murmured:

"I didn't see anything on my side."

"Not on mine either."

"Any sentries?"

"Didn't see any."

"Good, we'll wait."

As the columns became less and less frequent, the two men ventured once again onto the bridge. They passed a few stragglers who were running, while planes rumbled overhead at low altitude. Some isbas must have been burning somewhere, as gusts of acrid smoke swept over the bridge. Rifle-fire burst out on the main road. Kriegsheim was worried. They expected to see enemy sappers surge forward at any moment. How could only two men neutralise them?

His fears were justified. Coming from Lipsk across the fields, appeared a large platoon which was heading in column directly towards the bridge. Half of the men were carrying ten-litre petrol cans.

"That's it. They've come to burn the bridge."

Kriegsheim was livid. He threw himself, along with Kochs into a hollow, on the edge of which they positioned their submachine-

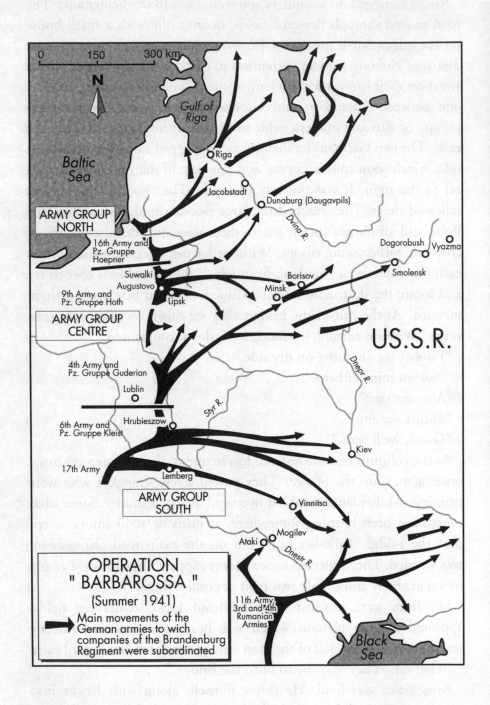

0   150   300 km

N

Baltic
Sea

Gulf of
Riga

Riga

Jacobstadt

Dunaburg (Daugavpils)

Dvina R.

Dogorobush   Vyazma

ARMY GROUP
NORTH

16th Army and
Pz. Gruppe
Hoepner

Suwalki
Augustovo

9th Army and
Pz. Gruppe Hoth

Lipsk

Minsk

Borisov

Smolensk

ARMY GROUP
CENTRE

4th Army and
Pz. Gruppe Guderian

Lublin

U.S.S.R.

Dnepr R.

Styr R.

6th Army and
Pz. Gruppe Kleist

Hrubieszow

17th Army

Lemberg

Kiev

Vinnitsa

ARMY GROUP
SOUTH

Mogilev

Ataki

Dnestr R.

OPERATION
" BARBAROSSA "
(Summer 1941)

Main movements of the
German armies to wich
companies of the Brandenburg
Regiment were subordinated

11th Army
3rd and 4th
Rumanian
Armies

Black
Sea

146

guns. The Russian officer had seen them and with one gesture deployed his men in extended order. The Germans waited until they were within effective range before opening fire. The Russians, lying flat on their bellies, retaliated. Their bullets hit the ground around the two Brandenburgers.

"I'm out of cartridges", announced Kochs.

Then he opened his hands, dropped his submachine-gun and collapsed.

"Kochs!" shouted the *Leutnant*.

He slid towards his injured comrade. From the road, bursts of machine-gun fire suddenly swept across the area. The Russians ran to the banks of the river for shelter, downwards from the bridge.

Kriegsheim gently lifted his companion to lay him on his back. A Mongolian soldier, who was also preparing to go down to the river bank, turned back and came to strike him with his bayonet. The blade hit him behind the ear and penetrated his neck. Kriegsheim collapsed, unconscious.

The German infantry now occupied the bridge. The two Brandenburgers were discovered by stretcher-bearers. Lance-corporal Kochs was dead. The lieutenant was lifted up and placed in a car, after a medical orderly had carefully bandaged his head and neck. The driver was nervous. He did not recognise the way. On reaching the main road, instead of turning left, they turned right, in the direction of Siolko.

The injured man had opened his eyes.

"Eh! Where are you taking us?"

The driver, clinging to the steering wheel, was red with shame and did not reply.

Kriegsheim made an effort and questioned him again.

"Has this road already been cleared?"

Obtaining no answer, he leaned once again against the back of the seat, and closed his eyes. The driver, relying on his lucky star, continued in the same direction. He overtook some infantry troops who where progressing towards the front in the ditches. There was a bend in the road and, suddenly, the driver saw an antitank gun aimed at him. He braked sharply. The wounded man held on with both hands as he was thrown forward. Two Russian soldiers lay dead on the road. Two stooping German soldiers approached. An NCO edged his way towards the car and shouted angrily:

"*Du Dummkopf!* The Russians are just behind the bridge!"

Then, seeing the shoulder straps of the injured man who had opened his eyes:

"My apologies, *Herr Leutnant.* We're on the point here. Don't stay exposed."

They helped Kriegsheim to get down in the ditch, where he made himself as comfortable as he could. His wounds were hurting him, but he could speak without pain provided he didn't move his jaw. He raised his eyes to thank the *Feldwebel* and saw in front of him, crouched down in the same ditch, two *Landsers* who seemed to be watching over a Russian prisoner in the same position.

The Russian prisoner had seen the officer and lowered his eyes. But Kriegsheim started. He stared at him intensely:

"Zöller, you're not alone? Where are the others?"

The Russian moved his lips without emitting a sound. He seemed in a state of shock. At last he managed to express himself in a toneless voice:

"There, on the road, *Herr Leutnant.* Wagner and Ottmann, dead, a *Pak* shell."

Then he placed his chin on his fists and his gaze became lost in the emptiness.

"He's speaking German now?" cried the *Feldwebel.* "What does that mean?"

Perturbed, the two soldiers got up and their gaze passed from the NCO to the wounded man.

"That means 'Völklabruck'", replied Kriegsheim.

"Völklabruck? Yes, I've heard that word several times, but I'll be damned if I remember when and why."

Kriegsheim muttered:

"What stupidity, my God, what damned stupidity!"

A rifle shot rang out, followed by a fusillade. The *Feldwebel* jumped

148

on to the roadway and took the two soldiers who were guarding the Brandenburgers with him. The second lieutenant and the NCO were left alone.

"Zöller, why are you here? Have you no mission to carry out today?"

Zöller looked at him, in despair, and turned his head towards the road.

"It's all my fault, *Herr Leutnant.*"

The gunfire stopped, the *Feldwebel* reappeared:

"They were simply covering their withdrawal, *Herr Leutnant.*"

Then, referring to Zöller:

"*So*, was it a Russki?"

"No", replied the lieutenant wearily. "Didn't you know that the Brandenburgers were committed round here?"

The *Feldwebel* shrugged his shoulders:

"We were told so many things at reveille, what we must do, what we mustn't do. We're a bit lost."

Kriegsheim turned towards the other NCO.

" Zöller, you left to fight against the Soviets on your own?"

The NCO got up and slowly, took off his Russian blouse. His German uniform appeared, against which the black, white and red of the ribbon of his Iron Cross, 2nd Class stood out clearly. He fought his exhaustion, came to attention, raised his head:

"Combat Team Zöller, one NCO, two men. Siolko bridge taken from the enemy. Losses: two killed."

Out of the eight bridges that 10th Company had to seize on the 22nd of June, five were taken without combat. The road bridge and the railway bridge situated to the north of Augustovo had been taken by Lieutenant König's team. König was killed. Rennkamp had failed at Holynka bridge, which blew up in front of his eyes.

Several days later, the 10th Company was at Minsk. Then it moved to Borisov. It did not reach Düren before October.

Subordinated to Army Group South, I Battalion prepared for its missions at Zakopane, in the High Tatra, until the 15th of June.

The 3rd Company under Lieutenant Werner John was committed separately, subordinated to the III Armoured Corps. On the 21st of June, it took possession of two bridges over the Bug River. On the 29th, it set up a bridgehead on the Styr River. In August, it seized some new bridges on the Dnepr, at Kiev, and did not rejoin Brandenburg until the end of that month, the last battalion to do so.

The two other companies of I Battalion reached Lvov, accompanied by a battalion of Ukrainian volunteers named 'Nachtigall'. The first to discover the summary executions perpetrated by the NKVD in the prison of the town, the Ukrainians took possession of the broadcasting station to proclaim an Ukrainian Free State. Following which, the Nachtigall Battalion was rapidly disbanded.

In July, the 2nd Company, under Captain Dr. Hartmann, scouted an attack route for the 4th Mountain Division. It was stopped by artillery in the village of Ljudowka and had to dig in. The following morning it was ordered to storm the Russian trenches protecting the east of the village. An attack was carried out under automatic weapon and mortar fire. The company stormed the position with fixed bayonets and entrenching tools. The position was rushed and the enemy pushed back to the neighbouring woods, but with catastrophic losses including twenty-eight dead, fifty wounded and all the officers killed except one. The company was sent to its home base to be re-formed. What did it matter, after that, if the Russians had left one hundred dead and wounded on the ground?

The Leutnant Lütke's parachute platoon, assigned to the 4th company, was also committed separately. Jumping on the 25th of June, the Brandenburger parachutists captured two railway bridges on the line linking Lida to Molodechno.

At Major Paul Jacobi's II Battalion, the 6th Company under Lieutenant Meissner took the bridges over the Dnestr intact, then marched to Crimea as the vanguard of the 22nd Infantry Division. It was not to leave the Eastern Front before the Summer of 1942.

8th Company, that Siegfried Grabert had temporarily left to Lieutenant Wolfram Knaak and that he took back on the 26th of June when Knaak was killed by the enemy, constituted three combat teams which preceded the *Panzergruppe Hoepner*. One of them had the mission of seizing the bridge over the Dvina in the town of Jacobstadt.

On the 28th of June, *Feldwebel* Werner's team was crammed into a Russian lorry, at the head of the columns of the 1st *Panzerdivision*. It needed to reach the bridge and cross it so as to cut the ignition wires without being unmasked. Standing on the footboard, Corporal Purwin, a native of the country and a Russian speaker, had put on a Russian uniform. He was to reply to any possible questions.

A sidecar, transporting a mortar, followed the lorry. The motorcyclist had kept his German uniform. Even though he was hidden by the bulk of the lorry, this was an extreme careless act. The Brandenburgers, whose repeated successes from the beginning of the Russian campaign had gone to their heads, had become foolhardy.

At the entrance to the bridge, the lorry had to stop in front of an unexpected obstacle, a barricade made out of paving stones and probably mined. It was at this point that the Russians smelt subterfuge. They opened up with very heavy gunfire, antitank weapons in support of small weapon fire. The Germans hastily abandoned their vehicle and dived to the bank of the river below the level of the road. Bullets mowed many of them down as they jumped from the lorry.

Only two escaped without a scratch: the driver, who pretended to be dead, and Werner who was extremely lucky.

Werner had scarcely hit the ground when he saw two Russians fire at him with a submachine-gun and come out of their hole to jump on him. Realising that he had not been hit, he shot them down with bursts from his own submachine-gun and jumped in their hole, only to see a young Russian officer coming to the aid of his men. He fired first, the Russian fell and his submachine-gun jammed. He stood up to clean it with his handkerchief, then put in a new magazine and sat down again, his weapon on his knees.

He risked taking a glance from time to time. Five Russians passed several metres away from him. Once again he heard Russian voices very near. There was a long silence, followed by an unbelievable noise and then pieces of steel and bits of masonry fell in a heavy rain: the bridge had been blown up. Werner, who had had too many brushes with death that day, flopped down into his narrow refuge. The moans of a comrade, who was dying slowly from a throat wound not ten metres away, added to his malaise. If he left would he be killed? One hour passed, then two. His mind empty, he waited. He thought of the cattle that he had seen at the abattoir stupidly waiting for death. Suddenly, he heard the sound of tank tracks.

Russians?

That was impossible as the bridge had exploded. He bucked up. A quick glance revealed the black uniform of a German tank crew member who had got out of his Panzer to help an injured man. He emerged from his hole and headed towards the tanks. Before leaving with them, he counted the dead: fourteen. His entire team was to lay there forever, even the driver who must have been killed trying to escape.

Marshal von Leeb, commander of Army Group North, spoke very highly of the Brandenburgers of the 8th Company in his Order of the Day of the 17th of July. The company was 80 kilometres from Leningrad at the end of the same month.

At the III Battalion under Major Franz Jacobi, the Lieutenant Kniesche's 9th Company did not reach the front before September. It marched as a vanguard of the SS Reich [2] Division and remained on the Eastern Front until the Summer of 1942, like the 6th Company.

11th Company, staying at Düren, was withdrawn from the Brandenburg Regiment in July to be allotted to the *Sonderstab Felmy*. [3]

2. Ex-*SS-Verfügungsdivision*, it was not to take the name '*Das Reich*' before May 1942.
3. See chapter VIII.

152

12th Company under Lieutenant Schader seized a bridge over the Bug, then cleared the way for the Guderian's tanks. It did not return to Düren before the end of August.

In September, Captain Benesch's 16th Light Company took part in a combined operation against the island of Ösel, in the Baltic.

It neutralised a Russian battery in the south of the island and lost eleven men.

Chapter X
Chase in Finland
(Summer 1942)

On the 26th of June 1941, Finland, anxious to free itself from the Soviet threat, entered the war alongside the Reich. As a result, the forces of the Wehrmacht were to support the Finnish Army.

Between June and September 1941, the repeated attacks of the German *Gebirgskorps Norwegen* in the north, linked to those of the Finnish Army further south, failed to reach their objectives. The dogged resistance of the Russians was not the only cause of this failure. It became evident to the German Command that the main obstacle was geographical. Immense stretches of territory devoid of lines of communication, dotted with lakes, crisscrossed with dangerous streams and rivers, covered with thick snow in winter, but infested with mosquitoes in summer, could not be conquered without meticulous preparation and tactical measures adapted for the purpose.

In January 1942 the Lapland Army was created, entrusted to General Eduard Dietl. The General now had a light company of Brandenburgers commanded by Lieutenant Trommsdorf at his disposal. Formed in the spring of 1941 on the training area at Zossen, to the south of Berlin, it remained for reasons of secrecy 'Trommsdorf Company', even though it was ranked fifteen among the companies of the Brandenburg Regiment. From October to December, Trommsdorf trained 80 to 90 men that he had chosen himself with care.

Among their number were to be found explosives and river navigation specialists from the engineers, as well as dog-handlers, wireless operators, medical orderlies and riflemen. They all had one thing in common, they were all highly skilled skiers and there was even an Olympic champion among them. Their polar equipment was impeccable. For the winter, they had Finnish *akjas* pulled by dogs. For the approach, they had two or three trucks and four *Kübelwagen*. In addition to the standard weaponry of the infantry, they had received a 75-mm recoilless gun and several sniper rifles. Naturally, almost all these soldiers were from Alpine regions.

They were now settled in a forest encampment near Rovaniemi, HQ of the new Lapland Army, one hundred kilometres to the north of the southernmost tip of the Gulf of Bothnia. In this high latitude, it was cold and dark. General Dietl was impatient to judge for himself this new company's abilities. He arrived without warning and inspected the ranks, standing at attention in two lines in snow that reached well above their ankles.

The general, himself a native of Upper Bavaria, discovered once again the angular profiles of the country men of his childhood underneath the visors of the mountain caps. As was his custom, he spoke to them in a Tyrolean or Bavarian dialect.

Then, he ordered a combat exercise to be carried out on the treacherous surface of a frozen lake. It took place not without a few incidents which revealed an insufficient knowledge with the land among the men. He turned towards Lieutenant Trommsdorf and said ironically:

"*So*, the Berliners have come to give us a demonstration of the guerrilla warfare in Lapland? Lieutenant, before imagining you can win your laurels, your company must first of all get accustomed to the country."

The officer's face turned into every hue, but he understood. Thirty Finnish auxiliaries henceforth accompanied the Brandenburgers in the field. They taught them to bivouac in temperatures of 40 degrees below, to build huts with fallen branches and to cover them with snow and then that the flame from one candle would be enough to

156

render them habitable, to make log fires that would last eight hours. The Brandenburgers threw themselves into nighttime reconnaissances on skis, using compasses, over 30, 40 or even 50 kilometres, with a pack of 30 kilos. They learnt how to harness and drive reindeer and to drink their daily dose of cod liver oil, while pinching their nose.

On the 6th of April 1942, they considered themselves to be ready. They were ordered to take part in a new operation set up by General Schörner's HQ, commander of the XIX Mountain Corps. The OKW had indeed drawn certain conclusions from the failure of the attacks of 1941 against Murmansk, the only port free of ice in all seasons in the Arctic Ocean, from where a railway line, called the 'Murman line', conveyed the supplies provided by the Allies in the lend-lease agreement to the USSR.

No frontal attack against this line was possible. Wherever troops had taken the offensive, they had been beaten. The enemy had the advantage of numbers and made use of short and rapid supply lines. The Lapland Army, in position inside the Arctic Circle, from then on restricted itself to a purely defensive stand. The Finnish, to the south, did the same. The bombing raids of the 5th *Luftflotte* had not produced the desired results either, as the damage caused by the bombs was always repaired within twenty-four or forty-eight hours. That is why it was thought that only the use of lighter formations, sent out unexpectedly in the hinterland in the direction of the railway line, would succeed. The operation was rendered possible by a 70 kilometre breach opened in the front inside the Arctic Circle, where the two enemies had set up only isolated strongholds.

There are 300 kilometres as the crow flies between Rovaniemi and the first Russian points on the Lutto River, which flowed to Kola and Murmansk. There the Brandenburgers had to join a battalion of mountain infantry, the *Gebirgsjäger-Regiment 136* III, commanded by Captain Stampfer, whose task it was to destroy the Russian strong points. A Finnish detachment in charge of fighting against enemy mobile units was to join them. Together they would form a *Kampfgruppe*, a battle group.

The Trommsdorf Company had to carry out an in-depth infiltration on the Russian rear to prevent them from accessing to supplies at the main depot at Ristikent, to the south-west of Murmansk.

When the Brandenburgers arrived on the Lutto, only the bodies of Russians and Germans occupied the position. The *Gebirgsjäger* battalion had not waited for them and had faded away into the trees.

Moreover, the weather centres had not come up to standard concerning the forecasts. The wind started to blow from the south, and the snow melted. Water flowed from everywhere and soaked the men to the skin. Building huts covered with snow was now of no use to them. They were stuck up to their knees in icy mud. It was impossible to make a fire. They ate their potted meat cold and standing up.

At night, it froze again and they lay on the ice, shivering with cold. Their tireless Finnish guide, a small, wrinkled man, seemed to have lost his self-confidence. He constantly hesitated on which road to follow. It started to snow heavily once again. The company doctor increased the number of pervitin injections to avoid frostbite in the feet and fingers. By the third day, they were out of rations. After another night of suffering, the snow started again. The doctor stayed at the head of the column. He encouraged those men who were collapsing and helped them up. Some of them said: "What does it matter if we die here or a little further on!" However, for a piece of chocolate they were ready to set off again.

Three or four times a day, Lieutenant Trommsdorf let off a red signal-light. The sky, grey and heavy, remained silent. The wireless operator had managed to drag his portable transmitter-receiver set. That night, for the fourth time, he put the aerial up and tapped out an SOS.

"*Herr Leutnant*, I have the battalion, it's replied!"

But the Stampfer Battalion did not know where the Brandenburgers were any more than they did. Probably a little more to the east, but that's all they could calculate.

The night fell for the sixth time. There had been nothing to eat for two days and six had passed without fire or shelter and the temperature was minus ten.

Trommsdorf sank down on the trunk of a dead tree. His company spread out over hundreds of metres. Only the doctor still seemed to be able to stand up.

"Doctor", he asked, "how many men have we left lagging behind?"

"None, apart from the dead bodies. Five or six, as far as I can tell without doing a roll call."

"In your opinion, how much longer can we hold out?"

"The last man will be dead within forty-eight hours."

"Look, doctor, it's my last signal-light."

A red bouquet opened up in the black sky. And, several seconds later, a volley of shots reverberated in the forest.

All the men cried out "Hurrah!". Other cheers could be heard echoing in the distance.

The patrol sent to look for them by the rear base did not take long to appear and brought with it a field kitchen. Hot soup, biscuits, dried fruit, dry tents and even some schnaps, they were saved.

On their return at Rovaniemi, the company was given a much needed rest. Trommsdorf left and was succeeded by Lieutenant Sölder. He was soon replaced by Lieutenant Hettinger, who was in command of a platoon of the 5th Company. In mid-April, the 'Trommsdorf Company' thus became the 'Hettinger Company'.

Summer had arrived. Endless nights were supplanted by days without end. The Russian attacks at the beginning of the month had temporarily brought back the Brandenburgers to the front line in the Kiestinki sector, with a great deal of success. Then they were taken back to Rovaniemi.

One morning, a goods train, whose flat waggons carried strange packages wrapped in groundsheets, arrived from Helsinki. Several metres long, the packages were however light enough to be unloaded by a single man. There was great mystery surrounding their storage in two barns requisitioned for the purpose. Something was being prepared.

The HQ of the Lapland Army, which had become the 20th Mountain Army, thought only a Brandenburg style raid alone could

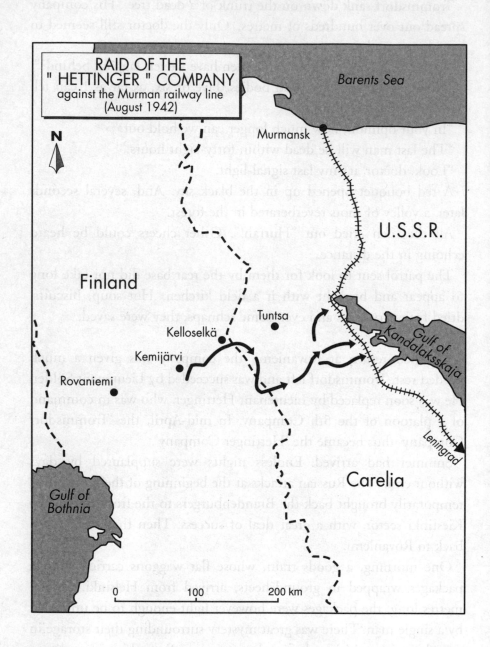

RAID OF THE
" HETTINGER " COMPANY
against the Murman railway line
(August 1942)

N

Barents Sea

Murmansk

U.S.S.R.

Finland

Tuntsa

Kelloselkä

Kemijärvi

Rovaniemi

Gulf of
Kandalaksskaja

Leningrad

Carelia

Gulf of
Bothnia

0   100   200 km

cause a sustained interruption of rail traffic on the Murman line. Bombs dropped from a plane hit a target as narrow as a bridge only once per thousand times; explosives placed by engineers would obtain a positive result 100% of the time.

The new commander of the company, Rolf Hettinger, was a typical Brandenburger. He knew that 80% of the success of an operation of this type depended on intelligence and the thoroughness of its preparation. He had brought back some Tyroleans of the 5th Company from Germany, some Souabs serving in the Brandenburgers from the beginning and some *Volksdeutschen* of the Balkans, because it was not enough for him that his men knew how to ski. He had discovered Russian speaking Germans from the Volga, Carelians who spoke Finnish and Ukrainians and Byelorussians in Soviet prison camps, practically all of them deserters from the Red Army. He selected from the regiment's home base the most highly qualified explosives specialists. He brought a batch of Russian and Finnish submachine-guns. Finally, fifty or so outboard motors, destined for the strange packages stored in the barns. They quickly realised that they were dismantled kayaks requisitioned at Wansee, the yachting resort of Berlin. They were in all different colours, blue, red, green, white and orange, too bright for some tastes, but they had no choice.

Training started immediately on the neighbouring waterways, building, dismantling, setting up and starting of the engines, and above all paddling. Hettinger was pitiless. The exercises lasted for hours. The men, with their shoulders and arms tired out, and the palms of their hands red-raw, moaned.

"There will be no respite until you have callouses worthy of a woodman on your hands and you are capable of paddling ten hours non-stop without losing your smile. If the Russians chase us, that's the only way you'll be able to save your skin. And remember: it is strictly forbidden to use the engines, unless it is absolutely necessary and on the orders of the section leader."

Hettinger faced with a dilemma as to weaponry. On the one hand, carrying heavy equipment would reduce the extreme mobility of his reconnaissance and destruction teams. On the other hand, the teams needed weapons and ammunition capable of resisting an enemy necessarily greater in strength. Eventually he considered that the success of the destruction missions was more important than the firepower and he dropped 80-mm mortars for the platoons and 75-mm recoilless gun for the company. However, each section was to be equipped with a rifle with a grenade launcher and a light machine-gun with 2,500 cartridges.

As for the uniforms, the now traditional formula of the *Halbtarnung* was adopted. The characteristics of the clothes and combat equipment which would enable easy identification were concealed. Each man received a pair of rubber boots, a lined parka, a Finnish dagger and a bag for ammunition and *Verpflegung* (field rations). The wearing of cartridge pouches, belts and rank insignia was forbidden. In addition each man was supplied with a mosquito net and mosquito repellent cream.

One of the primary conditions of the success of the operation resided in the proper functioning of radio communications, as much between the detached elements of a company on the objective as between the company itself and its support troops. In addition precautions had to be taken so that the transmissions did not betray their location. The ruse adopted consisted of using cyphers with four identifier groups of Russians instead of the cyphers with five groups of the Wehrmacht. Enemy listening stations did not pick up on this piece of trickery straight away.

On the 3rd of August 1942, the company started moving. In front of it, 160 kilometres of land and water to cross in eight or nine days, and as much on the return leg, which posed a problem concerning supplies. Apart from wild berries and mushrooms, this desert offered nothing to eat. Often, arctic hares, wild geese, hazel-grouse and reindeer were spotted, but they could not be shot at. Only fish were both accessible and abundant food supply. Seven teams, each one composed of three men, including one Finn, were in charge of equipping supply points on the return route. On the way there, the company carried its provisions.

One final strategem of war, the Finns would send patrols exchanging numerous radio messages intended to be intercepted by the Russians to divert their attention from the Brandenburgers.

Soon after having left Kairala, the first obstacle appeared. It took the form of high ground forming a watershed between the Gulf of Bothnia and the White Sea. The men had to carry their kayaks and their packs in their arms and on their backs over a distance of five kilometres.

That same evening, progress continued on the water, the kayaks were towed in groups of six. Dependent as it was upon a succession of lakes and rivers, the chosen itinerary naturally did not follow a straight line. They followed the Kutsan, a tributary of the Tuntsa, which, leaving the Vitsi Lake on the left, joined up with the Susi Lake that they had to cross after passing the village of Tuntsa. The Germans were now entering hostile territory.

A radio call from the Finnish battalion warned them that a Russian patrol went through Tuntsa very punctually, but that it was not expected before eight or ten days. Hettinger nonetheless found it more prudent to skirt round the village.

When the column reached the western bank of the enormous Kovd Lake, it had to overcome marshes and dense bulrushes which, over several kilometres, preceded free-flowing water. It was decided to cross the lake keeping an equal distance between the two banks. With the mist that floated just above the water, the convoy was absolutely invisible over a distance of up to ten kilometres.

It was planned to set up the base camp on an island that was thought to be deserted, near the western bank of the lake. A reconnaissance patrol having confirmed the absence of any Russian post, the landing took place. On the morning of the 9th of August, Lieutenant Hettinger sent some new patrols to reconnoitre the Murman railway line and the three chosen bridges, to hide the explosives nearby.

The northernmost bridge presented no difficulty in approach and did not even appear to be guarded. The one in the middle was 400 metres long and its destruction appeared particularly profitable but had to be well-guarded, a recent air attack having been repelled by the anti-aircraft artillery. The southernmost bridge also promised to give serious difficulties. Crossing a deeply embanked river, it could only be approached by kayak.

The patrols arrived at their destination on the evening of the 9th. They made the most of the clear moonlight to observe any movements and note the times when the relief of the guard took place.

On the 13th, the three platoons of the company started marching off at different times, so that each one could be in sight of their objective by nightfall. It was planned to place the charges in position between midnight and three in the morning, the time of night when the sentries were most likely to be drowsy.

The 1st Platoon, thinking the terrain to be clear, started to work without taking any particular precautions. Suddenly, a Russian sentry started pacing up and down the bridge and, noticing the Germans, gave the alarm. They no longer had the time to place their explosives and, seeing a reinforced party rushing forward from the other end of the bridge, had to beat a retreat. But the platoon leader had had the fortunate idea of bringing the outboard reserve petrol tank. He had the time to spread the fuel out over the bridge and set it alight. The retreat took place behind a curtain of flames. The Soviets, well lit up by the fire, were excellent targets and they lost a dozen or so men.

However, some others gave the alarm immediately by radio. Hettinger, who understood Russian perfectly, learnt that all the bridges and tunnels were alerted and he warned his platoons, enjoining them to do it as fast as possible.

The 2nd Platoon attacked the 400 metres bridge, after having left the little island where it was hidden at midnight. As the craft got nearer, three Finns and their watch-dogs took the sentries by surprise at the southern end and neutralised them. The explosives were set in three places, including the northern entrance where the Brandenburgers had not been seen. While everything was ready for firing, the guard was awaked by a radio call. The Russians pounced on the bridge. A light machine-gun of the platoon stopped them while the safety fuses were timed to three minutes. The withdrawal was naturally carried out rapidly and the bridge blew into pieces over

164

a length of 75 metres! Bodies were seen flying into the air. It was 3.15 a.m. when the kayaks got back to the little island from where they had left.

Only two men had been slightly injured and were brought back.

Even though the approach routes had been reconnoitered, the 3rd Platoon lost their way. It had however put its kayaks in the water early enough to be able to arrive in sight of the target at midnight, after coming very close to disaster as a result of the tumultuous current. The miners then worked in total silence, while the sentries slept. The delay igniters were set to function for 2.30 a.m.

With the alarm given, the Russians went out onto the bridge. At the designated time, the whole central part of the bridge flew into the air, along with a number of its guards.

The company reassembled at the base camp and preparations were made for the return. As he had not seen a Russian plane throughout the day, Lieutenant Hettinger ordered the departure for 6 p.m. An observation plane suddenly appeared at precisely that moment and swooped down to strafe them. The German LMG emptied belt after belt of ammunition in its direction and kept the plane at a respectful distance. Consequently, its attack was not very effective. It nonetheless caused two more men to be slightly injured.

Nightfall had not yet arrived when the rumbling of engines could be heard once again. Hettinger wisely brought his kayaks nearer to the bank. There they could shelter hastily among the bulrushes, which completely hid them from view. Soon their pursuers would parade in front of their very eyes. There were six large motorboats, each one carrying forty or so soldiers and with a heavy machine-gun at its bow, capable of wiping out the fragile flotilla in a trice. When they were further away, the lieutenant decided to abandon the direct route, by Susi Lake, and to go further north by Vitsi Lake.

In this sea of bulrushes, they now had to find the mouth of the waterway linking the two lakes. An imperceptible movement in the vegetation indicated it to them. They were far enough away from the bridge to use the engines without danger. The men, exhausted, abandoned their paddles and lay down in their kayaks.

The journey lasted all night; five craft disintegrated at the rapids that connected the lakes, but their occupants were saved. At the end of the afternoon, the company reached the mouth of Tuntsa Lake. Hettinger authorised a short rest. Then the convoy set off again, preceded by a scout kayak ahead.

When it was the least expected, the convoy was caught off guard by gunfire coming from both banks. The Soviets had preceded them by taking a shorter route and laid an ambush. The volume of fire betrayed the presence of the entire number that had passed them the day before. But the Russians, in position at water level, were obstructed by the bulrushes. Their fire was not as effective as planned, even less so as, right from the first salvos, the Brandenburgers had jumped into the river with their individual weapons. In water reaching their chest, they retaliated. A LMG had been saved and was fired. Under its cover, the company regrouped on the southern bank and got away on foot. It had lost all its kayaks, all its equipment and its support weapons. It left five dead and eight injured behind it, three of which were lying on improvised stretchers.

After the morning of the 15th of August, the Finnish battalions sent strong detachments to meet the Brandenburgers. Having heard the gunfire at Vitsi Lake, they attacked the Soviets just when they were reaching their motor boats. The Soviets withdrew and left no less than thirty-six bodies behind them.

The company could not indicate its presence to its allies as it had lost all its transmitter-receiver sets. By chance a Finnish reconnaissance patrol found it at daybreak on the 16th of August. Through the transmitter the Brandenburgers were able to link up with the Finnish battalions, 12 kilometres to the west of Siyeminki Lake. The following evening, the company returned to its departure point, at Kairala.

In spite of everything, the operation ended up being a great success. Rail traffic was interrupted for fifteen days. It was reestablished too hastily and resulted in some derailments. In addition, the NKVD believed there had been extensive collusion and carried out ferocious reprisals which disrupted the entire organisational set up of the units in the area and badly affected the traffic on the line.

Warmly congratulated by General Dietl, who henceforth baptised the Brandenburgers 'his German partisans', Hettinger's company would remain in Finland until December 1942, as reserve for the 20th Mountain Army, before reaching Neuhaus, in ex-Austria, in order to be reorganised.

Chapter XI

Operation Salaam
(1942)

In February 1941, Rommel and the first units of the *Afrikakorps* landed at Tripoli, to put a stop to the flight of the Italians.

The British, with an eighth of their strength but better armed, took 80,000 prisoners, at the cost of 133 killed. On the 11th of April, Rommel had taken again from the British all the ground lost and found himself at the Egyptian border. He stopped there, not only because he was weak in strength and supplies could not follow his lightning advance, but because he did not know what dangers which threatened his southern flank.

From 1940, the Abwehr had set up an outpost in Tripoli under the camouflage name of 'Wido', and a radio station at Nalut, 200 kilometres to the south-west of the city. The agents of Admiral Canaris had two missions: keep in touch with the Italian command in Libya and watch over the Algerian border with Tunisia. Both the radio operators in Nalut, *Wachtmeister* [1] Hans von Steffens and Corporal Holzbrecher, were Brandenburgers. They liaised on a daily basis with

1. NCO equivalent to a *Feldwebel* in originally mounted branches of service such as cavalry and artillery.

Berlin. Major Franz Seubert constituted an 'offensive' intelligence service within *Abwehr I,* which ran the affair.

It served at the same time as an advisory office for African affairs within the Abwehr.

In the Autumn, Seubert asked some specialists, the majority of whom were French, to bring together information which would give a complete geographical picture of the whole of North Africa. They were geologists, geographers, mineralogists and meteorologists who were going to form a *Sonderkommando* named 'Dora'. The information on Italian maps was not always correct, as the *Afrikakorps* discovered. No exploration or military action in desert areas was possible without precise knowledge of the nature of the terrain, meteorological conditions, tracks, water sources and human settlements.

With this aim, outside the usual specialists, Major Seubert made a request to the Brandenburg Regiment's Staff for all volunteers from German East and Southwest Africa, but also from Palestine. In June 1941, they were sent by plane to North Africa, to be put at the disposal of the Wido outpost at the same time as the Dora *Sonderkommando.*

One month later at Brandenburg, the new 13th 'Special' Company of the regiment became 'tropical'. It was commanded by Lieutenant Friedrich von Koenen, who was from a farming family in Southwest Africa. In October 1941, the first half-company reached Tripoli via Naples, to be placed directly under Rommel's Staff. From the viewpoint of the *Panzergruppe Afrika* command, to which from then on the *Afrikakorps* was subordinated, there was absolutely no question of them wearing any disguise. Von Koenen's men crossed the desert to reconnoitre tracks, identify targets or to act as watch-dogs at bridges and HQs.

During Winter, the Brandenburgers nonetheless started to don elements of the enemy uniform to protect bridges, open passages to motorised units, or to ensure liaison with agents of the Abwehr. They had few losses.

In 1941, General Rommel's lack of knowledge concerning the intentions of the enemy and its movements at the rear of the front proved costly.

It was true to say the Abwehr was well informed about the general development of the situation in Egypt by the Italian listening posts which managed to decode messages from the American military attaché in Cairo, but the *Panzergruppe Afrika* needed more accurate information affecting military operations.

An officer of the Abwehr detached to the *Korück*[2] in Tripoli, Major von Griesheim, arrived unannounced at the Tirpitzufer and declared:

"General Rommel entrusted me with informing you that there is a very urgent need to know what the British are up to. He wants a transmitter in Cairo. How you manage that is your problem. He wants it ready before he takes up his offensive."

Major Seubert replied patiently:

"My dear fellow, we have already made two attempts in that direction, the first one in May to extract the former chief of Egyptian general staff, Asis el-Misri Pasha, who is ready to collaborate with us against the British,[3] the second in July, to drop two radio operators in Lower Egypt, near Cairo, using a plane from Crete. Both these undertakings failed. But they taught us a lesson.

"The third will be set up so that any surprises are limited as much as possible. We have a very large operation in sight. I can promise you that in the spring of 1942 we will be in a position to satisfy the General's wishes. Tell him that from us."

That evening the two officers dined together and Major Seubert spoke to Griesheim of the new pawn that he had in his game:

"It was at the beginning of the war, in 1940. I was in Budapest, in civilian dress obviously, and I had gone to have a glass of tokay outside one of the many cafés on the avenue along the Danube. Do you know the place? When we got out of our austere Berlin it was marvellous to be among the flowers, the pretty women, the perfumed air and the gypsy melodies. Well, you can imagine my sense of euphoria. I started up a conversation with the man at the next table. I simply wanted to

2. Officer commanding an army lines of communications area.
3. This operation was given the code name 'Condor'. El-Misri Pasha was assisted by two lieutenants of the Egyptian Army, Gamal Abd el-Nasser and Anwar el-Sadat.

ask him where the best restaurant in the area was. By a stroke of good luck my neighbour was Count Laszlo Almàsy. A phenomenon. A former air officer with the *K.u.K.,*[4] a typical Hungarian of good stock, with his politeness and kissing of hands, but along with that, capable of touches of the most extraordinary daring. He practised every sport, including car racing and was no more afraid of the devil than of his own shadow.

"Almàsy lived for many years in the desert between Sudan and Libya as a land surveyor and cartographer, working for the Egyptian Government and with the collaboration of those British services that were interested. Thus he knew the desert perfectly, along with its every oasis, he had even drawn up a map of unexplored mountainous areas. As well as this he had established friendly relations with a lot of Egyptian officers and Arab leaders who were the enemies of Britain. It was he who had handled the liaison with el-Misri Pasha during the failed operation of June. He was ready to organise an expedition across the desert to lead our agents to the Nile."

"Be that as it may, it doesn't explain why he chose to risk his neck in the interests of Prussia."

"In the beginning, I couldn't explain it either. He made the first steps, without making any grand declarations however. These aristocrats of the old school are modest, they always seem to care about nothing. But he was talkative and told me a lot about his life. He held a grudge against the British who had always more or less regarded him with scorn. Also, he had already fought on our side once before. That created a habit."

"But I see a problem in incorporating a foreign citizen, and what is more a civilian, into a German military enterprise."

"Admiral Canaris resolved it. He was not a man to let such a rare bird fly away. He had incorporated him in the Wehrmacht on his own authority and got from the Luftwaffe take him on with the rank of captain, his former rank in the imperial and royal army."

4. *Königlische und Kaiserlische*, royal and imperial, the multi-ethnic Austro-Hungarian Army.

Von Griesheim left with the good news and Major Seubert set down to work. Before entering the operational phase, he thought it indispensable to make the count to put his cards on the table.

Captain Almàsy lived in a small apartment in an elegant boarding house in Kurfürstendamm. The Abwehr carefully provided him with his favourite brand of cigarettes, Queens, and a small reserve of French cognac, which he judged to be irreplaceable for regaling his friends.

"Sit down, *Herr Major* and dear friend," said the Hungarian welcoming his superior. "Would you be adverse to a drop of cognac?"

"Fill my glass! *Also!* I have thought about your proposition. I am not a specialist of Africa and don't claim to express a valuable opinion. However, I wonder how you will be able to cross a distance of 2,500 to 3,000 kilometres–that's the distance from Paris to Istanbul–crossing unknown territory for the most part, avoiding the most frequented places, water sources above all, and half the time in a hostile zone. And, to crown it all, in German uniform. Remember, as I have told you, General Rommel will not allow the use of camouflage as is used elsewhere with our Brandenburgers."

"For me it's child's play, my dear Major. I leave with heavy loads and lay depots of water and fuel along the way. Throughout the last part of the journey I have no heavy loads and can move more freely. On the way back, I find the depots and I have everything I need."

"How can you be sure of finding your depots again, in that great waste land, especially if they are hidden as they should be?"

"Do not concern yourself with that. I have not the slightest worry on the subject. Have the kindness to take my word, my dear major. Leave the responsibility to me, please. Another drop of cognac?"

It became clear to Seubert that Captain Count Almàsy would not be capable of setting the expedition up without assistance. He was too much of an individualist to adapt to the necessarily formal methods of German military administration. Seubert leafed through the Abwehr file and there he discovered the person he was looking for, *Wachtmeister* Hans von Steffens, one of the two Wido wireless operators in Nalut. He had a sound military knowledge, university education and experience in leading men and with Africa. He was in von Koenen's company in Tripolitania. All that was necessary was to call him in.

Several days later, von Steffens showed up in the Major's office, in his lightweight drill olive drab tropical uniform that he had not had the time to exchange for a *feldgrau* uniform in Naples, as was the rule for all personnel arriving from Africa in winter.

"I won't ask if you will volunteer for a special mission as you are a Brandenburger."

The major briefed von Steffens on the mission.

"Count Almàsy is indispensable to the success of the operation. But I don't want weapons personnel, radio operators or drivers who accompany him to be under his command. They will be under your orders and you will be accountable to me only. I'm granting you leave for the end of the week. Come back here next Tuesday morning at 8 a.m."

At the stated hour von Steffens was there, in his impeccable dress with pleats in his trousers that were sharp enough to cut a slice of bread. The major looked at him with a smile:

"A real fashion plate. Excellent, I like the dignified manners. But remember sometimes in special missions, you have to be careful not to overdo it. Let's go and see the Count."

Almàsy and von Steffens shook hands like men of the world, but without demonstration. With that, two aristocrats were brought together, or rather were in opposition. Friendship is difficult to develop when there is such a collision of rigidness and nonchalance. Both of the men had the feeling that their relationship would be difficult. However, when the Captain heard von Steffens enumerate the list of equipment that he judged necessary to assemble and how he counted on setting about it, he congratulated himself on having a collaborator at his disposal on whom he could shift the responsibility of an essential task for which he had neither liking nor capacity.

"We have several hundred British cars in our motor transport park in Tripoli. I think that two open-body Ford Deluxe for reconnaissance and two light lorries for equipment and supplies would be sufficient.

They are one and a half ton *Flitzers* [5]; they are light, which is what is needed for sandy terrain. I plan on having rope-ladders for when we get stuck in the sand. Camp beds and sleeping bags...

"Steffens, have you thought of getting yourself a good compass?"

"One per car, *Herr Hauptmann*, as we could be separated by some unforeseen event, an air attack for example. And, in addition a sextant for the command car. It will be necessary to prick the chart every day to know exactly where we are."

There remained the important problem of radio sets. Each car had to be provided with one and they had to be capable of transmitting over both short and long distances, and strong enough to withstand jolts, abrupt stops and starts and considerable variations in temperature. A contribution from the Abwehr at Stahnsdorf was requested. Installations and tests started immediately. Von Steffens got to know his colleague, *Wachtmeister* Abele, who had the task of training two agents who had to be transported by the expedition up to the Nile. The major had taken the precaution of informing Steffens on the subject of the two Abwehr recruits.

"We needed men already familiar with signals, who know Egypt well, speak English perfectly and also Arabic. We were only able to find them in the interpreter company of the *V-Abteilung*. We have two who are qualified and get on well. That's a gift from Heaven, there was not much choice! There was no shortage of Arabic and English speakers but none had ever set foot in Egypt. Now, the condition for the successful integration of these fellows in the Cairo environment is that they can be admitted without attracting attention. On that point we have everything that we could wish for: Eppler, Hans, 25 years, lance-corporal, Egyptian father, German mother, born and brought up in Cairo; Sandstede, Gerd, 26 years, German father, English mother, brought up in Cairo.

They are both volunteers. At first glance, they have neither the mentality or the bearing of soldiers. But, where they're going that's rather an advantage. There'll be no risk of them being taken for

5. German nickname for fast light lorries.

German soldiers! So we shall have to put up with a lot of mistakes. Remember what I told you: I didn't chose them, they were the only ones I could find and there's nobody else apart from them. Besides, Almàsy has met them and declared himself satisfied."

"Might I be allowed to have a differing opinion, *Herr Major*. Nobody can be committed to an adventure like this one without first having undergone strenuous physical training and without having acquired the reflexes necessary for the march discipline and battle discipline."

"Come on, Steffens, relax a little and try to get on with these two characters. You'll meet them tomorrow. Your colleague Abele, who will give them their last lessons on the radio, will take you to where they are staying. In civilian clothing of course."

The two NCOs showed up on the third floor of number 7 Tauentzinstrasse, a small street in a well-off area, where the Abwehr had requisitioned a comfortable apartment. Abele rang three times on the bell.

"Who is it?" asked a man behind the door.

"I've brought you some cigarettes."

The door opened and the two NCOs entered the darkened apartment. The sitting room in front of them was hot and the cigarette smoke formed a cloud. Glasses were strewn over the tables, along with ashtrays full of cigarette butts. The man who let them in noticed the backward movement of the two visitors and went to draw back the curtains and open the window, laughing as he did so. The harsh daylight showed up the dirt and untidiness in the room.

"I am Eppler, Lance-corporal if you please. You looked surprised both of you! But you must understand, we had a little party last night and we got up late."

In the embarrassed silence which followed von Steffens heard, on the other side of the door, little stifled giggles, words whispered by female voices, then the sound of the front door closing. The sitting room door opened and the second agent entered. He was as tall as the first one was small. It was Sandstede.

"Are you the new sergeant-major? I'm Sandy. What will you have to drink? Gin? Whisky? Nothing? That's a shame."

And he poured himself a glassful.

"Well we'll tidy up later. Get rid of the glasses Buddy, let's get on with the lesson. Bring the damned set."

When they were on the pavement outside once again, the two NCOs looked at each other.

"The major can say what he likes," said von Steffens at last, "those two will have to be watched."

"You said it," replied Abele, with a worried look.

Over two and a half months, supported by the Abwehr's influential friends called on whenever necessary, *Wachtmeister's* efforts continued. Von Steffens watched over everything. He was shown an example of a rope-ladder with stainless steel rungs, seemingly perfect. He felt its weight: "Too heavy!" He had the stainless steel rungs replaced by light and flexible wooden slats. He was not satisfied with any type of camp bed, they were either too impractical or too fragile. A new one was made according to his specifications. It was adopted only after being submitted to various tests.

At the end of February 1942, the equipment and the men supplied by Berlin could finally board the trains at Anhalter Station. Corporal Woermann and two radio operators, Lance-corporal Weber and Lance-corporal von der Marwitz, were joined by von Steffens and the two agents.

The journey took place without any problems, the two agents having accepted the authority of the head of the convoy although not without making a fuss. In Naples the team just missed a bombing raid which ravaged the railway station. Von Steffens strove in vain to find the two planes which would be needed to cross the sea. The answer was always the same: "In two weeks, when it's your turn." By sheer luck, the lieutenant in charge of air transport was an old comrade. He politely turned the officers that were waiting to be received to one side and listened to the *Wachtmeister*.

"Six men and five tons of equipment? For all that, we need two Ju 52s. At the moment I am short of fifty of these machines, which are at the bottom of the sea somewhere between Sicily and Tripoli, along with the men they were transporting. I haven't got the slightest idea where I would be able to get two for you."

Von Steffens emphasised the worrying situation of the *Panzerarmee Afrika*, whose fate depended on the resources he was asking for.

"Please, old chap, don't ask me any more, you'll make me betray a military secret. Believe me."

The officer was impressed. He thought deeply for a moment.

"Well, everybody that comes here says the same thing. But I know you and I trust you. Look, only the 2nd Air Fleet's Staff, in Rome, can free your two planes. It would amount to madness to telephone, the Italians listen to everything and the devil alone knows where all the tipoffs that they pick up would end up. Go there yourself. You'll take this afternoon's mail plane and go and see Lieutenant-Colonel von Trotha. Explain everything to him. If he can't help you out, then nobody else can."

The NCO was on his way. He clicked his heels and, with his eye fixed on the vanishing line, reported himself in the prescribed manner.

"Please don't bother! Reservist, no? Sit down...(He noticed the gashes on his cheeks.) Student? What association?"

"Wilhelmintana."

"I don't believe it! Me too! We are colleagues. Let's have a drink to celebrate."

He pressed a bell and, two minutes later, an orderly in a white jacket brought in a tray with a bottle and two glasses.

"You're not an officer, or not yet. Any difficulties?"

"I was a journalist. I didn't tow the line. They warned me, but I couldn't fit in with their policy. They withdrew my business card. I was so disgusted I went and joined the Foreign Legion. When I came back when the war started, the Abwehr fortunately took me back and gave me the same rank I had with the French."

"I see. Nobody can argue with the boys in the brown shirts. So there's no point in asking you what this special mission that you're asking me to pull two *Ju's* from nowhere is about. I've known about the Brandenburgers since the bridges over the Meuse. You were in tremendous good shape! I'll go and see if I can work a miracle for you."

He called a captain who handed him some lists.

"There are two old crates which have just received new engines and which have to go to Trapani tomorrow. Trapani can wait. Take careful note, Herr Schröder: the two aircraft return to Naples, after taking the *Wachtmeister* here present on board. In Naples, they emplane equipment and men that he, and no-one else, will indicate to you. No overloading. Then you'll be en route for Tripoli. Flight plan: outside the normal itinerary. Pass under Sicily, diagonally on Sousse. Follow the Tunisian coast sticking to the forbidden three nautical miles. In case of danger, do not hesitate to swoop into neutral territory, don't pay attention to all the agreements passed with the French. Because these planes must, are you listening, arrive safely and not take a bath. Is that understood?"

The flight over the sea left Steffens with a stubborn headache.

The Count was astonished at the arrival of the convoy. He refused to understand that the colonels had to wait for a plane three weeks in Naples, and an NCO managed to get two within twenty four hours. Von Steffens, with his usual propriety, explained:

"A colonel relies on his authority, an NCO has no power and it is quite natural that he is helped. A colonel orders, an NCO requests. There are a certain number of people who prefer to be asked rather than ordered."

Almàsy wondered if his subordinate was taking the mickey out of him or being serious. He opted for the second hypothesis. But he wanted to have the last word.

"You come round as regularly as clockwork. I won't expect you before two or three weeks. Nothing is ready for departure."

"*Herr Hauptmann*, I know to use the time. We have to test the radio sets, adjust the network that we are going to set up, carry out firing exercises and at the same time get ourselves used to the climate. That's just the minimum. The great thing is that the equipment is here rather than at the bottom of the sea, isn't it?"

With the arrival of the three new men that had come from the

179

Sonderkommando Dora, Feldwebel Munz, Lance-corporal Beilharz and Corporal Koerper, the staff was complete. The two new NCOs, both Germans from Palestine, were to be the drivers.

The captain realised, listening to von Steffens' detailed report, just how exceptional the NCO was. He decided to make his satisfaction known to Berlin. Then he spoke of the general situation:

"General Rommel could have advanced even further, if the Italians had followed. Meanwhile, the Agedabia-Gialo line is in our hands and will constitute, at least until any new order, the starting point of our expedition. Both sides will make the most of this respite to reinforce themselves. Rommel has gone hoarse asking for Malta to be taken from the British. With this 'aircraft-carrier' half way between transport routes, it is inevitable that half of our shipping goes to the bottom. We promised him. But the capture of Tobruk is a precondition. Afterwards the push towards the Suez Canal will follow. Of course that's my personal point of view. With Rommel, you never know what to expect. Come and see me tonight, we have still got to talk shop."

That evening, with two bottles of beer, Almàsy said more:

"On the terrain, we will be dealing with different British units, in first position the patrols of the Long Range Desert Group, the LRDG, which operate from the Siwa oasis. They are incredibly aggressive and composed of volunteers similar to our Brandenburgers. An encounter with them is to be feared."

"I wouldn't mind," remarked von Steffens, "crossing swords with them, once in a while, but that is not our mission."

"I absolutely agree with you. But there is another aspect of the action of the LRDG that I want to draw your attention to. They are positioning agents disguised as Arabs carrying false papers and a lot of money [6] in our lines of communications area. The Italian military police unmasked some of them and shot them on the side of the road

6. It was doubtless the work of Captain J.E. Haselden's services, a British intelligence officer born in Egypt of a Greek mother. He used Germans from Palestine who had changed sides. His unit was transported by the LRDG. whenover necessarily. The Germans, even Abwehr personnel, naturally did not have an overall accurate picture of the enemy which was carrying out the same type of war.

like dogs. Naturally they speak Arabic like natives and are sometimes only given away by the colour of their eyes. I am afraid that the British will try to introduce them amongst us. The fact that we are not a unit like the others gives us away like a blind man's stick."

"I have told the men to reply, if they are questioned, that our mission is to select landing sites in the desert, to carry out meteorological observations and conducting tests. It will be all the more plausible since, as far as supplies are concerned, we depend on the Luftwaffe."

This conversation interested the *Wachtmeister* greatly, but he had not slept for three nights and he fell onto his bed and didn't wake up until fifteen hours later.

The two months that passed between the return of the Berliners and the departure of the expedition were not at all restful. There were numerous incidents, sometimes serious, which highlighted the difference in training concepts between the Hungarian and the German. Steffens applied the famous precept of the German Army to the letter: *Schnaps ist Schnaps und Dienst ist Dienst*, which can be roughly translated as: rest is rest and duty is duty.

For his part, Almàsy had only one preoccupation: to succeed in his mission. A former aviator, he had never had responsibility for a land unit and did not appreciate the necessity for a minimum of discipline to hold it in line. He had, over a great many years, got used to setting off in the desert with civilians to whom it would have been out of place to give strict orders.

Eppler and Sandstede protested against their inclusion in training order under the same conditions as the others up to the point of open rebellion. Almàsy, instead of threatening them with the court-martial, accused von Steffens of provoking incidents by making demands incompatible with the special character of the mission. He considered the best thing was to ignore their wild behaviour, along with the incidents of petty theft from the magazine and the lack of cooperation manifested during the transmitting exercises.

There is however a limit that no army should overstep. Eventually the Count understood this. For his part, von Steffens chose to forget certain things and to close his eyes concerning others, while Eppler

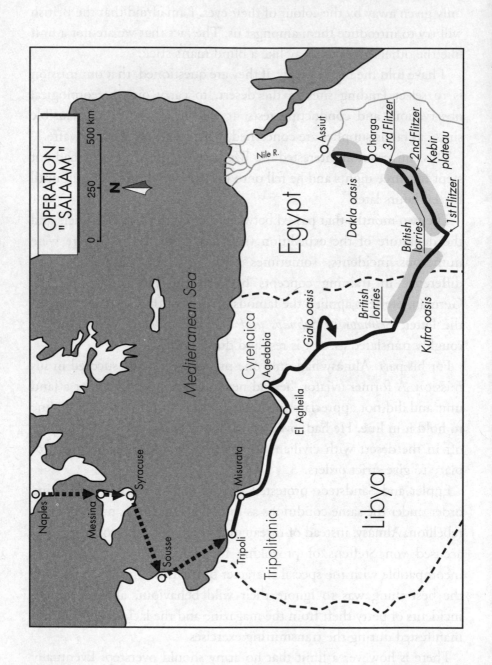

and Sandstede thought it wise to take every precaution, or at least give the appearance of doing so.

It was almost an harmonious team that went to look for the two Ford V8 Deluxe at the rear of the front. The cars were there, with full gasoline tanks, ready to leave. They had been taken in Cyrenaica.

At the end of April everything was ready. The machine-gun mounts had been set up so skilfully by Almàsy on the open-body cars that they were not seen from a certain distance and, nearby, they could be retracted easily. The radio sets worked perfectly, the weapons had at last been tested and the carburettors had been adjusted to reduce petrol consumption to a minimum.

One morning, Almàsy learnt that his secretary and factotum, *Wachtmeister* Endholt, was stuck in bed with a very high fever. The doctor said it was an infection and that several weeks of treatment would be necessary before he would be completely better.

Almàsy was stunned. All his life, even in the desert, he had always had a secretary-valet. Sandstede, who was listening to the conversation, joined in without being asked:

"Sir, why don't you take our Arab valet? Ahmed does everything in our room, he washes, irons, brushes shoes and clothes. You haven't got the time to find a replacement in Endholt, take him."

"Oh thank you! Sandstede, that's a very good idea..."

But Steffens interrupted:

"Not at any price, *Herr Hauptmann*. I let the two agents engage him, because I knew that you would have approved of them, but I made sure that this stranger would never enter our villa. He will not accompany us!"

"Are you saying, *Herr Wachtmeister*," sniggered Sandstede, "that you are in command here?"

"I am only saying one thing, that the orders from the Abwehr be respected. It is strictly forbidden to let an individual take part in a mission unless he has been subject to a meticulous investigation and been put to the test. I suppose that your lordship knows these orders?"

"Steffens, you're always the same. You invent difficulties. A harmless Arab!"

The NCO nonetheless had the last word. Sergeant Barrister, of the

British Intelligence Service, did not go with them...

Wachtmeister Abele and Corporal Weber, both wireless operators but married with children, did not go either. They were to maintain contact with Rommel. Corporal von der Marwitz was to stay in Gialo to liaise with the expedition.

On the 29th of April 1942, a column of two Ford V8 cars and three 1,500 kg *Flitzers* left Tripoli and took the Via Balbia, an endless road, which followed the coast. The Brandenburgers had to give up their usual camouflage, strictly forbidden by Rommel. They therefore painted black crosses on their vehicles. Was it their fault if the wind started to blow when the paint was still wet and the sand covered them up? In truth, they were not easy to see. The tropical uniforms were, of course, German. But they were provided with clothes from the Luftwaffe, whose background tint of khaki brown was more similar to British uniforms.

At the last minute, Almàsy had found a little medical senior ensign who was aflame with desire to know the desert. He integrated him into the column with, this time, the *bene placit* of von Steffens. A doctor is always useful and, if need be, can be used as a secretary.

It was only the pranks of Eppler and Sandstede that disrupted the journey as far as Gialo. They indulged in races over flat ground, without respecting for a minute the march discipline and skidded sharply at the entrance of the oasis in an effort to make Steffens' *Flitzer* land in a hollow of soft sand to avoid any collision.

Von Steffens spent his anger in digging like mad to free the wheels, in sand up to the hub. After two hours of effort, he suddenly collapsed. He was transported to the Italian infirmary, where all the doctors agreed: it was a heart problem, which required a long period of rest and repatriation. The NCO had paid the price of the hard efforts used to mount the expedition and too many nights without sleep.

He thought his departure would fill Almàsy with joy, but he was wrong. In reality, the Count was very affected by this. He judged the presence of his assistant to be indispensable. Besides he came and declared this to him with obvious sincerity. It heartened the *Wachtmeister* a little, compelled to give up at the last minute an undertaking to which he had given himself entirely.

He had too much a soldier's soul not to understand now that the Hungarian, by systematically covering the two agents, had not sought to ruin the authority of their German superior, but simply to save the mission. This could succeed without von Steffens, but had no more justification without the two agents. If an error had been committed, it was incumbent upon those who took the risk to constitute a team where too many incompatibilities clashed.

Almàsy went to seek information from the Italian commander about the extent of sand dunes which spread out to the east of Gialo. The commander suggested an air reconnaissance mission with the plane used by the fort. The result was not encouraging. The belt of dunes spread out over a distance of 300 kilometres. But, while they now knew its length, they did not know its width, as the pilot did not have authorisation from his superior to penetrate more than a distance of one hundred kilometres in the east. The only solution remaining was to attempt the passage with the cars.

A glance at the map showed the extent of the problem. Going east-south-east directly to Dakhla, an oasis not occupied by the British, was the shortest route to reach the Nile at Assiut, their ultimate destination, by Charga and the Yapsa Pass. Nonetheless, Almàsy wanted to consult von Steffens.

"I want to have your opinion as an experienced desert traveller. I'm not hiding from the fact that the route across the dunes would mean a lot of acrobatic feats. It would be simpler to go round them by the south, but that would take us near the British camp at Kufra..."

"That's not the only disadvantage. The new route by the south would lengthen our itinerary by a thousand kilometres. We have not planned enough supplies for such a long distance and length of time. I therefore agree with you that we must attempt the direct route."

Almàsy was anxious to take the head of the column, ordering to those who followed him to carry out exactly the same manoeuvres as him. The technique was as follows: rush on the dune at right angles, full throttle, then, near the top, aim hard right. To cross over the crest of the dune meant a sheer drop off the other side and certain death. They then had to descend the other side diagonally, to gain the maximum amount of terrain as possible. And recommence with the next dune.

All the drivers were skilled and there was no accident of any note. But by the end of the day the column had only progressed 40 kilometres in a straight line because of the constant zigzags and it put a great strain on the cars. The Count wondered if it would not be wiser to go back, when the medical senior ensign threw himself on to his neighbour, jumped from the car and started to dance on the dune shouting: "Water! Water!" It took two men to overcome him. Used to living in the cool atmosphere of an infirmary, the doctor could not stand a day under the hot, pitiless sun. It was an attack of desert madness.

They returned to Gialo. From a distance they were taken for camouflaged British, despite the vast Italian flag they were waving, they were greeted by two shots from a gun. With the misunderstanding cleared up, they took back the quarters they had had two days previously. Corporal Beilharz also fell ill. With von Steffens and the doctor, that meant three members of the team were out of action. Suddenly the problem of supplies for a long route went out. But another unpleasant surprise was waiting for Almàsy.

"I took care of the water," von Steffens told him, "it won't be drinkable for much more than two or three days. Here is the analysis I received by radio carried out from a sample that I sent them the day before yesterday by mail plane. Some more bad news: I checked the stock of rations and cigarettes again with Munz and Beilharz and we noticed that quite a few things are missing."

"Theft? Haven't you been watching over the supplies?"

"Yes, *Herr Hauptmann*, but you personally authorised your two protegees free entry into the magazine and you would not have tolerated it if I had searched them when they came out."

"That's enough, Steffens, you've quite understood that I can't do without those two rogues. Concerning the rations, I'll ask the Italian cook for some more and I'll pay for them out of my own pocket.

What bothers me most is the water."

"Don't worry, *Herr Hauptmann*. This afternoon I had the cans emptied, disinfected and then filled up with pure water from a spring 20 kilometres to the north of the oasis."

"Thank you, *Wachtmeister*, once again you have been invaluable. What else?"

"A recommendation, if I may be allowed. In your team, you have some weak members and some...kids. There are only two men who you can really count on, Corporal Woermann and Lance-corporal Koerper. All I can do is wish you good luck."

The following morning they set out again. The Count, flanked by Woermann, took the head of the column. Koerper brought up the rear. On the evening of the fourth day, a quite unexpected wall of dunes was encountered. Almàsy undertook a reconnaissance and entrusted the convoy to Woermann. The NCO was a good watch-dog. He constantly swept to the horizon with his field binoculars. Suddenly, he made out several flashes from very far away. He recognised immediately that it was the reflection of the sun on the lenses of another pair of binoculars. He did not delay in identifying three vehicles of the type used by the Long Range Desert Group, and remembered that each one had a three man crew, a machine-gun or a 37-mm gun. "If they discover our tracks, they'll be here within ten minutes," thought Woermann. He acted quickly to conceal the cars in a hollow in the terrain and to put their machine-guns in firing position. He continued to follow the movements of the enemy with his binoculars. The British got nearer and then stopped. One of them got out and examined the ground.

"That's it", thundered the NCO, "they've found our tracks. We've had it."

The British set off again, heading towards the Germans. The machine-gunners had their fingers on the triggers. But suddenly, the British turned off to the west and got further away. Soon they disappeared over the horizon.

When Almàsy came back, a retrospective shiver went up his spine.

"In my opinion," confided Woermann, "they saw, from the tracks of the tyres and wheel-base, that they were British vehicles."

"The day will come," smiled Almàsy, "when the British will know that we came by this way. I know one of His Majesty's little lieutenants who will get a good ticking off."

The column started on its way again and succeeded, before nightfall, in getting round the obstacle. They set up camp without making a fire and, in spite of their blankets, their teeth chattered following a sharp drop in temperature of 40 degrees. They set off en route the following morning. Scarcely one hour after their departure, Woermann's trained eye made a new discovery:

"A group of enemy vehicles!"

The binoculars were trained and revealed fifteen or so lorries arranged in a circle, the bonnets facing the middle.

"Obviously a British depot" thought Woermann, out loud. "It's essential that we go and make sure. In any case, I smell a rat."

Their approach did not provoke any reaction. From twenty metres no human being was visible. A search of the vehicles began. All were totally empty. But - how wonderful - a tanker lorry was full of petrol. The column filled their tanks and the reserve tanks. The rest was left to flow into the sand. They did not leave before Koerper had taken out the sparking plugs, several new batteries and numerous spare parts. He asked for a further hour to put sand in the gear boxes.

Around midday, they reached a *garet,* which is what the Arabs call a field of volcanic rocks. This one was immense. its real size would only be known after having crossed it. The blocks of basalt were all different sizes, as small as an apple to as large as a house. In parts they were so tight together that the column was forced to make a detour to be able to pass them. In fact, detours were constant. Fortunately Almàsy had carefully adjusted the compass between Tripoli and Gialo and constantly kept his course reliably. After six hours of effort, at low speed to spare the tyres, they eventually got through only to find themselves faced with another obstacle at nightfall, one that this time the Count had known about since the days of his past explorations, the high plateau of the Kebir mountains.

"In 1937, coming from the Nile, I was here with some English colleagues, at the top of the cliffs that you see in front of you," he told his companions. "I discovered a valley which descended from the height of the plateau at eight hundred metres to the plain, to the north-west of here. At dawn, I will reconnoitre alone to find it and I will give you a light signal to come and join me."

He did not have to look for very long and everybody gathered at the entrance of the surmountable passage.

"Hang on," said Almàsy, "when I came here I buried a sealed iron water cannister. It must still be here."

Under the incredulous and astonished stares of the Germans, Almàsy moved forward slowly, peering into the large walls of the jagged rocks, as if he was trying to find his bearings, then suddenly he quickened his step, stopped and shouted: "A spade!"

Somebody ran forward with one and he started digging for a moment, stopped, looked at the cliffs again, then moved about two paces and started digging again. Then he cried out joyfully:

"I've got it! Get your drinking cups ready!"

This was good news for men who had to be content with two litres each, for cooking, washing and drinking. The cannister was pierced, Almàsy was the first one to taste it. It was warm, but drinkable. Only Woermann insisted on not having any.

"Now let's find a recess somewhere which will be a good hiding place for the first of our *Flitzer*-tankers. We'll be very happy to find it on our way back."

Then the uphill climb started. With frequent stops so as not to overheat the engines. When they arrived at the top, the plateau, 250 kilometres long, was spread out before them.

"This is the most fabulous aerodrome that nature could give whoever wants to take it, one and a half hours flying time from the front. I have already measured it but my notes have gone astray. I can't return without bringing back a plan of it. It will take several days. I'll take two helpers every morning, the others will rest."

Eppler and Sandstede were the first two volunteers to carry the survey poles and the theodolites.

Five days later, they were back on the road, hiding a second small petrol tanker two days later, and the following day the third one. They were within sight of the Charga oasis, the route took them down a slight hill.

"My dear fellows," said the captain solemnly, "tonight is our last bivouac away from the enemy. From tomorrow morning, approaching Charga, we will be in hostile territory. Let's make the most of this opportunity to wish that everybody returns to Europe safe and sound. I think this is the moment to empty the bottle of Scotch that I have been protecting from certain individuals in my uniform-case. Tomorrow morning we'll split up so that each driver speaks English and Arabic, at least during the passage across the oasis. So, Eppler with me and, in the other car, Koerper and Sandstede in the front."

The morning of Sunday 24th of May 1942 dawned clear and calm. When they reached the barrier which blocked the road to the entry of the oasis, an indigenous sentry of the Sudan Defence Force asked for papers. Eppler was in his element:

"What's that," he said in Arabic, "showing him the PASS [7] on the bumper, "can't you open your eyes? Vanguard of the division commander! And if you are thinking of stopping the general when he shows up, Allah have mercy on you! Come on! Open!"

The sentry raised the barrier, muttering to himself. They crossed the oasis without seeing a living soul, then followed the winding road of the Yapsa Pass without passing another vehicle. They arrived at the top of the pass at midday, from where they saw the panorama of the Nile in all its splendour. They all looked at each other with justifiable pride.

---

7. A reversible plate bearing *STOP* on a yellow background on one side and on the other *PASS* on a white background. According to H. von Steffens in his work *Salaam*, this plate was solely destined for liaison and staff officers and indicated that the vehicle could not be checked. It is acknowledged however that, according to British handbooks of the period, it had another purpose, indicating to vehicles in a column that the vehicle which displayed it, temporarily stopped, must be overtaken. Was the *PASS* plate only temporarily and locally used for another purpose? This is likely.

They were 1,500 kilometres, as the crow flies, behind British lines.

"We have arrived," announced Almàsy, "we will go no further. Eppler and Sandstede will descend the pass by foot. Let's leave the road and go and hide behind these rocks."

They soon formed a circle, smoking their cigarettes in silence. The two agents knew their mission. They got their trunk down, got rid of their German uniforms and put on civilian clothes. Eppler wore the ordinary outfit of an inhabitant of the working-class towns, half-Arab, half-European, with a garish coloured tie and, on his head, a red fez. Sandstede gave himself the appearance of an American globetrotter, a rather bohemian one, as his English accent confirmed, as well as his perfect knowledge of South Africa and Uganda from where he claimed to originate. Needless to say, on the inside of their clothes, tailor's labels from Dar es Salaam or Alexandria had been sewn. Before giving them several rolls of Egyptian gold coins and twenty thousand pounds sterling in notes, the captain asked them to turn out their pockets. It was a good thing he did, for they contained the Italian and German money that had been given them.

"That's a mistake that could have cost you your head. When, in God's name, are you going to be serious?"

He spoke for another half an hour, entering into the detail of the mission, and reminded them of the errors they must not commit.

"You had a good time in Berlin and Tripoli. I don't blame you for that. But think carefully about this: if you live it up in Cairo, you will attract the attention of the British police and they'll get you!"

They left, taking the radio set in a shabby suitcase, and their two silhouettes disappeared round the corner.

"Tonight, they're going to swim in the Nile," groaned Woermann.

Almàsy consulted his watch: "Good, they've gone. If we set off right away, we can still cross Charga before sunset. Let's go!"

The two cars carefully started to descend the hair-pin bends of the pass. Suddenly, Woermann — it was always him — let out a flurry of swear words and pressed on the brakes.

"What's the matter, *Unteroffizier?*"

Woermann merely indicated a bend in the road further down:

"A military convoy!"

Almàsy thought for a moment and showed proof of his legendary sangfroid.

"Nothing can happen to us with our plate. Drive unhurriedly. Think intently: 'I am a British general' and everything will be all right."

As soon as the first British car saw them, the *PASS* plate worked wonders. The vehicle pulled over to the left. The lorries that followed did the same. An officers' car, which was driving along in double file, got in between two large lorries. When they passed them, all the officers saluted. As the Germans were passed the last vehicle in the column, a medical car decorated with a red cross, Woermann let forth a sigh of relief, while Almàsy muttered without understanding : "A Sunday! A Sunday! I can't get over it!"

The crossing of Charga was carried out without incident. They had the time to cover another thirty or forty kilometres before setting up camp.

Over the following days, the third *Flitzer* was found, but not the second. Fuel was beginning to run desperately low. Almàsy, now that his mission was accomplished, seemed to undergo a nervous collapse. He even envisaged giving himself up. Woermann roared:

"Never! The Brandenburgers never give up!" Koerper backed him up. Almàsy remembered von Steffens' last words: Woermann and Koerper... He tried to pull himself together. The incredible toughness of these German soldiers filled him with new strength. He looked confidently at Woermann, who had climbed on the roof of the car.

"This blasted *Flitzer* must be around here somewhere...But, am I seeing double, or triple?...It's not one lorry I can see over there, but three...no, five!"

They cocked the machine-guns, left the road and rushed towards the vehicles. They were unnecessary precautions, as the lorries had been abandoned. They found them filled with rations, cigarettes, schnaps...and petrol. They took everything they needed, filled all the petrol tanks and let the surplus fuel flow into the desert sands.

Munz suggested sprinkling the remaining food with petrol and emptying the water tanks.

The Count replied: "That would be against the law of the desert, that friend as well as foe respects, for both of them have no greater enemy than hunger and thirst."

On the 4th of June 1942, the small column was back in Gialo. The Italian commander received them with a guard of honour. Hot platefuls of *pasta asciuta* were washed down with one or two flasks of chianti. This was heaven for the four men with their bodies bruised by the road, their faces and arms ravaged by the sun and whose stomachs revolted at the idea of another tin. The following day they still felt exhausted. But Rommel was expecting them. They arrived at his HQ on the outskirts of Bir Hacheim.

The General stood by the door of his command truck. He congratulated the Count and pinned the Iron Cross 1st Class on his chest. Then he asked him if he recommended one of his subordinates. Almàsy named Corporal Woermann.

"Come this way, *Unteroffizier*. Your captain recommended you for the Iron Cross 1st Class, you already have the 2nd, as you are not a conscript . There is only the *Feldwebel's* star missing on your shoulder straps. I know, I'll give you two of mine!"

He went to get them from his greatcoat.

Almàsy had something else to add. Rommel gave him permission to speak: "We tried several days recently to communicate with you, by means of the two radio operators that we left at your HQ. They never replied."

"They couldn't reply. They are in a British prison camp. And I am the cause of that. I took them and all available men with me to fill out my offensive. During the course of that confounded night of the 27th of May, we stumbled on a British column. I managed to escape but not them. They were captured along with all their documents. After that, Eppler and Sandstede's role was finished. The High Command ordered their messages to be ignored if they sent any. If they are ever captured, they could be turned against us."

Rommel was not mistaken. The lively night life of the two rogues had rapidly attracted the attention of the police services. They were arrested on board the luxury boat that they had hired on the Nile, and the documents discovered in Abele and Weber's car had unfortunately compromised them.

Chapter XII

The Caucasian Dream
(1942)

At the same time as the companies were toing and froing, Berlin Staff continued to mould the regiment. In January 1942, the 11th Company was thus reconstituted out of the 16th 'Special' Company. The following month, a light engineer company was set up in the port of Swinemünde, on the Baltic.

At the end of Spring 1942, while Lieutenant Hettinger's Brandenburgers were fighting against mosquitoes and the Russians in the forests of Finland, and Lieutenants von Koenen and von Leipzig were drying up under the Libyan sun, the majority of their comrades were once again on the point of departure in the garrisons in Germany.

In July, the entire I Battalion under Captain Walther left Brandenburg; II Battalion left from Baden, with the exception of its 6th Company which had just come back from Russia; III Battalion left Düren not including the 9th Company still in the East, and the 11th, which was not ready.

Hitler knew that his victory over the Soviets depended on his oil supplies.

Resources coming from Rumania and its synthetic fuel factories were too limited to enable his air force and armoured troops to operate at full potential. For this reason the Soviet wells in Batum, Maykop, Grozny, Baku and the Caucasus became essential targets. The withdrawal of the Russians before his offensive on Voronezh at the end of June 1942, that he mistakenly took for a rout, persuaded him that he could now divert large forces towards the Caucasus, without jeopardising his push towards the Volga. The capture of Sevastopol, on the 3rd of July, freed the new Marshal von Manstein's 11th Army to join forces with the operation.

Forces committed in the south of Russia were henceforth divided between two army groups: Group B (former Army Group South) which had to take Stalingrad and go down the Volga as far as Astrakhan; Group A, entrusted to Marshal List, which had to make straight for the large Euro-Asiatic mountain range from Rostov.

The distances to conquer were enormous. With the fact that Baku was 1,100 kilometres as the crow flies from Rostov, it was essential that the German Army finished off the enemy rapidly in this theatre of operations, so as to be able to concentrate once again its forces on the main front, in Russia itself.

The Army Group A was therefore formed essentially of rapid units, which had to form a spearhead, and mountain infantry units, suited to progress in hilly areas.

Given the number of rivers to cross, a dozen between the Don and Kuban, the capture of their bridges intact was vital. The Brandenburgers were naturally given this mission.

I Battalion, the first to arrive there, assembled at Poltava. Its four companies were divided between the two army groups. Leaving from Bogoyawlenskaya, the 1st Company under Captain Babuke had to open the way for the 14th *Panzerdivision*.

The 2nd Company under Lieutenant Gerhard Pinkert, whose brother Helmut was the intelligence officer of the regiment marched ahead of the XL Armoured Corps towards the Don. Captain Kurschner's 4th Company, now a whole parachute unit, had to be employed by General Ruoff's 17th Army. 3rd Company, under Captain John had to be deployed primarily in aid of the 3rd *Panzerdivision*.

The Major Dr. Paul Jacobi's II Battalion, divested of his 6th Company, alighted at Kichinev, in Moldavia, then moved to the region of Nikolayev, on the Bug River.

The 5th Company under Lieutenant Zülch had to open the way south for the III Armoured Corps, and the Lieutenant Oesterwitz's 7th Company the same for the LVII Armoured Corps.

Initially, the 8th Company under Captain Siegfried Grabert, like the 5th, had to free the Maykop route for the III Armoured Corps. The 7th and 8th Companies were noticeable as the two companies of mountain infantry of the regiment in Russia. Their men wore, not without pride, the mountain cap and the edelweiss, like their comrades in the Hettinger Company in Finland.

8th Company was sent to Rostov in July. It received the mission of deploying in advance of the infantry to take possession of the major bridges which led to Bataisk on the other side of the wide, marshy Don delta.

The battle was still raging on the 24th of July 1942 in certain areas of Rostov, when Captain Siegfried Grabert led his company across the town. With his strength reduced by half, he crossed the northern branch of the river in inflatable boats. Lieutenant Hüller, leader of the 2nd Half-Company, followed him with the remainder of the unit.

The marshy areas spreading out between Rostov and Bataisk could only be crossed by means of the very large embankment which supported the road and the railway line. Five or six bridges stretched across the branches of the river. Only the largest was mined and guarded. The Russians had established their posts immediately beyond it, opposite Bataisk itself.

As always, they had a formidable artillery at their disposal, which let forth a shower of shells onto anything that moved. The crossfire of machine-guns swept across the surface of the water and fired at the level of the embankment at the slightest alarm. To attempt an approach during the day would be suicidal, as neither the artillery nor the German air force were yet ready.

So the Captain waited for dusk.

The Brandenburger mountain infantrymen followed the roadway in two lines, ten metres apart. Every time a light flare went up, they lay flat on the ground. After two hours, they reached their target, an enormous wooden road bridge, 400 metres long. There, they relieved a platoon of motorcycle troops who, thanks to their well-aimed firing, had prevented the Russian engineers from approaching with their cans of petrol. But they had not been able to preserve the rail bridge. On their left, 200 metres away, it was burning, throwing up high flames which caught the clouds in a red light. After having hidden his company in a ravine which preceded the branch of the river, Siegfried Grabert could not wait for daylight to pass over to the other side and put a solid bridgehead in position. Addressing Corporal Fohrer, his machine-gunner, one of his recent fellow students from the university of Tübingen:

"You're going to build me a good parapet for your heavy MG with stones. You'll fire above our heads when we launch an attack on the bridge."

"That's a good one, *Herr Hauptmann!* Where can I find some stones here? Up there, I'll serve as a shooting gallery target for the Russians. Me and my squad, we'll be shot down in no time."

"What do you suggest?"

"Setting up my firing position at the base of the embankment, a little further along on the right. I'll fire parallel to the bridge, which will mean I can protect you crosswise as well. Nobody will be better positioned than you to fire directly on the bridge."

"You're right. Get on with it."

Ivan had realised something. His mortars made the shells rain down, which eventually reached the ravine: two killed. 80-mm mortars of the Brandenburgers responded and with such accuracy that the Russian mortars soon stopped their fire.

At 2.30 a.m., ghosts advanced on the bridge, hugging the railings, light machine-guns at their hips, fingers on the trigger. Enemy fire rang out at the same time as Fohrer's heavy MG 34 roared. A flare lit up the area. It showed up the deserted roadway of the bridge. They had succeeded!

Rifle fire now crackled at the end of the bridge. The bulk of the company rejoined the leading squad. The ammunition followed. Only a half-company remained on the line of departure, to ensure supplies, liaisons and also to prevent any possible encircling movement by the Russians.

By losing the bridge, the Soviets had lost the stopper that they had created on the Caucasus route, the equivalent of being defeated in a pitched battle. Recapturing it would signify a great victory for them and they spared nothing to achieve it.

Their shells burst continuously at the entrance to the bridge and on the embankment. One after the other, the German heavy machine-guns were silenced. The antitank guns were subject to the same fate. The wounded piled up. The doctor and medical orderly were overburdened with work. Some voluntary helpers, including two ex-medical students from Tübingen, assisted them until they in turn were hit. The wounded were stoical. Not a shout was to be heard, only occasionally the sound of stifled groaning.

The Russian infantry went on to the attack, believing they could remove everything without any difficulty. The survivors were knocked down and blown back in disorder. A mortal silence fell heavily on the bridgehead.

A call disturbed it: "Ammunition!" The men started to get edgy. Where have the supplies gone? What are they doing at the rear? Where's the relief? So many questions which the Brandenburgers could not answer. They did not know that the Rostov route was cut off by a battalion of Russian partisans who had come by the river at night and benefited from constant artillery support which would not let even a mouse get through. An infernal day was beginning for the Brandenburgers. The link between the two bridgeheads was becoming ever more precarious. The telephone line was cut, the signal flares had run out, the passage for runners practically impossible. A barely visible pocket lamp signalled in Morse: "A shot of morphine for the company commander."

Medical Captain Weber decided to swim cross the branch of the river, with his medical case fixed on his head. Corporal Fohrer volunteered to accompany him.

The Soviets had a great many sites for snipers. However they had no high position and their fire was inaccurate. The two men, paddling and swimming in turn, progressed under the bullets which whipped up the water around them.

Captain Grabert was only slightly injured in the head and the morphine was not for him. He explained the situation to the NCO, who left with a message for the rear, while the doctor busied himself with the wounded. Fohrer had the same luck as when he was coming over, even though the Russian antitanks had started firing.

At the other end of the bridge, he found the commander of an infantry battalion and an artillery observer officer, their uniforms shiny with sludge, who had managed to pass across by making a large detour. Their presence gave hope to the combatants. The doctor had also managed to come back. There was nothing left in his case. The merciless bombing started up again. It was at that point that Captain Grabert appeared, staggering. Even he didn't know how he had managed to cross the bridge. This time, in a weak voice, he asked for some morphine for himself. He had an open wound in the stomach and was pressing it with both his hands. The doctor tried to reassure him by dressing it. Grabert looked at him:

"It's a waste of time doctor, I've studied medicine and I know that I am going to die."

The intensification of the shelling was most certainly the preparation for a new attack. This one was on a large scale. Assault waves followed one another across the water and the marshes, aimed at taking the bridgehead from behind. The half-company that had remained on the north bank no longer existed as a fighting unit. Shouts of "Hurrah! Hurrah!" were heard.

The wounded did not want to be massacred in their holes. They came out, scraped around in the mud to try and extract cartridges that might have fallen during the fighting, and fired in a frenzy. These brown silhouettes with the red star, which moved clumsily over the

200

marshy terrain, were ideal targets. The Brandenburgers were first class shots. Every bullet hit an assailant. Demoralised, the Russians surged back in disarray while the dive-bombers swept down. There was a massacre.

Night fell on a scene of carnage. In the bridgehead, where Lieutenant Hüller was dying, the captain had left the command to an NCO. During the night, he drove back all Russian attempts to progress by infiltration with a handful of able-bodied men. They fought with the weapons and ammunition taken from the Russian bodies. In the morning, when the German tanks streamed over the bridge, they greeted them by waving their helmets.

"Long live the Brandenburgers!" a tank commander cried out to them. The infantry followed and, after a preparation by the artillery, launched the attack on Bataisk.

The NCO and ten of his men who were still able to stand up accompanied them. It represented a derisory reinforcement, but the gesture proved to themselves that their might knew no limits.

The legendary Captain Grabert was dead. His men, almost all of them wounded, staggered along one after the other to salute his remains. Corporal Fohrer had wanted, at the time of handing over, to bring back the body of his commander wrapped in a tent quarter as the old Goths used to do with their King who died in combat. But today the Wehrmacht made no distinction between its dead and Captain Grabert would rest among his soldiers at the edge of this bridge that had become their most intimate property by virtue of the sacrifices granted to it. Grabert's company had lost 87 men in twenty-six hours, including 33 killed and missing.

Throughout the following days, two companies of Major Franz Jacobi's III Battalion alighted at Stalino. They then got to Rovenki, to the south of Voronezh. Lieutenant Ronte's 10th Company was subordinated to the V Army Corps which was advancing on Novorossiysk, while the 12th Company was put at the disposal of Army Group Centre to fight against the partisans with the 9th Company. Now under Lieutenant Wülbers, the 9th had been deployed in the central sector of the Eastern Front from the summer of 1941. It had been brought back to Dorogobush, between Vyazma and Smolensk, and had been continuously tracking down partisans for a period of months. These Brandenburgers did not know that they were forerunners.

The reconstituted 11th Company under Lieutenant Hütten did not arrive before August, in Armavir. In the month of October, it was to precede the III Armoured Corps in the Caucasus.

The German Army flowed like a river towards the south. Marshal Timoshenko put his new tactic into effect, which consisted of, by means of rapid retreats, escaping the encircling manoeuvres so dear to the Germans and which had already cost the Soviets millions of prisoners. The Germans, who had passed the Don on a large front, from Rostov to Zimlianskaya, continued their advance in three directions: Krasnodar to establish the link with the Crimea and reach the Black Sea at Novorossiysk; Armavir, to reach the oil field of Maykop; Mineralny Vody to continue along military routes which crossed the mountains of the Caucasus and emerged into Georgia, then, if all went well, to push as far as Baku. Then all dreams were permitted.

Minds were already racing in the bivouacs. The *Landser* from the Caucasus stretching his hand to the *Landser* of the Africa Armoured Army across Turkey, Iran and Palestine!

The forces, having crossed the Manych River, then descended towards the south following the Tikhoretsk-Kropotkin-Kurgannaya axis, where they encountered the barrier of mountains. From there, some turned off to the east and the Terek, others towards the west, in the direction of Maykop and, if possible, Tuapse on the Black Sea. The 13th *Panzerdivision* with, on its right, the SS Wiking Division, was committed opposite Maykop. Both formations had to cross a tributary of the Kuban River, the Belaya, which flowed in a north-westerly direction. In both cases, an appeal was made to the Brandenburgers of II Battalion to provide crossing points by preventing the Russians from blowing them up.

On Saturday the 9th of August, Reserve Lieutenant Ernst Prohaska, from the 8th Company, got his small troop under way, just after the midday meal. He preceded several half-track armoured vehicles of the 66th Motorised Rifle Regiment's I Battalion, which belonged to a battle group of the 13th *Panzerdivision* with the task of entering Maykop by force to take possession of the bridge spanning the river at the exit of the town. In the unbearable heat, the column moved off lethargically.

It was not easy to obtain from the petulant Major-General Herr, division commander and insensible to any variation in temperature, that he also hold back his tanks in the rear until the Brandenburgers had completed their mission.

Prohaska's team had four vehicles at its disposal taken from the Russian and the men had slipped on a Soviet blouse over their uniform. Everybody wore also the side-cap set with the red star. Those among them who were called on to enter into verbal contact with the Soviet check-points had been chosen among Germans from Russia or rallied Soviet citizens.

When the last Russian runaways were in sight, the Brandenburgers broke away ahead, while the tanks followed at a careful distance. They easily managed to get between the retreating cars that very often came to a halt causing hold-ups, thereby playing particular havoc with the men's nerves; it was at times like this when the risk of being questioned was the greatest. At last, the men from Prohaska were in front of the bridge over the Belaya, after having crossed Maykop from one end to the other at a snail's pace.

In front of them was the traffic control post of the Red Army. A sentrly stopped them. When he gave the signal to set off again, a starter did not work. But the driver, a rallied Russian, confidently called the post commander, asking for a starting handle. No sooner was it in position than the truck set off again. They nevertheless did not get off so easily.

At a crossroads, a Soviet general officer observed the passage of his forces. The Brandenburgers' cars had to make a stop level with him. "Who are you?" the officer asked one of the drivers. But he did not

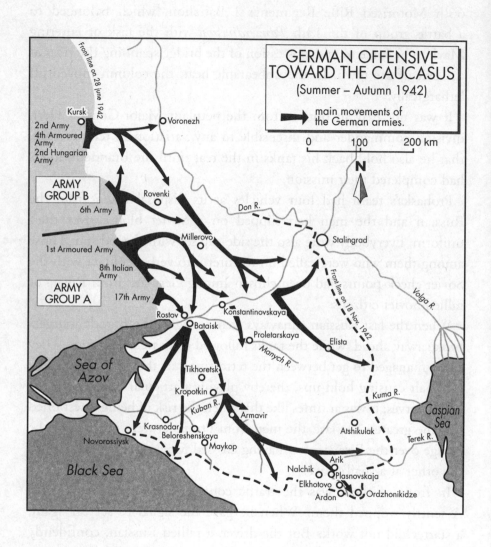

**GERMAN OFFENSIVE
TOWARD THE CAUCASUS**
(Summer – Autumn 1942)

→ main movements of
the German armies.

0   100   200 km

N

Front line on 28 June 1942

Kursk

2nd Army
4th Armoured Army
2nd Hungarian Army

Voronezh

ARMY GROUP B

6th Army

Rovenki

Don R.

Millerovo

Stalingrad

1st Armoured Army

8th Italian Army

ARMY GROUP A

17th Army

Rostov

Bataisk

Konstantinovskaya

Front line on 18 Nov 1942

Volga R.

Proletarskaya

Manych R.

Elista

Sea of Azov

Tikhoretsk

Kropotkin

Kuban R.

Armavir

Kuma R.

Caspian Sea

Krasnodar

Beloreshenskaya

Maykop

Atshikulak

Terek R.

Novorossiysk

Black Sea

Arik

Nalchik

Plasnovskaja

Elkhotovo

Ardon

Ordzhonikidze

leave him the time to reply. "My word, it's you! You were a cyclist at my HQ, last year. I thought you were dead or taken prisoner. What happened?"

The man had a story all ready. He slowly spouted it out, so as not to leave any time for the general to take an interest in his companions, none of whom spoke a word of Russian. The signal to restart the engine spared him from some dangerous questions.

The four cars of the Brandenburgers entered the bridge which crossed the deeply embanked river in one go. Leutnant Prohaska understood better than he could from any map the importance of the operation whose success depended on his keen eye and his decision. If the bridge was blown, the obstacle was insurmountable with the usual ways and means of the engineers.

The team now arrived at the other end of the bridge. A tanker stood there, possibly containing the petrol needed to destroy the bridge by fire. Several Soviet soldiers were waiting, leaning casually against the tank which protected them from the sun. The officer did not need to give an order. Each man knew what he had to do. In one swift movement, the men threw down their Russian side-caps and blouses, leapt to the ground and opened fire on the enemy soldiers, without giving them the time to seize the revolvers hanging from their belts. Prohaska then divided his troop into two, putting light machine-guns in position at every entrance to the bridge. Simultaneously, the ignition wires which went under the abutments were ripped out. As a precautionary measure, the Russians had made provision for two different ways of destroying the bridge.

Meanwhile, tanks of the 13th *Panzerdivision* had opened up a path through the crowd which blocked the streets of Maykop. Amongst the clouds of dust, nobody identified the German Panzers, whose characteristics were no longer visible. Lieutenant Morell, who was in command of the point knew that any exchange of fire would jeopardise the element of surprise in taking the bridge. He had given strict orders to that effect to the tank commanders. Consequently, he could not believe his ears when he heard distinctly in his headphones *"Nicht schiessen! Nicht schies...sen!"* (Don't shoot! Don't shoot!).

The Lieutenant, who immediately feared that this mad carelessness could cause a catastrophe, thought:

"Who is the damned imbecile..."

The tanks eventually arrived opposite the bridge eighteen minutes after the Brandenburgers had occupied it. The roadway was covered with vehicles that their occupants had hurriedly abandoned when they saw the Brandenburgers open fire. Lieutenant Morell tried to move a big Limousine out of the way with his tank, but only succeeded in damaging his clutch. The stalled vehicle prevented the *PzKpfw IV* behind from freeing the bridge. Fifty minutes went by before the passage was cleared and the tanks were able to relieve the Brandenburgers.

Not understanding the reason for the delay, Ernst Prohaska, who heard them firing from the other side of the river, slipped between the vehicles which were obstructing the bridge to go and stimulate some movement. He passed literally between the projectiles. But, when he arrived in front of Lieutenant Morell's tank, a bullet went through his head. He was to be the fourth officer of the Brandenburgers to receive the Knight's Cross on the 16th of September, awarded posthumously.

On the 11th of August, the tank battalion of the SS Wiking Division was moving a little more to the west, preceded by a camouflaged detachment from Lieutenant Oesterwitz's 7th Company.

The men had slipped Russian greatcoats over their German field blouses and some had wrapped their head or arm in a bandage. Several caps bearing red stars completed the disguise. They mounted on board three trucks taken from the enemy. The small troop made it their duty to catch up with the head of the tank column, which had not waited for them. Just when they were overtaking them, two Panzers which mistook them for escaping Russians turned their guns towards them. Lieutenant Oesterwitz was only just able to warn them in time by radio!

The three trucks were now travelling on a clear road, and soon reached infantry and artillery positions. Waving their arms, they cried at the top of their voices: *"Tanki! Tanki!"* Panic stricken, the Russians started to run and in turn shouted *"Tanki! Tanki!"* Panic reached the infantrymen who were digging a trench. They threw down their pickaxes and spades and scattered. The rumour spread throughout all the positions: *"Tanki! Tanki!"* The Brandenburgers could hardly contain their laughter, seeing the batteries put to horses and dart off at a gallop and the motorised guns being limbered and leaving at full throttle.

Some Russian officers attempted to react. A high-ranking political commissar jumped onto the running board of the first truck.

"Are you mad in there! You're making everyone run away! Stop immediately! There's not a single tank in sight!"

The only answer from the Russians of the group was to start up again: "Run for your life! We have been betrayed!"

And the commissar shoved out of the way, fell backwards onto the side of the road.

At Pshechskaya, they caught up with a Soviet heavy artillery battalion, which was quietly positioning behind the river. The Brandenburgers overtook it in the main street in the town. At point blank range, after having, as always, removed their Russian greatcoats and putting their own grey-green mountain caps on, they shot the gunners down. Those who escaped fled and the guns were abandoned.

The Brandenburger mountain infantrymen now arrived at the railway bridge. The guard was taken completely by surprise and offered no resistance. Lieutenant Oesterwitz took a group to go and take possession of the road bridge.

At a short distance from the target, he was stopped by a control post. A commissar asked to speak to the officer in charge.

The interpreter of the group, disguised as a Soviet officer, came down to explain to him that they were all that was left of a unit which was cut to pieces on the Kurgannaya road. The commissar shook his hand and let both the trucks through.

The bridge was stormed in pure Brandenburger style, costing them only three wounded.

From the first months of the Russo-German war, many German units used Soviet prisoners as helpers by supply troops. Battalions of volunteers had even been formed mainly to fight against the partisans.

From the 6th of October 1941, this process was made official by Major-General Wagner, the Army Chief Supply and Administration Officer.

The idea of also using dominantly Muslim ethnic minorities arose relatively early, the first units of volunteers from Turkestan and the Caucasus being formed in November 1941 on the lines of communications area of Army Group South. The year 1942 gave rise to ethnic legions regrouping existing battalions, referred to under the generic term of *Osttruppen,* Troops of the East.

Like several others, the services of Admiral Canaris thought that the weakness of German total strength faced with the Soviet multitudes could be compensated by the support that certain native populations would lend to the Germans if, instead of treating them as the defeated and inferior, they offered to arm and lead them.

Reserve Captain Oberländer was the most well known advocate of this theory. Several months earlier, he was acting as a political adviser to the 'Nachtigall' Battalion, a formation of Ukrainian volunteers attached to the Brandenburg Regiment's I Battalion. Disgusted by the way in which the German Government behaved towards Ukrainian Nationalists after the Galician campaign,[1] he was one of those who pushed the Abwehr to seek allies among the peoples of the Caucasus: Georgians, Armenians, Chechens, Abkhazians, Ossetes, Circassians and others, some of which had not been subjugated by the Russians for more than a century, and considered the Germans as liberators.

Thus a fugitive from the Caucasus paid a visit to Tirpitzufer, a young Chechen by the name of Hamdi Mansoura, who had been clever enough to reach Berlin without papers. He proposed assembling volunteers to transport them with arms and ammunition as far as the valleys occupied by his compatriots. It was certain that the uprising would gain ground among the neighbouring peoples equally hostile to Moscow.

1. See Chapter IX.

208

Approached by *Abwehr II*, Colonel von Haehling, commanding the Brandenburg Regiment, gave his agreement after taking the advice of his intelligence officer, Lieutenant Helmut Pinkert. He designated Lieutenant Erhard Lange to draw up the plan of operation and to proceed to its realisation. Lange was one of the longest serving Brandenburgers. He had been in the Poland campaign as an NCO and commander of a *K-Trupp* of the *Kampverband Ebbinghaus*. In 1940, he commanded one of the two platoons of the *Nordzug* sent to Scandinavia. He then took over the head of the 1st Half-Company of the Siegfried Grabert's 8th Company. The first thing the officer did was to consult the history books. He learnt that a near-general uprising of the people of the Caucasus against the Russians had taken place in 1834, that the war lasted five years and that the Tsar's forces only succeeded in subjugating the mountain people by devastating their country and massacring entire villages. The great leader of the rebellion was called Shamil-Effendi, and his name was still revered in the Caucasus. Lange therefore named his operation 'Shamil'.

He travelled through Soviet prison camps looking for volunteers. He was approached by such a number that he soon understood that the majority of them only wanted to leave the particularly harsh conditions of life in the *Stalags* and of seeing their native land at any price. They were not the type of men he wanted, but real patriots possessing enough political intelligence to know that there are Germans and Germans, and with enough character to remain loyal to the oath that they would have to take, whatever hand fate dealt them.

The assistance of the young Chechen, who knew his people, was invaluable. When he had brought together twenty-one men from the Caucasus, already with basic military training and being possessed of all the required qualities, he put an end to his search and immediately started collective training at the school at Gut Quenzsee. Lange decided to parachute his volunteers with their weapons and ammunition onto a high plateau that Hamdi had described to him and which they had recognised together on the map. But it was imperative for the operation to take place in summer, as in winter the whole region was shrouded in snow. When the order to depart arrived, the Caucasians had only carried out one single training jump at Spandau.

Taking off from Crimea, where the guns still thundered at Sevastopol, they flew on board a Junkers 52 in the direction of the Caucasus.

The Black Sea flowed beneath them with waters of a blue so dark that it seemed to merit it's name. The plane, which could theoretically transport only seventeen fully-equipped paratroopers, was overloaded. It had just enough fuel to reach the plateau and come back.

Lange had planned for his men to jump at dusk, so they would have a complete night to escape any possible pursuers. When the plane arrived in sight of the coast, the barrier of mountains was nothing more than a dark mass whose features were not clear. Lange did not recognise any of the landmarks that he had chosen. He asked the observer who looked alternately at the landscape and the map spread out before him:

"Are we on the correct route?"

"The devil if I know. The map does not correspond to what I see. You are the commanding officer. What do we do?"

"Keep your course, perhaps we'll find a landmark eventually."

The mouth of a river faded from view behind them. What river? They had no idea, there were so many of them. There was a river in every indentation along the coast and they all looked the same.

Hamdi Mansoura had said nothing up until then, but he observed the landscape attentively. He went to the lieutenant:

"This is not the area where we have to go."

For Lange, the situation was disastrous but clear: it was better to go back to Crimea than to jump into the unknown. Then he thought about the welcome he would be given at the base, with its veiled sarcasm. The Luftwaffe would find any excuse to refuse him a plane for any new attempt. No, it was now or never. He asked Hamdi for his opinion and the Chechen, after consulting his comrades, returned solemn but determined:

"We can't postpone it, the season will be too far gone. Let's jump now, we'll manage."

Opposite the barrier of high mountains sparkling with snow, the Ju 52 turned round and went back towards the coast. The distance was soon covered and the sea was already reddening under the last rays of the setting sun.

"We're jumping", Lange said to the captain.

"Now? Take the trouble of looking down. You'll break your backs on those rocks. I'll try and find a flatter terrain. Look, down there, along the coast, there's one, big enough. Make your mind up. I haven't got enough juice to carry on looking."

"All right."

The men understood and put their helmets on again. The terrain was coming too quickly, the plane had to turn and after having taken a wide turn, straightened up. At the signal, they all jumped, one after the other. The Junkers carried out the same manoeuvre a second time to release the containers of weapons, rations and ammunition.

Lange, who was swaying gently in the air, looked at the twenty-one other chutes.

In front of the disappearing sun, they took on a blood-red hue. But, as the parachutes neared the ground, he saw down there hundreds of tongues of fire that pierced through the growing darkness.

Terrified, the lieutenant heard the whistling of bullets. The descent, that no human power could accelerate, became an endless agony. When at last he touched the ground, and had assembled his men, he counted only eleven, four of whom were wounded. The others, including Hamdi, were lying under their parachutes, dead. Except one who groaned quietly. His almost hashed leg was at a strange angle to his body. "Adieu!" he cried before the dry crack of his pistol was heard.

Night had fallen. The Russians fired at random. A heavy machine-gun joined in, then a second one. No one returned fire because the rifles were in the containers. The Chechen Hanefi eventually found one. Underneath the bullets which passed just above his bent back, he extracted four rifles and a case of ammunition. Now, to the left and to the right flares went up into the sky.

"Hell, they're everywhere," groaned Lange. No time to look for the other containers. They had to flee before the encirclement was complete. Running like rabbits between each flare, the men fled towards the mountain.

One of them stayed behind. Lange retraced his steps to bring him back. In the raw light of a flare, he saw him on his knees, his head lowered, then he saw his elbow moving up, and heard a small bang. The body collapsed.

They reached the first escarpments. Spontaneously, Hanefi had taken the lead. The others, as trained mountaineers, formed a silent file behind him. The German looked intensely, but could distinguish nothing, not even his hand in front of his face. He tripped and fell. A hand lifted him up, then held him under the arm to help him walk. His first reflex as an officer was to get rid of this help which humiliated him. He stifled it and let the Caucasian, who seemed to see in the dark, hold him up.

The exhausting march lasted the whole night, sometimes climbing steep slopes, sometimes tumbling down ravines with no visible bottom. And there were always stones which came away under their feet, causing falls which wounded their limbs and tore their clothes.

At dawn, they made a halt. No one was missing. Their hands bore traces of dried blood. They rested.

"*Herr Oberleutnant*, can sleep one hour only?" one of the men risked asking in his pidgin of bad Russian and German.

Distant voices, further down the slope, meant the answer to the question was unnecessary. Everyone got up without a word and set out again. As long as they knew the Soviets were on their trail, there would be no respite. After three days and three nights, every hour of which had been a cruel and silent struggle, they thought that their pursuers had lost their tracks. In this lunar landscape, made of loose stones, they had left none behind them.

They at last allowed themselves, just as nightfall was approaching, to look around to find a place where they could sleep, sheltered from the freezing wind. A slit in the rocks opened out into a sort of cavern, which they could slip into and lie down. Hanefi stayed at the entrance, while his comrades plunged into sleep. Crouching down he slept in his own way. The slightest noise, the faintest echo in the mountain made him open an eye. Then he fell back into unconsciousness.

In the morning they left, their stiff muscles making it difficult to move their legs. Near midday, while they were descending into a gorge, they found a spring surrounded by a little vegetation. The oldest of the Georgians among them searched in the plants and uncovered the roots. He handed them out and recommended chewing them well. They had no taste. They drank the crystal waters with delight and filled their field flasks. They were surrounded by majestic mountains. In their rifts, snow sparkled. That evening they found another hole which could provide shelter while they slept.

Lange had a guilty conscience. He was not carrying out the mission that he was responsible for and which involved stirring up, with the help of his handful of determined men, an anti-soviet revolt among the Chechens. "We are off mountaineering," he thought, "while our comrades are fighting."

He spoke to Hanefi:

"Chechens? Soon Russki *kaputt?*"

Hanefi made a gesture of powerlessness:

"Chechens far, very far. Walk a lot. Nicht eat. Perhaps dead! *Inch' Allah!*"

The others around him repeated: *"Inch' Allah!"*

They set off again and the absurd odyssey continued. The wasted faces of the men, their pallid complexions, frightened Lange. Their eyes, which had kept their sparkle aroused by suffering, seemed to be popping out of their heads. The wounded had particularly suffered from hunger. One of them, that very morning, had died in his sleep. They buried him under some stones. A second one was very weak. Only the third one had rallied, and completely recovered. Between themselves, the men spoke a simplified Tartar which served as a common language among all people of the region whatever their origin. The officer did not understand a word, but the tone of the conversations, calm, devoid of emotion, reassured him. Lange admired the depth of the culture, of which these plain men were the guardians, and which enabled them to confront the spectre of death so impassively!

However, they had to find food to eat and to establish some kind of contact with the local population. For that, they would have to go down into the inhabited areas of the north side of the mountain. The descent began, just as eventful as the journey up. When they came across a shanty, it was empty, there were traces of goats, but no goats. In a hut, they found a fresh cheese and a pile of griddle-cakes. They shared the find with exclamations of joy. Lange asked Hanefi:

"The people here, where are they?"

"Them believe we Russian."

And he shrugged his shoulders.

From then on, every morning, the lieutenant sent two or three men out on reconnaissance. Their ten-day old beards, their hollow cheeks and their tattered uniforms scarcely gave them a reassuring appearance. While waiting for the patrol to return, the men, lying on the grass, started to sing very quietly, a melancholy chant that they all seemed to know, which expressed their frame of mind. Suddenly, one of them stood up:

"There they are."

Their comrades had indeed returned.

"*Herr Oberleutnant*, we arrived village. A man come ask papers. He say he is NKVD. The people come around. We take the man, look for rope and hang the man to a tree. Now people know we not police. They come."

The following morning, when they were waking up, an old peasant was standing in front of Hanefi. They conversed in Circassian. Lange approached. Showing his shoulder straps, then his blond hair:

"Me, German. Me, friend."

The Circassian made it clear to him that he did not understand.

Lange had an idea. He got a small German flag out of his pocket, scarlet with a swastika in the middle, that he had brought along as a possible sign of recognition. He put it under the eyes of the old man, who felt it and said something. Hanefi translated: "Good material." Two young men arrived. They saw the swastika and laughed. Then, animatedly, explained something to the old man, who in turn laughed very loudly.

214

Hanefi translated the old man's words: "You are our brothers. Welcome!"

A sort of agreement was accepted with the village council. The Shamil group was to continue its march towards the east, but without appearing in inhabited areas. They would always be provided with guides who would take over one from another in each valley. Every day, a place would be indicated to them where they could find enough to eat. The march continued uneventfully. Where there was a Soviet Army post indicated, they made a careful detour. They calculated that, within a week, they would have attained the goal of their expedition.

The fourth evening, two young Georgians of the group left, as agreed, heading for a village to meet up with some promised guides. The street was deserted, with their suspicions aroused, they turned around. In front of them were soldiers, rifles at their hips.

"*Stoi!*" (Halt!).

The two young men bounded towards the nearest low wall. One after the other, they were shot down.

In the camp, at the edge of the forest, the others heard the gunshots. They hastily gathered their things together. Lange and Hanefi thought the matter over. The Chechen was someone who understood quickly and knew how to take courageous decisions:

"*Herr Oberleutnant*, Shamil business *kaputt*. We go to the north, straight to the Germans."

Lange agreed. It was obvious that the forces coming from Terek, to the north-east, were going to complete the encirclement formed in the south by the soldiers that were following them from the sea. The route into Chechen country was blocked. The only way out was to find a route north.

Suddenly, Hanefi seized a rifle from the hand of a comrade, jumped off to the side and plunged into the undergrowth. Three others bounded off and followed him. A gunshot, then silence, the branches opened up and the four men appeared. Hanefi, the last one, leaned over and wiped his knife, sticky with blood, on the grass.

They got away rapidly and followed the edge of the wood to be less visible. Lange, at the front with Hanefi, did not allow anyone to go into open country until an examination with his binoculars had revealed the absence of any khaki silhouettes. It was a succession of marches and countermarches, of detours and hideouts. The Soviets were everywhere. They were covering the area with a fine tooth-comb.

It was not before the third day that the runaways felt they had escaped the encirclement. The soldiers may have lost them, but one of their dogs had found them. The animal was well trained. It did not let them get near. They could shoot it, but that would put their pursuers back on their trail. The dog rushed into a field of wheat and barked for a long time. The next day, the dog was there again, and started barking once more.

And so the kill began. The Russians took their time, they did not show themselves. They set traps everywhere. One shot and a Caucasian fell. The survivors continued, with no thought save to flee and escape from the killers. In the evening, there were four men left, Lange, Hanefi and two Tartars, all wounded. But they all had a rifle and cartridges. The Russians knew that and did not approach them. Only the cursed dog appeared. Hanefi aimed carefully and shot it down. They feigned a smile and collapsed on the ground. They slept, except the younger of the Tartars, who had been shot through the throat and was slowly dying. In the morning they found him cold. During the night, he had dragged himself off into a bush like an animal to breathe his last. They discovered that he had also been shot through the shoulder.

The three set off, in their hearts they felt condemned men. Could they escape this? They didn't believe it any more. A single thought obsessed them: to sit down and eat. Just then, they saw a peasant's house in front of them. "There!" they said together. They entered. A long table, and all around it were Soviet soldiers. They had seen so many these last few days that the company seemed familiar. They had, when crossing the first friendly village, exchanged their uniforms for peasant blouses and trousers. Their appearance did not give them away.

"We tired," said Hanefi in his bad Russian. "We thirsty. Please, we tea?"

The Russians kindly handed them some steaming beakers. One of them addressed Lange.

"He no understand," interrupted Hanefi, "he from Birobidzhan, not know Russian."

The soldiers burst out laughing:

"Neither do you!"

"I am Chechen."

"It doesn't matter," said a fat Corporal. "We are all fighting against the Fascist occupier."

A young Russian asked them if they were going to Kolniki. They said they were but admitted they did not know the way. When they were leaving, the young soldier came out with them and offered to put them on the right road. Lange thought with disgust that Hanefi would have to kill him in order to get rid of him. When they had been walking for a half an hour, Hanefi turned round towards his guide quickly and punched him under the chin. The young Russian fell down, stunned. Hanefi got out his knife. Lange seized his arm:

"No!"

A dull sound. The Tartar had shattered the Russian's skull with one blow of his rifle butt.

They pricked up their ears. They heard a distant roll of thunder. The front! Lange calculated that being against the wind, the distance could not be great. Hanefi put his hand on his arm.

"Hanefi not go with you. Hanefi stay here. Hanefi go with the Chechens."

Lange hugged him.

The last two members of the expedition edged their way towards the front. They avoided positions held by the units without too much difficulty. The isolated Russian soldiers that they passed did not pay any attention to them. Leaving a copse, they saw some Soviet soldiers from behind. An officer gave an order. The soldiers got up and advanced in a line. The two fugitives followed them bent over then hid in a bush and waited for nightfall. When it arrived, step by step, they started their advance again. A field pocket lamp suddenly shone on them.

"What are you doing there?"

"Patrol", replied the Tartar coldly, shooting at the Soviet at the same time.

217

They ran. A flare shot up. They lay down then started to run. The sound of rifle fire rang out behind them.

"*Wer da?*" (Who goes there?).

They were saved, they were Germans. Lange presented himself to the commander of the company:

"Lieutenant Lange, of the Brandenburg Regiment, with the Tartar Seyd Timarkaiev, sole survivors of the failed Operation Shamil."

"Ah, it's you? We should thank you. You were doubtless small in number, but you did us one hell of a favour. The Reds withdrew an army corps from the front to capture you. They feared a general uprising among the peoples of the Caucasus."

Lieutenant Erhard Lange was at peace with himself. Operation Shamil had not been a total failure after all. On the 15th of January 1943, he was awarded the Knight's Cross of the Iron Cross, the seventh one for the Brandenburgers.

Chapter XIII

Captain von Kœnen's Tropical Battalion (Winter 1942-1943)

The crushing victory of the British at El Alamein, followed, three days later, by the Allied landing in Algeria and Morroco, seemed to sound the death knell of the Armoured Germano-Italian Army in Africa. The concentric Anglo-American advance coming from the west towards the Tunisian coast and the British advance threatening to overrun rapidly the whole of Tripolitania caught them in a pincer movement from which it was difficult to escape.

The Führer, despite the opinion of his generals on the terrain, in the first place Rommel, decided to do battle on Tunisian soil, using the new 5th Armoured Army, formed in December 1942 with the help of new divisions hastily transported across the 'brook', the Mediterranean in the language of the day. This 5th *Panzerarmee* joined up with the Germano-Italian Armoured Army retreating from Libya, which was to be later replaced by the 1st Italian Army having overall responsibility for the same German units.

The Germans, whose inferiority in strength and weapons was dismaying, nonetheless delighted in one certain advantage. They had experience of war. Their officers, of every rank, were used to facing up to the most critical situations and their courage and determination, along with their refusal to accept defeat, was a source of amazement among the 'boys', who did not have the same reasons for fighting to the last as they did.

The attack by the British, landed at Bône and Philippeville, against the defences at Tunis, had been pushed back by relatively weak forces. The Tebourba counter-attack had been a victory, as another surprise counter-attack at Sidi Bou Zid proved to be, further south, two months later opposite the disoriented Americans. These obvious short-lived victories showed nonetheless that the wildcat, however badly injured, was still capable of lashing out fearsomely. A desperate situation encouraged daring.

At the end of October 1942, the Lieutenant Friedrich von Kœnen's Tropical Company left Libya for Tunisia, via Murzuk. At the same time, in Brandenburg, Captain Plitt's 9th Company was becoming 'tropicalised', and it left for Africa in November. Following this, von Kœnen's company became a battalion, and the lieutenant a captain. His unit was still reinforced with a platoon from the Coastal Raider Company of the regiment, which became the 5th Company. The following few weeks were dedicated to coastal surveillance tasks and the shaping up of the battalion.

Colonel-General von Arnim, commander of the 5th Armoured Army, eventually decided to appeal to von Kœnen to cut two railway bridges to the north of Kasserine, on the Oran-Tunis line, an important supply line for the Allied troops, originating in Algeria.

On the 26th of December 1942, on the Bizerte airfield, two groups of Brandenburgers each boarded three DFS 230 gliders towed by Ju 52s. Captain von Kœnen's glider, whose target was the bridge at Sidi bou Bakr, took two Arabs to guide it on the way back. The men, nine in each glider, were seated on a central boom which ran lengthways along the narrow fuselage, with 150 kg of explosives, weapons and ammunition between their legs. They were forbidden to make any movement. After three hours, they were suffering from cramp and their nerves were beginning to disintegrate. Their main fear was encountering night fighters which would prove fatal.

Just as they were approaching the landing zone, they realised that they were flying in the middle of a formation of other planes. Captain von Kœnen's voice rang out:

"Prepare yourself for a dive! Emergency landing!"

But the order was almost immediately taken back. The formation in question was German and its mission was to cover the approach with the sound of its own engines.

The landing on a terrain recognised from air photos went off uneventfully; however, there was a glider missing and there was a light shining a short distance away. The group immediately settled themselves in a hedgehog around the gliders, weapons at the ready. It was a false alarm. The Arab guides sent on reconnaissance reported that some of the locals had lit a fire in front of a hut, just to warm themselves. As for the absence of the third glider, they would have the explanation for that later. The pilot of the Junkers towing it had followed one of the planes of the formation encountered en route by mistake. After straying off course without finding the target, he released the glider on the off chance, fortunately in the German zone.

Captain von Kœnen left with two men to reconnoitre the bridge, whose outline rose high up in the moonlight. Approximately 300 metres long, it consisted of two iron beams in the shape of a T, onto which cross-sleepers of the single track were bolted, and supported by stone block piers. Not a sentry to be seen. The guard of the bridge must have retired for the night to Sidi bou Bakr station, at the eastern end of the bridge. The officer sent a message to the other Brandenburgers. They arrived bringing the equipment with them.

A protection squad went upstream of the wadi, and another, downstream. The positioning of the explosive charges began. The central pier was heavily mined. Other charges were positioned further away on weight bearing beams in order to bring about other breaks in the structure.

It only remained for the ignition wires to be fitted. Consternation broke out, they were in the third glider! The Captain, seething with rage, was about to order the removal of the charges, when *Feldwebel* Dormann, an old engineer used to taking precautions, announced that he had a packing box of primers and a small roll of safety fuse in his own kit. There was exactly 60 cm per charge, in other words the man lighting each fuse would have forty seconds to seek shelter.

While the artificers of the group carried out the link-ups, one of the men had climbed up to the top of one of the telephone poles. He couldn't manage to cut the cables with his wirecutters. He became impatient and started to sever it with blows from his hatchet. The cable bent without breaking. The man became enraged and swore at the top of his voice in a Bavarian dialect, without realising he could wake the guard up. He did not see the officer making desperate gestures for him to be quiet. At long last, the cable broke and fell.

The station still showed no signs of life.

"They are sleeping", said student Hoffner sarcastically, as he distributed boxes of matches to the three men responsible for lighting the fuses.

While the fuses burned, the Brandenburgers distanced themselves with long, firm strides, taking care not to run into the shingle on the wadi bed. The Bavarian distinguished himself once more by catching his feet in some telephone cable and falling a distance of two metres very noisily. Another *"Sakrament!"* echoed in the conniving silence of the night.

Practically at the same time, three bursts of flames followed by powerful explosions and a rain of debris gave the signal to depart. The detachment had to vanish before daybreak.

The pilots still had time to set light to the gliders before the French arrived. The Brandenburgers ran behind their Arab guides, when automatic weapon fire was heard in the direction of the bridge.

Two men did not answer their names. The burning planes had not rallied them. When the day broke, the group penetrated the Djebel bou Ramli, and found themselves in temporary safety. The men had 180 kilometres to cover before reaching Maknassy, the first Italian stronghold.

But it was out of the question to march during daylight. The Brandenburgers gathered at the bottom of a small gorge where there was a little shade and tried to sleep.

Von Kœnen was not tired. He wanted to see that the bridge had been destroyed for himself and went up to higher ground. From a distance of three kilometres, his binoculars gave him an excellent view. At 9 a.m., he saw a spitting, steaming train arrive and stop abruptly in front of three collapsed spans, a destroyed pier and another one knocked over. Around 10a.m., some trucks stopped at the landing site and loaded up the remains of the burned gliders.

In the afternoon, several Arabs showed up in the gorge. One of them, who looked badly rigged out in his burnoose, suddenly threw it off. It was Berger, one of the missing men.

At nightfall, they began walking again. The Captain had planned a distance of 35 kilometres. They covered it in seven hours. The men started to stumble. The day was beginning to break, when, after crossing two roads and a railway line, they headed once again for the protection of the mountains.

The guide moved away to reconnoitre the surroundings, while the captain positioned the sentries and had the weapons prepared. After an hour, the Arab came back with a basket of dates and some news. The region of Sidi bou Bakr was crawling with American patrols. At Gafsa, there were French Spahis, British and Americans troops. Then, without waiting for the nightfall, he set off, to get back home as quickly as possible. He feared that his absence would be detected, but left the Germans with an inhabitant of the village where he had obtained the dates, who replaced him.

The group still had five days and nights of marching ahead of it. From then on the Brandenburgers made progress during the day. They were exhausted and staggering. Not one of them had the strength to carry the MG 42 light machine-gun that had been stripped so as to divide up the parts among them. The majority of them had cut the uppers of their ankle boots as their swollen toes hurt them so much. They had beards like scarecrows.

In the afternoon of the sixth day, they reached Maknassy, and drank their first hot coffee. The following morning, as they at last got some sleep, an Arab entered the village leading a donkey ridden by Feldmann, the second missing man.

The High Command in Africa rapidly decided that a third similar operation had to be carried out by Captain von Kœnen's Brandenburgers. On the 10th of January 1943, Lieutenant Luchs, commander of the company posted to the southern front, received the order to go to the headquarters of the Germano-Italian *Panzerarmee*. There, he received the mission to blow up the railway bridge crossing the Wadi el Melah, this time to the south, on the line linking Tozeur and Sfax. Means of transport: gliders once again. He was shown air photos.

"*Herr Oberst*", he said after having studied them, "I don't think a discreet approach is possible by air. The photos show there is a French camp 300 metres from the bridge, with cavalry and armoured cars. The planned landing zone is too near this camp. I think an approach by the Chott Jerid would attract less attention from the enemy. We occupy the east bank, the Allies the west bank. Between them is a vast no man's land, the salt desert where we can circulate freely."

"That's an idea," replied the Colonel, "but what transport are you thinking of using. Camels?"

"No, *Herr Oberst*, dromedaries are not acceptable. The heat and the reverberation are infernal. Only rapid light trucks could risk it, steering by compass. They could cross the Chott in less than an hour. Reaching its north-western limit, the bridge is only 30 kilometres away. Using the night as cover, we can do it without being detected."

"That's good, *Leutnant*, you seem to be certain of the matter. One must either have confidence in the Brandenburgers or do without them. I will give instructions for you to receive explosives. The bridge is not long, only 50 metres. The difficulty will be with the two high masonry piers. The engineers have made the necessary calculations. You will need 750 kilos of special explosives. Here is a sketch-plan of the laying-out to set up and here is the order which will give you full powers to draw the explosives. Don't waste time. The bridge must be blown up no later than the 18th of January."

Luchs returned to his company and selected seven experienced 'desert foxes', plus a very good interpreter, Lance-corporal Kaspar, who had swiftly learnt how to adapt his Palestinian Arabic to Libyan and Tunisian dialects. He had two British *Flitzers* overhauled at the motor transport park and set off without wasting any time for El Hamma, to the west of Gabes, where the engineer equipment park was to be found. The store-keeper shook his head:

"This explosive is not very common, we haven't got any here."

Luchs went back to Gabes.

"An aircraft? You might as well know, *Leutnant*, that no aircraft flies between Italy and Tunisia anymore. Your 'full powers' are useless."

Luchs stayed loitering about on the airfield. He saw a Ju 52 on the edge of the runway. He approached it, feigning indifference, and after chatting with the pilot learnt that he was going to leave for Naples where his plane had to receive a new engine. Luchs persuaded the pilot that his full powers gave him the right to emplane with him.

The following morning, Luchs was in Naples at 8 a.m. But he did not find any special explosives. At midday, in Rome, the same thing. There was only one hope left, Berlin. On the runway, a *Stuka* was having its tanks filled. The mechanic informed him that it was going to Germany.

The Lieutenant went to see the colonel in command of the airfield.

"You're going to Berlin? I'm extremely sorry, this crate is going to Munich. You may go, I'm busy."

"*Herr Oberst*," persisted Luchs, after a deep intake of breath, "I have an order from *Generalfeldmarschall* Rommel and I must leave for the Reich immediately. If you stop me, you will bear full responsibility."

The colonel let forth a torrent of choice words on the subject of greenhorns wanting to give lessons to their elders, then he angrily signed an emplaning order.

In Treviso, in Venetia, the plane landed to take on more fuel. But there was a storm over the Alps and the control tower denied permission for take-off. Luchs went to see the commander. He took advantage of a moment when the commander was absent to put a stamp on a petrol coupon and put the paper in his pocket. The commander came back.

"As I was saying. Nothing can be done. You'll have to wait for fine weather."

Thirty minutes later, the tank was filled and the plane taxied on the runway under the disapproving stares of the ground staff. A journey through hell began: gusts of down-wind threatened to flatten the plane against the mountains, a layer of snow on the canopy which blinded the pilot, whirlwinds which threw the plane in every direction. Both men were shivering with cold. The ordeal lasted four long hours, during which time they had no idea how long they had left to live.

Munich, at last! On the ground there was a strong hailstorm. Luchs telephoned Berlin to obtain authorisation to continue as far as Tempelhof. On landing, a car was waiting for him and drove him to Tirpitzufer.

Colonel Piekenbrock had planned everything ahead. The second lieutenant received his 750 kilos of 'special'. It was the 12th of January. The following morning, he had a fever of 40 degrees. The medical officer ordered him to bed. Luchs, after swallowing half of a tube of tablets, went off, unsteadily, to the Anhalter Station. He was lucky enough to get a fast train leaving for Rome and, luckier still, to find a seat. The following day, the 14th of January, the train arrived at Termini. A taxi transported him to the aerodrome.

At 6 p.m., he was in Trapani, Sicily. An unpleasant surprise was awaiting him. Because of the absence of fighters protecting the crossing of the 'brook', all takeoffs were forbidden for twenty-four hours. Luchs went to plead his case to the commander.

"Are you completely mad? To fly without protection with a cargo like that!"

Then shrugging his shoulders, he had Lieutenant Luchs sign a release form, recognising that he took to the air having been duly warned and under his responsibility alone.

At 8.30 p.m., the plane took off, passing two metres above the waves and soon arrived in sight of Tunis, but right in the middle of an air attack.

The parachute flares lit up the town like daylight. Burstings of flak filled the sky and exploding bombs covered the earth with lightning and smoke. The Junkers turned to the east to seek another airfield further south.

The flak crew mistook him for an allied plane and opened fire. One engine caught alight. Both men's hearts stopped beating when they remembered they had 750 kilos of explosives on them. The pilot did not hesitate. He dived on to the small airfield and pulled on the joy-stick in time to land.

The Italian soldiers surrounded the plane and called on the Madonna to witness that the two Germans had lost their heads. They were interrupted by the throbbing of enemy engines.

A sense of paralysing despair took possession of Luchs. He wanted to embrace his plane in protective arms. At the same time he wanted to run with the others to the underground shelter. And that is what he did, while the bombs opened up craters on the runway and lit fires here and there.

When the alert ended, Luchs and his pilot came out into the open air, expecting to find a horrible emptiness where their plane and its formidable cargo had once been. The plane was still there. "Another miracle", thought Luchs. In fact, the Junkers was in quite a bad state riddled with splinters, but its cargo remained intact.

The Italians, anxious to get rid of this dangerous presence, hurried to load the explosives on to a truck, that they had readily put at the disposal of the Brandenburgers. At El Hamma, *Feldwebel* Klima had put the last touches to the preparations. The two British *Flitzers* bore their original registration plates and tactical signs and each one was supplied with the German National War Flag ready to be used. The men were issued with sand-coloured clothing, the international uniform of the desert. Luchs used the evening of the 15th of January for a final rehearsal of the operation, using the topographical information that had been provided by local members of the *Destour*.[1]

1. Tunisian Nationalist movement led by Habib Ben Ali Bourguiba, future President of the Tunisian Republic.

The following morning at 6 a.m., they left for Kebili, swastika flag unfurled, then the crossing of the Chott, flag rolled up. They arrived at the Italian post of Djebel Morra late in the afternoon, flag unfurled once again.

The Italian *capitano* had information concerning the French camp. According to him there were 80 to 100 horsemen and a dozen armoured reconnaissance vehicles.

At 1 a.m., on the 17th, Luchs and his men were on their way to their target, flag once again hauled down, but ready to be hoisted at the first shot. After ten kilometres, the two lorries became stuck in the sand up to the axles.

It took their eight passengers one and a half hours of hard labour to get them out. When they were ready to leave it was too late: the operation would have to be put back twenty-four hours. In the meantime, they could try to get nearer to the target. Around 5 a.m., the distant whistling of a locomotive prompted them to be more prudent, and, at the same time, made the feverish urge to fight rise up in their blood. They looked for a hollow of a wadi to conceal their vehicles, which they covered with camouflage nets.

Two men were posted on sentry-duty, the others lay down to sleep. At 11 a.m., Luchs, who had detected no human presence since dawn, decided that a reconnaissance was possible. He left, flanked by Klima, disguised as Arabs. At around two kilometres from the bridge, they were able to observe with binoculars at ease. The camp was not visible. It had to be behind a hill that hid it from view. Suddenly, the *Feldwebel*, who had just made a careful scrutiny of the horizon, murmured: "*Herr Leutnant*, down there, two horsemen!"

Luchs turned round and watched.

"They've seen our tyre tracks and are going to discover the *Flitzers!* We must warn our comrades!"

The two men reached the camp in time to make the men sight their rifles. In fact, it was not two horsemen, but six, fifteen, soon a large platoon. At 50 metres the Brandenburgers opened fire, hoisting their colours. They aimed for the horses. Three mounts and two horsemen fell. The others withdrew to 200 metres, beginning an encircling movement. Rifles were no longer enough. The light machine-gun was brought to the firing position. As a result, the French moved back 500 metres. An encirclement was no longer possible, for its perimeter would have reached 3 kilometres.

The horsemen were now attempting to assemble. Heavy fire from the rifle grenades dispersed them, but two of their number left at a gallop for the camp. Luchs made a swift decision. He was not there to fight and die heroically, but to accomplish a mission. They therefore had to take advantage of this respite and disappear.

Covered by several bursts, the *Flitzers* took the route by which they had come at great speed. When the wind had blown away the dust that their wheels had swirled up, they saw a swarm of horsemen and several reconnaissance cars a way off, but they soon abandonned the pursuit.

At the Italian post, Luchs conferred with his NCOs.

"It's the 18th today, the deadline that the *Generalfeldmarschall* gave us. He must have his reasons. We'll set off again tonight at midnight, in order to make doubly sure. We must risk the lot."

Feldwebel Klima smiled.

"The French will never think that the 'Boches' they put to flight will have the cheek to come back. The champagne must be flowing in their camp!"

Kaspar agreed and added:

"Tomorrow would be too late. The French will be sober again and will have their eyes open."

They took the route they had taken the day before once again and, because of the knowledge they had acquired of the terrain, managed to position themselves one kilometre from the target, darkness rendering the use of any camouflage needless. They approached the bridge, climbed onto it, looked around them, without seeing any sentries. A confused sound of singing rose from the camp. Totally reassured, they went back to the two lorries. The explosives were loaded onto one of them, which advanced slowly towards the bridge, preceded and followed by security details one hundred metres apart.

The lieutenant and three of his men, including the irreplaceable Klima, carried out the work, while the five others were deployed as lookouts on either side of the bridge.

The charges were set to the engineers' specifications and the ignition wires grouped at the base of the bridge, on the bed of a wadi, where the long delay igniter was set for ten minutes.

Two men got in the *Flitzer* and returned to the other vehicle at full throttle and with all its lights on. Once they were gathered together and ready to leave, the Brandenburgers looked alternately at their watch and the bridge. Five minutes went by. Ten minutes: nothing. Fifteen minutes: nothing. Twenty minutes, still nothing.

"The mechanism didn't worked," concluded Klima. "Do we go back?"

Luchs agreed. They set off again. But they had scarcely crossed half the distance when a gigantic burst of flame rose up, followed by an enormous crash. Mission accomplished.

"That was a close shave!" murmured the two men.

This time, the enthusiasm of the Italians was at its height. Kindheartedly, the Brandenburgers raised their glasses with them.

When the group got back to headquarters, the air reconnaissance photos revealed to them that a train had fallen into the breach opened in the bridge. The locomotive and two waggons could be seen upside down on the bed of the wadi.

"That's not all, *Herr General*," specified Leutnant Luchs.

"All around the bridge, while my *Feldwebel*, my interpreter and myself were laying the charges, the others placed mines with delay igniters on either side of the bridge."

Then turning to the officer of the engineers:

"What I don't understand is that the delay lasted twenty-five minutes instead of ten."

"I must take some of the blame," admitted the engineer. "I should have realised that this British chemical igniter, containing acid, was adjusted for an average temperature of 30°. When you used it, it couldn't have been more than 10°. Under full sun the ten minutes would have been reduced to four."

230

In the same month, the 5th Company of von Kœnen's battalion made a name for itself by capturing a crew of four British men who had landed from a submarine on the coast. With the radio equipment seized, the Brandenburgers could indulge in a *Funkspiel* with the British, who sent them a second crew from Malta, and were taken prisoner like the first!

In February 1943, the new Brandenburg Coastal Raider Battalion delivered reinforcements of boats and men to the 5th Company in order to survey the coast around Bizerte. The new commander of the Brandenburg Division, Colonel von Pfuhlstein, made a personal visit to von Kœnen's battalion in Tunisia. He brought the captain back with him and left the unit to Lieutenant Hoffmann.

April announced the end of the Army Group Africa. The Brandenburgers of the *Tropenabteilung* were used as ordinary infantrymen with Major-General von Manteuffel's division, while the coastal raiders of the 5th Company pursued their surveillance of the shores. But the Brandenburgers had no intention of remaining stuck in Tunisia. The majority of them would manage to leave Cape Bon by boat to get back to Sicily.

PART THREE

THE BRANDENBURG DIVISION (1943-1945)

Chapter XIV

The *Abwehr* loses control of the Brandenburgers (Winter 1942-1943)

In the Autumn of 1942, while the Tropical Battalion under Captain von Koenen was being formed in Tunisia, Hettinger's company was still maintained in Finland and the 6th Company stationed in France was at the disposal of Marshal von Rundstedt's HQ. The main body of the Brandenburg Regiment was committed in tough fighting in the southern field of operations on the Eastern Front, on the spurs of the Caucasus Mountains.

I Battalion was reduced to *Kampfgruppe Walther* formed from the 2nd and 3rd Companies, who were fighting on the southern bank of the Terek River. In October, Lieutenant Schulte's 1st Company got back to Freiburg/Breisgau.

As for III Battalion under Major Franz Jacobi, only the 10th and 11th Companies were still committed in the Caucasus. As it was the turn of the 9th to become a 'tropical company', it had come back to Mödling, south of Vienna, in August. The 12th Company was still fighting against the partisans in the central sector between Smolensk and Vyazma.

The 5th and 8th Companies of Major Paul Jacobi's II Battalion were fighting in the Chikola sector, the zone of action of the III *Panzerkorps*.

On the 2nd of November, at 5 a.m., Operation 'Darg Koch' began. This was the name of the village, situated beyond the Terek, which had to be crossed.

The 5th Company, reinforced with a group from the 13th Antitank Battalion, an organic divisional unit of the 13th *Panzerdivision*, had the primary mission of capturing Ardon, which gave access to the river, and then to rush the four rail and road bridges. They were under the direct orders of the commander of the II Battalion. Lieutenant Kurt Steidl and thirty men forming the «shaking out» unit were responsible for the road bridge, on the Ardon-Darg Koch road. They quickly cleared the entrance to the bridge, which was weakly defended, but, crossing over to the other bank, they ran into a fortified area, with a large blockhouse in the middle of the position. During the deadly hand to hand combat, the bridge fell. The position was impossible to hold out any longer for the Russians; they fled in disarray towards Darg Koch. The Brandenburgers, accustomed to firing enemy weapons, made shells and grenades rain down on the fleeing enemy. By radio, Steidl informed Lieutenant Zülch, commander of the 5th Company, that the bridge had been taken. White flares were let off.

He saw however that several bridges were still held by the Russians a little further away. But he had too many casualties to be in a position to attack them.

It was particularly urgent to obstruct the end of the bridge since he saw through the binoculars that the Russians were reorganising themselves in front of Darg Koch. Their artillery started up and rounds were falling dangerously near.

Steidl requested *Nebelwerfers*[1] support by radio but their aim was too short and the rockets fell on to the German position inflicting more losses.

When the smoke lifted, Steidl saw a formation of Soviet tanks and trucks, loaded with infantrymen, arriving. It was a strong counter-attack clearly with the objective of taking back the bridge. After two

1. Multi-barreled electrically fired rocket-launchers.

238

hours, ammunition was beginning to run short and there was no relief in sight. The enemy subjected the Ardon road to curtain fire, in order to stop the Germans from progressing. The only thing the lieutenant could see through the binoculars was a thin cordon of infantrymen, lying flat on the ground, seven or eight hundred metres behind him. As he had no more than ten able-bodied men to use one antitank rifle and two light machine-guns, he hoped it was Zülch. Soon he would have no more than 7.92-mm cartridges and some hand grenades left. Crouching down amongst the dead and wounded of both the intermingled armies, the Brandenburgers felt irreparably lost.

The Russians had got sufficiently near to be able to throw grenades. The three men remaining with Steidl were injured one after the other. The last survivors had to withdraw so as not to be killed. The shells which fell ceaselessly on to the bridge had started to destroy it. However, coming from the other bank, in successive bounds, a lieutenant and a corporal had managed to get through and jumped in the trench next to Steidl. They had brought from the company the order to fall back immediately! The survivors shook their heads. To die in their hole or to die while falling back, it was the same thing.

"No", shouted Steidl to them, "even if we have one chance in a hundred of getting through, we must take it. On my signal, up and forward in ten metre bounds, at intervals of fifty metres. You!" he said to the youngest, who seemed to be the most demoralised, "you leave first. I'll leave last."

So everyone stood up, including the lightly wounded, and set on their way. They got back to Ardon miraculously unscathed.

Immediately, Lieutenant Zülch worked on dividing the remainder of his men up in order to form, come what may, four platoons with reduced strength. For the moment, the Brandenburgers were alone in holding the village. The Russians did not seem determined to capitalize their advantage and cross the river.

Then, one night, a little before dawn gunfire rang out:"Russians!"

Zülch was one of the first in the street, his submachine-gun in his hand. He ran barefoot, having had only enough time to slip on a pair of trousers. He gathered his men together, who were coming out of the houses half-clothed but all holding their weapons. Their crossfire was so effective that the attackers moved back to the outskirts of the village.

At that moment a captain appeared, claiming the authority to command the defence. He was the head of a battalion hurried to the scene and demanded that Lieutenant Zülch subordinate his troops to his command. Zülch replied with the outspokenness typical of the Brandenburgers:

"*Herr Hauptmann*, I have the situation completely under control and I know the area perfectly. By taking away my command, you will disorganise the defence!"

It was a waste of time.

"*Was?* We are in front of the enemy! I demand your total obedience!"

Zülch, seething with rage, submitted. To prove to him who was in command, the captain ordered him to form a patrol straight away and go and observe the enemy from the top of a nearby hill.

Zülch was astounded.

"What for? To expose ourselves to any shelling? Why do we need to know if the Russians are being reinforced? With the arrival of your battalion, we are strong enough to give a warm welcome to all those who show up. What is urgent is to strengthen our defences and to pre-position your companies. My place is here and not on that hill."

The Captain bawled:

"Be quiet! That's an order! *Los!*"

Zülch shrugged his shoulders, assembled a dozen men and left the village by a side footpath. He was scarcely out of sight of the irascible captain when he sent the majority back to their positions and continued with his orderly and a runner. He hadn't gone a hundred metres when a shell hit him right on the head. The decapitated body remained standing for a moment, then, like a felled tree, tumbled to the ground in one piece.

One of the finest officers trained for special missions had died, because of the fault of one of the too many superiors who refused to admit that the Brandenburgers were not soldiers like other soldiers.

A company formed from troops of II Battalion, which was protecting the withdrawal of the 13th Armoured Division, was surrounded by the Russians at the same time in the region of Alagir on the 11th of November. To escape the shelling that was decimating them, the Brandenburgers dug themselves in, digging desperately in the mud with their hands. They held out three days and pushed back all the attacks with the two light machine-guns that they had left. Brown bodies covered the ground in front of them. However, the Russians had penetrated to the right and the left of their defensive layout and their liaison with the main forces was becoming more and more difficult. There was nothing left to eat, the injured were dying because of lack of medical aid. In the morning, a white frost covered the numb bodies.

At last, the High Command decided to make the front fall back. That evening, gigantic fireworks announced the withdrawal. Eight hundred vehicles, petrol and ammunition reserves blew up. A number of the forces managed to sneak away by a breach, leaving all the injured that the Soviets finished off as they advanced. The Brandenburgers set off walking last at the first rays of dawn. The enemy, behind them, fired with all their barrels. Their path was scattered with corpses and moaning bodies. A small handful managed to get back to the exhausted remainder of the 13th *Panzerdivision*.

At the same period, the *Abwehr* was disrupted by harsh disputes concerning the use of the Brandenburgers. The regiment had been neglected more and more by its parent organisation and the dependence of companies on the units to which they were temporarily subordinated increased in proportion.

Division or army corps commanders at that time considered the Brandenburgers as their skivvies, without seeing to their replenishment of weapons, equipment and vehicles. For its part, the General Army Branch of the OKH, [2] normally directly involved with this type of problem, declared itself to be incompetent.

2. *Oberkommando des Heeres*, High Command of the Army.

In fact, the *Abwehr* was out of date and the conflicts with its opposite number within the SS, the SD, became more and more animated. The Office VI of the RSHA,[3] equivalent of the *Abwehr* II, even created a *Lehrbataillon zbV* at Oranienburg whose tasks were strangely in common with those of the Brandenburg Regiment. The command was to be entrusted to an, as yet unknown, SS officer of the name of Otto Skorzeny.

It was in November 1942 that an important decision affecting the Brandenburg Regiment was taken at the OKW. From the 1st of January 1943, it was to be changed into a *Sonderverband* (Special Unit) *Brandenburg* and increased in strength. The existing companies had to give rise to battalions and battalions to regiments in order to form a division in the Spring.

The Staff of the existing regiment became the *Sonderverband Brandenburg* from November, I Battalion was soon to become the *Sd.Vd. 801*, II the *Sd.Vd. 802*, III the *Sd.Vd. 803* to which a newly created *Sd.Vd. 804* had to be added.

This change in organisation was accompanied by a much more fundamental one. The new unit was no longer placed under the direct command of the *Abwehr II* as it had been previously, but, as from the 1st of April 1943, of the Wehrmacht Operations Staff, headed by General Alfred Jodl. He wrote: *"The Wehrmacht Operations Staff lacks a unit of its own for the OKW war theatres. We have to go begging to the Army High Command for every division, a tiring and often annoying practice. This is an unworthy and at the same time unbearable situation! The newly-formed Brandenburg Division will therefore be placed under the direct command of the Wehrmacht Operations Staff as its sole house unit and will be deployed by it."*

The measure was officially justified by the concern of preventing the Brandenburg units from being improperly employed by the divisions to which they were subordinated in the context of their missions. But it was also the tangible manifestation of the loss of influence of the *Abwehr* to the advantage of the SD.

3. Reich's Main Security Office, to which the *SD* (Security Service), the *Gestapo* (Secret State Police) and the Criminal Police were attached.

In practice, the transformation would not take effect in a short time. The Brandenburg units committed in the East were temporarily kept there and wore themselves out in the cold and the snow like ordinary infantry companies. The remainder of the *Kampfgruppe Walther* did not return to Freiburg, where the 1st Regiment had to be formed, until the beginning of April 1943. The *Sonderverband 801's* I Battalion that was created in the meantime had been dispatched to the Eastern Front on the 30th of January. Landing at Idriza, near the Latvian border, it was to be brought to fight against the partisans.

In December 1942, Captain Horlbeck formed a *Kampfgruppe* with the companies of II Battalion, to which was added the III Battalion's 11th Company. Handed over to Lieutenant Weithoener afterwards, this *Kampfgruppe* was the last German unit to cross the frozen Don delta in February. In April, the remainder of the unit was ordered to the new Austrian garrison, before joining Baden-Unterwaltersdorf where the new 2nd Regiment was being organised.

First unit of the *Sonderverband 803* to be set up, II Battalion, created in Düren from the 6th Company that had come back from France, left Germany in February to go and quarter in the Pyrenees.

In April, the two remaining companies of old III battalion, Brandenburg Regiment arrived in Düren, while the 9th and the 12th remained in the East.

The *Sonderverband 804* was created in Brandenburg and entrusted to Major Heinz who assembled some new volunteers, defaulters and loners coming from former disbanded units sent to the barracks.

On the 9th of February, Colonel Haehling von Lanzenhauer, whose own destiny had been linked to that of the regiment since the Autumn of 1940, died in hospital in Germany of a lung illness. A newcomer replaced him, Colonel Alexander von Pfuhlstein. He wore a Knight's Cross about his neck that was won in 1942 as commanding officer of the 154th Infanterie Regiment on the Eastern Front, in the Demjansk pocket. Incidentally he was reputed to be an anti-Nazi, a conviction obviously instilled by Colonel Oster, the head of the Central Department of the *Abwehr* with whom he had begun contact around 1935.

The new Brandenburg Division had to comprise a staff formed in Berlin, four light infantry regiments each of three battalions, the Tropical Battalion under Captain von Koenen, a coastal raider battalion and a signals battalion. The remaining units were made up of a training regiment and a battalion of Russian volunteers.

The new 1st Regiment, was naturally entrusted to Major Wilhelm Walther and had its home base in Freiburg/Breisgau.

In May 1943, while Captain Plitt's I Battalion was fighting against the partisans in White Russia, the Captain Gerhard Pinkert's II Battalion was sent to Yugoslavia. In June, the regimental staff moved to the Eastern Front, with the Orlino marshes as its destination. In August, I Battalion returned to Freiburg.

The 2nd Regiment, commanded by Lieutenant-Colonel von Kobelinsky, got itself organised in Baden. In July, it was dispatched to Greece.

The 4th Regiment under Lieutenant-Colonel Heinz was the only one to be maintained in the historical barracks in Brandenburg. It was also the first to be transported to Yugoslavia, from the month of April 1943.

The new Coastal Raider Battalion, the *Küstenjäger-Abteilung*, was created in January from the former Light Engineer Company which had returned from Kerch, on the banks of the Sea of Azov. Its four companies were equipped with heavy assault and inflatable boats. Commanded by Captain Conrad von Leipzig, who had been on duty in Africa within the *Sonderkommando Dora*, the *Küstenjäger* Battalion was intended either to fight the partisans from the sea by landing rapidly to carry out quick raids, or to neutralise port installations. But the unit was not set up until July in Lindau.

The Brandenburg Signals Battalion organised itself slowly in Berlin-Zehlendorf under Captain Eltester.

The battalion of Russian volunteers was created at Freiburg, home base of the 1st Regiment, but trained in Krapenuhl, near Brandenburg. Entrusted to Captain Alexander Auch, it was christened 'Alexander' in honour of its leader. It was comprised of a 'white' company composed essentially of Ukrainians and Byelorussians, and a 'black' company principally made up of Caucasians. In addition, five of the twelve battalions that formed the four light infantry regiments had the use of a 'legionnaire' company usually made up of Russian volunteers. Considering the tasks that awaited the new division, essentially the fight against partisans, the natives knowing the country well were now more useful than English or Czech speaking Germans.

The *Abwehr II* had made a last attempt to keep some control over the Brandenburg Division by obtaining that the divisional training regiment, named 'Kurfürst', be made up of training personnel from the school at Gut Quenzsee. But it was withdrawn from the division after the 1st of April 1943 and a new *Lehrregiment Brandenburg* was formed the following month.

Finally, the new division did not include any organic support, medical or transport troops, unlike conventional units. As before, the units using the Brandenburgers would have to provide for them.

Chapter XV

Lieutnant Kohlmeyer's Legionnaires

On the 6th of July 1943, the 3rd Regiment's I Battalion of the new Brandenburg Division, having left Düren by train, arrived at Pustoshka, to the west of Velikiye Luki and to the north of Nevel. There it relieved I Battalion, 1st Regiment committed on the Eastern Front since January and in that zone from the month of May, which was now moving to Orodesh. Its mission consisted of protecting the supply road which crossed a region of forest and marsh in a south-north direction, where the particularly active partisans were slowing down the military traffic on a daily basis and inflicting perceptible losses to the units in charge of reducing them.

The companies were divided up between the strongholds chosen according to their mission. Lieutenant Kohlmeyer's 4th, one of the 'legionnaire' companies in the division, composed of Soviet volunteers recruited in the *Stalags* and trained by the Germans, set up in a large farm in Sarethsje.

Lieutenant Herbert Kriegsheim, commanding the battalion and former head of the Coastal Raider Company, gathered his unit commanders together at his Pustoshka CP for an analyse of the situation.

In the late afternoon, Kohlmeyer went back to his stronghold in his *Kübelwagen*. On this occasion, he had taken the wheel and his driver, a lance-corporal, was next to him.

As straight as a die, the road which crossed through the forest was in good condition and the car was moving at great speed when, in the middle of the roadway, a helmeted *Feldwebel* of the *Feldgendarmerie* flanked by a lance-corporal armed with a submachine-gun asked to see the papers of the vehicle, after presenting himself in the prescribed manner. The *Feldwebel*, as well as his gorget in silvered sheet-metal, wore the prestigious German Cross in gold on his chest.

"What is the meaning of this?" replied Kohlmeyer curtly.

"My apologies *Herr Oberleutnant*, this area is infested with bandits. [1] We are obliged to carry out strict checks of any vehicles."

Kohlmeyer had not had wind of any checks of this type and it was most abnormal that two totally isolated men were in a zone "infested with bandits", unless they had a death wish. And how would they have got there? The lieutenant saw no car anywhere that could have brought them from Vitebsk or elsewhere. However, the *Feldwebel* was quite obviously German. His language was impeccable and he even spoke in rather educated tones.

"This is a comical situation" commented Kohlmeyer as he handed over his papers. "Are you taking me for a partisan?"

"Of course not," replied the *Feldwebel* laughing.

He handed back his papers. But the lieutenant had noticed a shocking detail in the military policeman's dress. His German Cross in gold, surprising enough in his case and which had to be worn on the right according to the regulations, was pinned to the left pocket of his field blouse, in the position reserved for the Iron Cross. He was overcome by an indefinable malaise. A glance in the wing mirror showed him that the other provost had taken up position behind the vehicle, his *Maschinepistole* in firing position.

"You should tell your colleague to move. He's making me nervous," said Kohlmeyer.

1. Official German term for partisans from August 1942.

"Müller," shouted the *Feldwebel*, "everything is in order!"

The lance-corporal did not seem to understand and did not change his bearing. Kohlmeyer's suspicions became clearer.

"That's a very beautiful award you are wearing there," he said to the NCO, calmly pointing out the sparkling German Cross adorned with a large swastika in black enamel.

"At the front since the first day of the war, *Herr Oberleutnant*," replied the fellow as he clicked his heels together in true Prussian style.

"*Donnerwetter!*" continued Kohlmeyer. "You well deserve a couple of cigarettes." Then he turned to his driver: "So can you pass me the box by your feet?"

There was no box at the lance-corporal's feet but a submachine-gun with a loaded magazine inserted into the feedway. An intent stare from his lieutenant made him grasp the situation. He bent down casually, disengaged the operating handle from the safety notch and threw the weapon into his hands.

The false-provost was no novice. He nodded to his companion who also raised his weapon. But Kohlmeyer would not have been a Brandenburger if he had not been the first to fire. Sawn in two, 'lance-corporal' Müller collapsed onto the road. A second burst settled the score of the *"Feldwebel"*, who had leapt away to seek shelter in the forest.

"Load up his body", said Kohlmeyer, "as proof."

Once at the farm, a search revealed the contents of his pockets. He was an ex-German Communist.

In the night of the 18th and the 19th of July, Lieutenant Kriegsheim was standing with his adjutant in front of the hut which sheltered the CP of his battalion at Pustoshka.

"A beautiful night," murmured the adjutant, a young second lieutenant native of Riga. "A magnificent night..."

Then he turned his head to listen out. "It sounds like a motorcycle," he said. In the distance a revving sound could be heard.

"Who could possibly go for a ride on a motorbike through the woods in the middle of the night", said Kriegsheim, ill at ease. "It's coming from the direction of Sarethsje."

They listened without saying a word. A few seconds later, a motorcycle stopped in front of the hut. The driver hurriedly turned off the ignition, let his machine fall on to its side and ran towards the entrance.

"Hey!" shouted the adjutant. "What's happening? Come over here."

The man turned round and walked quickly towards them.

"The stronghold has been attacked by surprise", he called out in Russian, distraught. We were asleep, when suddenly gunfire broke out outside. And, when we went out, it was already over. Just dead bodies, bodies everywhere..."

"*Verflucht!* Partisans?"

"I don't know. Who else? Outside everything was turned upside down. I escaped as quickly as I could with my motorbike."

"Put the 2nd Company on alert immediately", ordered Lieutenant Kriegsheim to his adjutant.

The telephone line with Sarethsje had been cut. While waiting for the 2nd Company to reach Pustoshka, the Russian legionnaire was questioned once again. He continued to splutter out his story of heavy and sudden rifle fire, of the innumerable deaths.

As the moon was growing dim, the 2nd Company was now going towards Sarethsje in combat order. The stockades of the stronghold emerged from the dawn mists. In the middle of the track, a shape lying on the ground could be made out. It was Lieutenant Kohlmeyer. A pistol had fallen from his open hand, his body had been awfully pierced by the projectiles.

When the Brandenburgers entered the farm, their weapons ready to fire, they discovered a heap of intermingled bodies, German NCOs and Russians shot together and stretched out lifelessly. The sound of groaning rose up from all around. Some other legionnaires, stupefied, were crouching in hidden recesses.

The different isbas where the Germans were able to quarter were searched straight away. Their doors had been riddled with bullets and hand grenades had been thrown inside. Everything pointed to an act that had been prepared down to the minutest detail, as all of the fourteen Germans of the company had been shot. Forty-six Russian legionnaires had disappeared, but eighty-two remained, a good half of which were dead or wounded. Two lorries were missing. No trace could be found either of the legionnaire Alexander Lewa, a Russian who had emigrated to Serbia after the Revolution and had even married a German woman. He had just formed an intelligence service within the 4th Company, taking two men in each platoon.

As there was every indication that the attack had not been directed from the outside, one thing was becoming certain: it was a mutiny!

A reinforced platoon followed the tracks of the two lorries. They were discovered in the forest, pushed behind a bank edging a side road. Around midday, the pursuers came under violent fire. The Brandenburgers realised that they were exposed to German weapons, notably the MG 42 with its fearsome rate of fire, for the moment turned against them. After a short combat, they had to break off the attack, a considerable group of partisans having evidently joined the mutineers. They had to retreat.

In Sarethsje meanwhile, the wounded were being cared for and the survivors were giving their accounts. Fire had indeed been opened from the outside by legionnaires from the company who had mutinied. When it had stopped, the mutineers had entered the farm, holding pocket lamps, to finish off all the wounded Germans. They had all recognised the leader, the legionnaire Alexander Lewa, who was naturally believed to be above all suspicion. The person who the battalion commander really mistrusted following revelations made by the Chechen legionnaire Seynal was another member of the 4th Company named Kirin, former captain in the Soviet Army having even commanded an artillery battalion, and what is more an ex-member of the Communist Party. In actual fact, he was only the second in command. Only two legionnaires also exposed by the same Chechen, Prishwin and Khanow, had been apprehended during a train journey and handed over to the Field Security Police of the German Army.

In Pustoshka, blue smoke rose up in large clouds inside the I Battalion's CP. The officers were seated, motionless, puffing nervously on their cigarettes, while Lieutenant Kriegsheim related to them in minute detail the development of the mutiny. When he had finished, he remained silent, staring at the ground.

"Who is to take care of the execution of the surviving legionnaires?" asked the commander of the 1st Company finally, a young lieutenant originating from Thuringia.

Kriegsheim lifted his head, his eyes sparkling with indignation, his hands clenched.

"Why must they be shot?"

"There is no warrant for such a question!" replied the young officer. Lieutenant Mertens, commander of the 2nd Company, added further:

"If we don't take severe measures in such a case, our men will be under the impression they belong to a relief committee and not a military unit. It will be felt at the first operation."

"These old Soviet soldiers are really all traitors, every single one of them," added another senior officer. "They come with us to escape the prison camps, play the game long enough to beguile us into trusting them, then go back to the Reds after doing in their German comrades. It seems to me that what has just happened is sufficiently eloquent. If we don't put all the survivors against the wall we would show ourselves to be irresponsible!"

"Anything else?" asked Kriegsheim.

Silence was restored. The air was stifling, the tension and the heat unbearable. One officer tapped his fingers interminably on the table, another tirelessly sharpened his pencil. Through the openings, the sun gave off a harsh light.

"Only the mutineers can be punished," he continued. "Khanow and Prishwin were already killed by a *Feldwebel* going back to their cell, following a so-called escape attempt. Without an investigation, my belief is quite clear on the matter..."

"It would be the last straw if the *Feldwebel* were worried," retorted the young lieutenant from Thuringia angrily. "In that case I would ask for an immediate transfer!".

Lieutenant Kriegsheim now had to control himself in order to speak calmly.

"This matter is closed! But if other suspects are discovered among the legionnaires, they will be court-martialled in accordance with the rules. The truth is that we have been beaten on our own ground, that of lies and dissimulation. Incidentally, I wonder, gentlemen, if you are still in your right minds. Who prevented the Russian legionnaires remaining in Sarethsje from going over to the partisans in their turn? They were even massacred by the mutineers as savagely as our German NCOs. What greater proof of faith can you give me?"

Naturally nobody could give one.

"It is out of the question to execute the legionnaires that did not mutiny," concluded Kriegsheim with such authority that no officer challenged him.

The 4th Company was disbanded, but a new platoon was formed with the available Russian legionnaires. However the affair went up as high as Berlin, making a distinct threat hang over the head of Oberleutnant Kriegsheim. As a result he shortly lost the command of his battalion.

With the Alexander Legionnaire Battalion also sent to the East, the 3rd Regiment's III Battalion under Captain Grawert had to participate in operation 'Zitadelle' and seize the bridges of Kursk as the vanguard, but his mission was called off at the end of the month and he was to be committed in a purely defensive fighting on the Desna River, winding up in heavy losses. On the 2nd of October, he was withdrawn from the front, with just 360 men answering the roll-call, and sent to the south-east of Minsk.

I Battalion, from then on commanded by Captain Wasserfall, who was to be succeeded by Captain G. Pinkert, fought its toughest battles in the early Autumn, this time against the Red Army. It was widely used on all sides, like a fireman of the front line. On the 6th of October it was subordinated to the 246th Infantry Division to the east of Vitebsk. At the end of November, from then on subordinated to the 211th Infantry Division, constituting with other units the *Kampfgruppe Nord*, it counter-attacked on the Polotsk-Vitebsk road.

On the 9th of December, the battalion was withdrawn from the front and sent to Koslovo. It was swiftly thrown into battle again, until such time as the front became stabilised in the Vitebsk region.

Sent back to the zone of operations at the end of 1943, III Battalion was committed to the south of the Beresina River opposite regular Russian formations reinforced with partisans. It was soon brought back to the east of Pinsk with the Regiment's Staff, while I Battalion was committed south of Polotsk before being sent to Horodno in order to be joined to the prestigious Feldherrnhalle *Panzergrenadier* Division. The two battalions freed the supply routes and did not join up with each other until mid-March.

I Battalion was held in the Derevna region until the Spring of 1944. It did not leave the Eastern Front for Italy until the 30th of May, where it arrived with III Battalion in June.

II Battalion under Captain Bansen had been sent to France, where it was the first to leave for Italy in October 1943, [2] put at the disposal of the Supreme Commander South in the Abruzzi. There it protected the supply lines against the partisans and kept watch over the Adriatic coast where the High Command feared an Allied landing would take place.

2. With the exception of the 8th (Legionnaire) Company, mostly composed of French volunteers. Quartered in Pont-Saint-Esprit (Gard) it was to be held in France to fight against the maquis, administratively attached to the signals battalion of the 11th Army.

Chapter XVI

Colonel Branto
(1944)

The first unit of the Brandenburg Division to reach the Balkans was the 4th Light Infantry Regiment under Lieutenant-Colonel Heinz. In April 1943, he spread his units around Sjenica, in Serbia. In June, Captain Hollmann's I Battalion was transported to Greece, in the Peloponnesus.

In July, two battalions of Colonel Pfeiffer's 2nd Regiment went to Greece.

The 1st Regiment under Lieutenant-Colonel Walther met up with the 2nd there in September. It protected the Athens road and at the same time had to keep a close eye on the Gulfs of Corinth and Euboea, both suitable for an Allied landing. In the Autumn, the Coastal Raider Battalion was involved in many attacks of islands occupied by British and Italian forces.

On New Year's day 1944, the 1st Regiment's I Battalion protected the Thermopylae Pass by the south and II Battalion protected it by the north.

In the 2nd Regiment, I Battalion was resting in Prijepolje in Serbia, after fighting against Tito's partisans. II Battalion left Tirana, in Albania, and joined I at Prijepolje, as did III Battalion. The regiment was subordinated to the V Mountain Corps.

The 4th Regiment continued to provide security for the major communication roads in Yugoslavia, where the attack by the Titist brigades failed to wipe it out. Two battalions of the 3rd Regiment were still in Russia, a third in Italy.

The *Küstenjäger* Battalion under Captain von Leipzig had assembled its *Sturmboote* in the northern Dalmatian islands and was reorganised, while its 1st Company patrolled in the Aegean.

If the Reich had had an inexhaustible supply of men, it doubtless could have imposed its law on the peoples of the Balkans by force. But, while it had to control enormous fronts in Russia where its armies suffered bitterly from lack of reserves, it was impossible for it to provide its lines of communications forces in Yugoslavia with the reinforcements they were clamouring for.

Large areas were left completely neglected through lack of strength.

Such was the case in the area that straddled the border between North Albania and Kosovo, Serbian territory inhabited by Albanian, Muslim and Christian mountain people, passionate about their freedom and indifferent to the political conflicts of the modern world to which they refused to belong.

The Germans did not have the means to invade by force the inextricable mountains where the Albanian groups hid. In addition, faced with a powerful attack, these groups would withdraw to the south and come back after the departure of the columns. The Abwehr considered that subversive action by its agents could, on the other hand, obtain definite results. It had a local station in Pec, in Kosovo, at its disposal from where its operations were to be conducted, principally in the Pec-Prizren-Scutari triangle roughly in the area of the Drin basin.

The situation presented some major difficulties owing to the fact that there were numerous antagonisms which existed at that time in Yugoslavia. The forces initially opposed to the Axis were divided between the monarchist Chetniks, grouped around General Mihailovic, and the Communists, allied to Russia and controlled by Tito. The Chetniks allied themselves to Tito's partisans, then the two leaders separated and from then on their forces clashed.

At that period the Abwehr was still trying to evade a complete takeover by the SD and, although the Brandenburg Division had got away from Canaris, the collaboration between the Abwehr and the Brandenburgers went on to lower levels.

That is how the division came to provide the cadre and command officers and NCOs of the station at Pec, which in addition to a company of Byelorussians, was made up of a troop of two hundred Tadzhiks, mountain people from Pamir recruited by the Abwehr in the Soviet prison camps. Their hatred of Communism made them very reliable allies. A chrome mine in Dakovica was guarded by two hundred Turkomans brought together in the same conditions. To establish strongholds in a line surrounding the danger zone was the only thing the Abwehr could strive after. Faithful to its tactics, it did everything possible to ensure the sympathy of the population.

Learning that the inhabitants of the neighbouring area of Gusinje, to the south-west of Pec, wanted to be protected from the Titist encroachments coming from the north, it sent a detachment of Tadzhiks and Turkomans, two-thirds Muslim, to the area, commanded by a mere *Obergefreiter* of the Brandenburgers, Fred Brandt, who had scarcely risen the ranks at all since 1941. [1] He was familiar with central Asian countries and knew their dialects. In addition he spoke Russian, because of his Baltic origins it was easy for him to assimilate Serbo-Croat rapidly. In the eyes of those organising special missions it was his merit as a person and his abilities as a fellow-soldier which were important and not the rank stated on his *Soldbuch*. That was why Brandt had been sent as advanced guard to Gusinje as a *Stadtkommandant*, and not an ordinary field grade officer.

On the 3rd of December 1943, the first Friday following his arrival in the village, Brandt went to the mosque with his Muslim soldiers. After presenting arms to the building, they entered it in their socks, rifles in their hands, following the Albanian custom. Brandt, along

---

1. Period when he undertook a first mission in Afghanistan as a Gefreiter, a rank just below his current rank. See Chapter VIII.

with the others, took part in the prayers and prostrations. He knew the suras of the Koran as well as any Imam.

The following Sunday on the other hand, he summoned the Christians following the Greek rite to go to church and attend Mass.

When the Germans paid for services rendered and provisions handed over by the population not in money but in cartridges, their popularity knew no bounds.

The high Dukagjin plateau stretched to the south of Gusinje, and separated the Albanian part of Yugoslavia from Albania itself whose inhabitants called themselves, like all Albanians, *Shqipetars*. They were recognisable by their clothing, the most typical feature of which was a skullcap of white felt, worn at the back, leaving the forehead entirely free.

Brandt had manipulated a meeting with San Nikola, the leader of the *Shqipetars* in the Theti valley, on the other side of the mountain. He secured his alliance against Tito's Serbs by providing him with Italian carbines for his troop. When, in order to conclude their agreement with a flourish, he gave Bairaktar an Italian Beretta submachine-gun for his personal use, the leader embraced him and invited him to spend Christmas at his home.

Brandt felt that by responding to this invitation he would learn some interesting things about what was happening on the other side of the Dukagjin. Climbing the 2,000 metre high barren plateau, under the snow and an icy north wind and struggling for ten hours without being able to stop was not exactly a relaxing excursion. Brandt, his guide and his two companions were on the point of exhaustion when they reached San Nikola's house. They took care to confine themselves to their role as guests, to be celebrated and pampered, without asking any questions and without uttering the slightest word resembling an order, intolerable for the *Shqipetars*. Salvos saluted their departure just as they had done for their arrival.

On his return, Brandt obtained a meeting with his superior in Pec, to whom he confided what he had learnt in Theti, by putting together all the snatches picked up during the course of the conversation. He had quite simply discovered the origin of the enemy attacks against the chrome mine at Dakovica, which had continued repeatedly over a period of several months, in ever more intensity.

Between the Albanian border and the town of Dakovica lay the Bytyce forest, where the precious mine was to be found. To the south west of the forest, clinging to the high, arid slopes separating the Albanian Drin basin from that of Serbian Morava, was the miserable village of Dega, without any access roads and which had not, until then, attracted anybody's attention. However, it was the largest outpost of the Intelligence Service in the Balkans where about ten British officers, including two colonels, had set up their quarters and their radio posts. Weapons, ammunition, equipment, provisions and money were regularly parachuted there and gathered together in a large warehouse. The surrounding population took direct advantage of this manna from heaven and it was in their interests to keep the existence of this British base of operations a secret.

In mid-February 1944, a strong attack was launched against Dega, carried out by a German mountain infantry regiment. It was a success and the spoils exceeded the expectations that Brandt's information had given rise to! But they had to wait two months for the arrival of Captain Plitt's I Battalion, 1st Regiment of the Brandenburg Division, coming from Larissa in Greece, which divided its companies between Pec and Dakovica.

On the 8th of March 1944, Brandt took the Dukagjin road again, this time with six Tadzhiks and an Albanian interpreter, with the mission of establishing a permanent forward stronghold in the south, behind the mountain.

Leaving Theti, where he had friends, he carried out reconnaissance in several directions. In the Nikaj valley, he came across the tracks of the partisan chief Nik Sokol, who had pledged allegiance to the British. Brandt, who understood the psychology of the Albanian mountain people did not make the mistake of believing that Nik Sokol served the British by political choice any more than any other partisan leader. He knew that for the leaders of the Albanian groups, that the only thing that counted was the advantages they could obtain. He therefore considered he had some good cards to play.

He asked the inhabitants of Nikaj to provide him with a guide. He couldn't find one. The villagers were afraid. He made up his mind to venture alone and one evening, openly placed his weapons on the church square, then set off in the direction that he had been shown. After several mishaps, he arrived at the chief's shelter, protected by a hundred or so partisans some of whom were in British uniforms and carrying British submachine-guns and light machine-guns as well as Italian carbines. The majority had the silver encrusted grip of a revolver sticking out of their belts.

When he found himself face to face with Nik Sokol, Brandt strove to show him that a German presence at Nikaj had nothing but advantages for him. He promised not to impede the parachute drops and even to contribute to them. He was anxious above all to be considered as a simple visitor and guest by the Albanians. Delighted, the chief held out his hand and kissed him.

Then, in order to distinguish him from ordinary German soldiers, he gave him his white felt skullcap as a gift, which he pushed well back on the nape of his neck, and he called his subordinates to inform them of the agreement which, like all diplomatic undertakings, contained a secret clause. Nik Sokol's troop would end all hostility towards German troops, while continuing to claim credit for what would then be imaginary attacks to the British. In this way, he would not only have nothing more to fear from the Germans, but the airdrops would continue as in the past.

Their return journey took them through Dega and then by the Dakovica road to Pec. Before reaching sight of Pec, Brandt removed his white skullcap and replaced it with his regulation *Tropenfeldmütze* in olive drab cotton twill. The leader of the Abwehr station was waiting for him impatiently. Brandt informed him of the agreement struck with the Albanians.

"You were wrong trusting a man sold to the British to that extent", the Captain declared.

"An Albanian does not sell himself, *Herr Hauptmann,* he pockets shamelessly what he is offered. For the partisans, a British officer is a milch-cow. They dispute among themselves for it and don't hesitate to kill. The officer in command of a British mission is the big man."

"The British are handing out gold and you have none."

"That's my advantage. The Albanians have no respect for the one who pays. They respect the guest who obeys their customs and who does not want to give any order, something that neither the British nor our own army does."

On the 4th of April, Brandt occupied his stronghold with his six Tadzhiks. On the 11th, he was at Nik Sokol's home. When he entered, he found a large gathering sitting cross-legged in front of low tables loaded with food and drink.

The host made Brandt sit down beside a friendly guest who shook his hand like everyone else and introduced himself:

"Major Anthony Neel, of the British Army. Would you like some Scotch?"

The German understood that the meeting had been arranged intentionally. He joined in. When the guests got up, the Albanian drew the two enemies aside.

"We three must be in absolute agreement on what has been decided. My friend Brandt here will promote British airdrops. In exchange, my men will not attack the Germans."

The Brandenburger was not really surprised by the acceptance of the British officer, who feared for his safety. He had seen the authority that Brandt wielded. In the mountains of Albania, his potential enemies were the rival Albanian troops, who could attack at any moment to seize weapons and a variety of equipment parachuted in, rather than the distant German forces. A realist, typical of his race, he considered that an arrangement, even an unnatural one, which allowed him to fulfil his mission — of arming the Albanian partisans — was, after all, an excellent one.

Neel took the protection of the Abwehr very seriously and wanted to obtain the *bene placit* of his superior. He suggested to Brandt that he should meet the British officers who had been able to get out of Dega. The German accepted. On the 12th of May, a strange column set off on its way composed of Major Neel and his Italo-American interpreter Napoitani, Nik Sokol and five of his men, regrouped under *Obergefreiter* Fred Brandt, who was himself accompanied by two Tadzhiks and two Albanian partisans. After four days of walking, the group reached the British base of operations, north of Dibra, where there were nine officers of the Intelligence Service and two radio operators amongst a heap of weapons and produce of all types, that they seemed totally incapable of protecting by themselves. At their head was none other than Winston Churchill's special plenipotentiary in the Balkans, Colonel Fitzroy Maclean.

Major Neel set out the facts. A British base of operations in Nikaj could only exist if Fred Brandt, who had the ear of the leaders of the Albanian troops, promised his protection. The British plenipotentiary did not immediately assimilate the subtleties of the situation.

"In short, *Mein Herr*," he said to Brandt, "you agree to work with us. I understand you! Berlin is crushed under the bombs. The Russians have almost completely freed their territory. We are at the gates of Rome. You have lost the battle of the Atlantic. It remains for us to lay down the conditions..."

Brandt interrupted him very sharply: "You are mistaken, Sir! I am neither a traitor nor a defector. I consider that the agreement I'm entering into with you is in the interests of my country, even if it does not conform to the main lines of the Wehrmacht. However, I shall do nothing without referring to my immediate superior in Pec." The Colonel beat an instant retreat.

"Of course my dear fellow. I did not make myself clear. We are very happy to enjoy your protection since, in this out-of-the-way place, we are without forces. But do you think that six men are enough to defend a strong point against an attack of well-armed sets of partisans?"

On the 25th of May the *Obergefreiter* had returned to Pec. Informed of the situation, Belgrade sent a lieutenant-colonel from the Abwehr to examine his report.

"I don't understand," the officer told him "that a British colonel, as formalist as they are, has accepted to negotiate on equal terms with a simple lance-corporal."

"It's because they don't believe I am a simple lance-corporal. A message from their head office in Bari, Italy, informed them that I was a colonel in disguise. They ended up calling me 'colonel' despite my protestations," replied Brandt.

"Brandt, I know and trust you. I give you carte blanche to carry on in the same way. Go and set up your strong point at Nikaj. The Englishman is right: six men is pathetic. I'll give you twenty other Tadzhiks. But aren't you afraid that Nik Sokol will drop you for the British, so generous with money?"

"The Albanians, *Herr Oberstleutnant*, are people of honour. Nothing is more important for them than the laws of hospitality. During my first visit, last Winter, I vowed to observe their customs. They held me as one of their own. The British, who keep them at a distance, even when they want to be friendly, are of no importance for them. They only deal with important chiefs. I, on the other hand, am full of esteem even for the less important ones. They all respect me. I can cross *Shqipetar* country alone and unarmed, from east to west and from north to south, and no-one would touch a hair on my head. Why do you think that the British military mission requests my protection? They have seen the power I hold although they don't understand the reason for it. Their dominating and money-grabbing mentality is too far removed from the spirit of these mountain-dwellers."

"You are really not afraid that these troops will attack us? After all, they are armed for that reason."

"No. The *Shqipetars* understand nothing of the subtleties of European politics. They believe what they see, observe that those who wear a German uniform live on good terms with those who wear a British one. They realise that they can receive everything they need, weapons, cartridges and gold, without risking a bullet.

"They don't want to die uselessly anymore than we do."

On their return to the Anglo-German strong point at Nikaj with his reinforcement of twenty Tadzhiks and two light machine-guns, Brandt found a new British officer there, Captain John Hibberdine, who

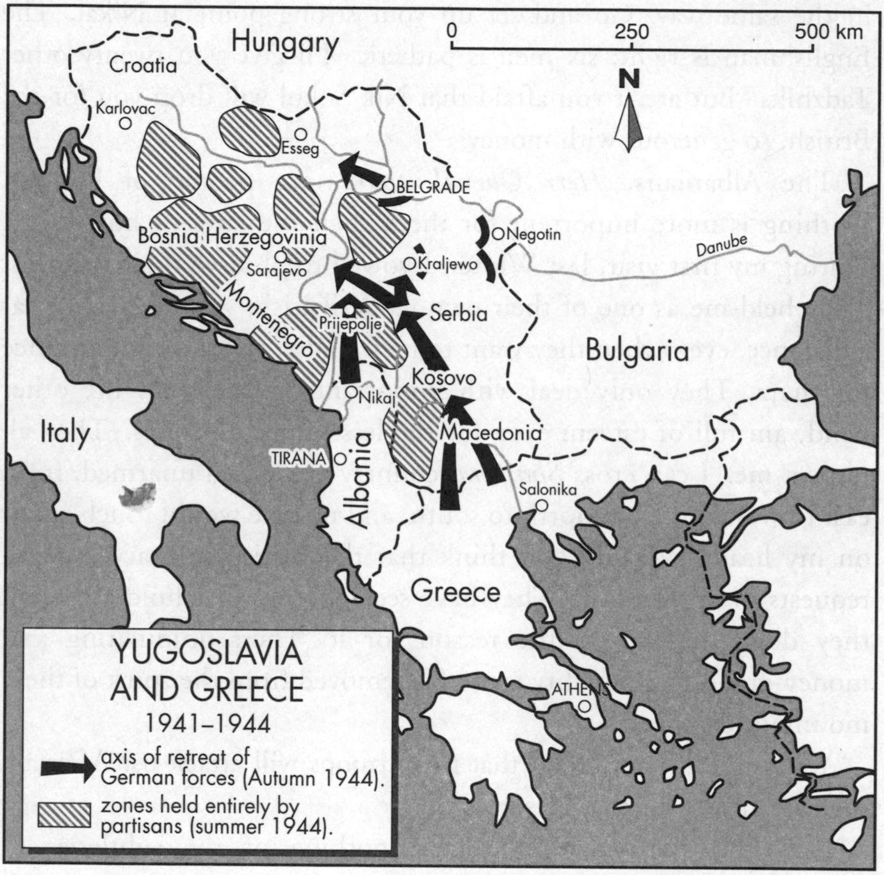
0
250
500 km
N
Hungary
Croatia
Karlovac
Esseg
BELGRADE
Negotin
Danube
Bosnia Herzegovinia
Sarajevo
Kraljewo
Montenegro
Prijepolje
Serbia
Bulgaria
Kosovo
Nikaj
Italy
Macedonia
TIRANA
Albania
Salonika
Greece
ATHENS
YUGOSLAVIA AND GREECE
1941–1944
axis of retreat of German forces (Autumn 1944).
zones held entirely by partisans (summer 1944).

spoke German perfectly, which made relations easier, and a radio operator. From that day on, the liaison with the head office at Bari, on the Italian coast, was on a daily basis and the airdrops increased. A consignment of brand new tents allowed a comfortable camp to be set up, that Nik took into his safekeeping along with a hundred of his own people. For the Albanians, the big boss was 'Colonel Branto'.

Scarcely four weeks had gone by since his journey to Pec, than he was summoned once again.

"There is some unease at the Army Group HQ concerning this accumulation of weapons at Nikaj. In Belgrade, they are asking why we are permitting it. Naturally, it's up to me to provide an answer. What must I say?"

"It's an effective way of stopping the troops of mountain-dwellers from harassing us. Since I have been in Albania, all attacks against the chrome mine and our lines of communication have stopped. So, a positive result. It is also in our long-term interests to see a fiercely anti-Communist and anti-Serb military force formed in Albania. It could play the same role as the Ustasha Army in Croatia."

"Is that also the ultimate aim of the British?"

"Colonel Maclean is an admirer of Tito. He is a man of cynical calculations. But in the meantime, the important thing is he's playing into our hands. And he is satisfied with the fictitious combats fought against us as told to him by Nik Sokol."

On the 10th of July, Major Neel asked Brandt to escort him as far as Scutari, a well-supplied town where he wanted to buy some articles that the containers never had in them, such as handkerchiefs, slippers or whisky. The three day walk necessary to cross a hostile mountain needed the protection of some good rifles and 'Colonel Branto's' white skullcap. They left therefore with five Tadzhiks, three mules and the two partisans that Nik had instructed to escort the major. On the way there, the journey went off uneventfully. On the way back, Brandt chose another route further to the north where their column had not been spotted. Everything went well as far as Bogë, where the local gendarmes invented a reason for confiscating the load that the mules were carrying.

A brief order to the Tadzhiks and, in less than a minute, the four Albanian gendarmes were disarmed, tied up and left on the ground. The Tadzhiks carried them to the gendarmes headquarters and locked them up in a cell, taking the key with them as a souvenir. But the alarm had been raised. The group set out for Theti in haste. Non-identifiable units were giving chase to them, shots rang out. The pursuit ended with nighfall.

In Theti, Brandt gave the weapons taken from the gendarmes at Bogë away to Bairaktar San Nikola. A memorable evening ensued where the spirits, bought at Scutari with Bari Intelligence Service funds, flowed.

Until the end of August 1944, the airdrops went on regularly. Brandt was now handling the beacons and collecting the containers.

One after the other, the troops rallied to Nik Sokol in order to have their share of the armaments that had fallen from the heavens. The British were very satisfied, having learnt that deadly attacks had been launched against the Germans in Macedonian Morava. Brandt was enjoying himself, for he knew the attacks were characteristic of the Communist partisans. He was also satisfied, as his dream of seeing a national Albanian army set up was beginning to take shape through British generosity.

Throughout the Summer, things started happening quickly in the Balkans. The German Army had evacuated Greece and was going back up to Belgrade as quickly as possible to avoid being cut off from its bases by Soviet forces who would reach Serbian territory on the Danube, at Turnu Severin, on the 4th of September.

At the end of August, the British military mission decided to get closer to Scutari, the activity of the Titist partisans in Serbia rendering its presence in Nikaj useless. Major Neel asked Brandt if he would agree to carry on applying the same policy.

"I think," he said "that the decision depends on you alone. Since the assassination attempt against Hitler on the 20th of July, the Abwehr has been dismantled and a lot of officers arrested. We know that your station at Pec has disappeared and the one in Belgrade must be in the process of being relocated under the Russian guns. Come with us. Who knows what the future holds?"

Brandt thought he could still play a useful part and he accepted. What else could he do? He pitched his camp on a plateau at an altitude of 1,800 metres in a very good strategic position, in the Shillaku mountain, a one day walk east of Scutari. Nik Sokol, who did not want to be separated from his 'milch cow', came with a hundred or so men. Once operational and with their safety ensured, the British threw off the mask. They had the order to destroy the large Scutari fuel depot and the bridge over the Drin, and counted on the Albanian partisans to carry out the work. 'Colonel Branto' secretly opposed his will to that of Colonel Maclean's. He therefore tried to persuade Nik Sokol's mountain dwellers that they had better things to do than serve British military ends. And he was heard!

The lance-corporal was recognised by everyone, without having been named by anyone, as the camp commander. His role set him at the same level as the highest ranking British leaders and the Albanian Bairaktars. His influence was spread throughout the many troops formed from anti-Communists which gathered round the camp, demanding a North Albanian National Army to be formed. They volunteered, in order to keep Durazzo and Tirana, to fight against the Communist army of Enver Hodja, which was coming up from the Epirus.

The Bairaktar council gave Brandt the responsibility of asking the British leader at Bari, on their behalf, for the massive aid they required to form a complete fighting troop, Major Neel was convinced and transmitted the list of necessary equipment to Bari. Meanwhile, the Albanians made up a national defence council, which the lance-corporal was part of, this time as an Albanian colonel, as Germany was no longer anything in the Balkans.

The answer was much awaited. At last, it arrived in the form of an invitation made to the leaders of the future Albanian Army to go to Bari to discuss the methods of delivering the armaments requested. But the transport of the delegation across the Adriatic posed some problems. They were resolved by the British who offered to go to a British airfield in Montenegro from where an RAF plane would take them across the sea.

The Albanians protested. Nobody would make them go into the Serbs' country, their mortal enemies. But if Colonel Branto wanted to represent them...

Brandt accepted and set off for Montenegro with the major, three Tadzhiks and the interpreter. Five days of walking through valleys and over mountains ended with the crossing of the Dukagjin, which led them to Gusinje. They continued in a northerly direction to Kuti, in the heart of Titist country. There, Brandt found an old partisan on his route who owed him a debt of gratitude. While a man from the region was sent to Kuti to establish contact with Serbian bands, the old partisan beckoned Brandt into the undergrowth to speak to him confidentially:

"Listen, my brother, one of Tito's firing squads has arrived in Andrijevica, to seize a German officer who is to come in the company of a British man. When I learnt that a British man, coming from Albania, was requesting an escort of partisans from Kuti to be taken to Berane and that there was a German with him, I immediately knew it was you. This is not a chance meeting. In the name of the Lord, Be on your guard! Somebody has set a trap for you. If you are not killed here you will be handed over to Tito. You know he never spares anyone."

Major Neel seemed to be entirely unaware of this ambush. He persisted in waiting for the return of the messenger for four days, while *Obergefreiter* Brandt and his Tadzhiks stood on their guard, like at the outposts of a front line unit. Eventually, the messenger returned, but with bad news. The Albanian SS Skanderbeg Mountain Division [2] was occupying the area and the airfield had been evacuated. The Serbian partisans had struck camp.

On the 29th of September, the small troop returned to the camp at Shillaku. During its absence, great quantities of provisions had been

---

2. Created in April 1944 in Kosovo from Albanian volunteers. In August took twenty-first place among the 38 divisions of the Waffen-SS.

parachuted in, but not one single weapon or cartridge. The following day, Brandt assembled the Bairaktars and set out the situation clearly to them. The feeling was unanimous. "We are betrayed! The British have gone over to the Communists!"

That same afternoon, the Albanian troops struck camp and withdrew to the east. Before leaving, the leaders came as a body to offer sanctuary to Colonel Branto. The last ones to take their leave were Nik Sokol and the two partisans who had faithfully guided him across the country throughout the last few months.

"You are wrong not to accept our offer straight away," said Nik Sokol to Brandt as he was leaving. "The SD at Scutari have put a price on your head, and on the heads of the Tadzhiks as well. In return, don't trust the British, they are cheats!"

Brandt, in truth, did not know what to do and, with the prospect of the disaster threatening Germany, he didn't care. Whether he lived or died, who would know?

The British mission received the order by radio to go immediately to the Adriatic coast, where a gunboat would take them. Neel suggested to the Brandenburgers to come with him with his Tadzhiks, and gave him his word as an officer that they would be treated as prisoners of war. [3]

Avoiding Scutari by the south, they reached, four days later, the Kenete Salu Lukeive lagoon, and they landed at Bari the following day. They got into a military truck with their weapons. On arrival at Intelligence Service HQ, Colonel Branto was separated from his men and asked to lay down his weapons, then to empty his pockets. He carried this out, without managing to strangle an alarming dread.

Behind the table, a beardless lieutenant put a series of questions to him, in order to fill out a personal card.

"Turn round," said the voice of a military police sergeant next to him. "Hold out your hands!"

Handcuffs were slapped around his wrists and he was pushed towards the prison. He stayed two days without food.

3. Fred Brandt and Major Neel met again several years after the end of the conflict and established friendly relations.

On the 15th of November, he was taken to London by plane. Incarcerated in the premises of the Intelligence Service, he was sworn at by the guards: "Dirty pig! You'll be hanged!"

Four months of endless winter went by in absolute isolation. One day the guards extracted him from his cell and led him on his trembling legs in front of the war council. After ten minutes he was acquitted because of lack of proof! He was then sent to a prison camp as a war criminal.

At the beginning of the Summer of 1944, the Brandenburg Division's 1st Light Infantry Regiment continued to fight against Tito's partisans during constant operations often ending in failure, with the imbroglio of relations between the Serbs and the Croats in the background. In August, it withdrew to the north-west with the entirety of German forces.

The 2nd Regiment was committed in the same battles. In August, it came up against the attempt at a breakthrough towards Serbia that Tito undertook with the equivalent of thirteen divisions through the 2nd German Armoured Army. On the 20th of August, Soviet forces made contact with the Titist offensive in the Balkans. The regiment then withdrew to Belgrade.

The 3rd Regiment's I Battalion had been sent to Venezia Giulia in May, and was soon joined by III Battalion. These two units fought against the partisans in the Gorizia-Udine region and on the coast between Fiume and Abbazzia. The Regiment's II Battalion was still fighting in the Abruzzi, further south, then was sent to the French-Italian border to keep the passages in the Alps open.

The 4th Regiment, commanded by Major Helmut Pinkert, had a ringside seat during Operation 'Rösselsprung', aiming to capture Tito in his CP. Some units from the 1st Regiment were also committed, but the operation only just failed. The 4th Regiment was the most involved in the Balkan intrigues and collaborated closely with the Chetniks. In March, it was put on alert for Operation 'Margarethe I', when the Wehrmacht occupied Hungary, and in August after the defection of Rumania.

The Brandenburg Parachute Battalion took part in Operation 'Trojan Horse', in Hungary. After further training the unit was sent to Yugoslavia. In August, it took the airfield at Otopeni, near Bucharest, following the reversal of the Rumanian alliance. But it soon found itself encircled.

The Coastal Raider Battalion went on with its raids along the Dalmatian coast. Its *Sturmboote* were now being confronted by a fleet organised by the partisans.

After the Brandenburg Division had been in existence for one year, Lieutenant-General Fritz Kühlwein succeeded von Pfuhlstein in April, who had been thrown out by Jodl. Now he could assess the situation and for that purpose wrote a memo addressed to the Wehrmacht Operations Staff. He pointed out that the division had been created as a special formation intended for offensive operations but, since the German army was forced to pull back and lead essentially defensive combats, the Brandenburgers were barely used except in partisan warfare. General Kühlwein therefore suggested modifying the way the division was made up and to create *Streifkorps*, patrol corps used in co-ordination with the existing light infantry regiments. General Jodl gave his agreement. The first unit of this type, intended to serve in France, was named *Streifkorps Südfrankreich*.

But it was already too late. German armies were in retreat everywhere. On the 20th of July, a bomb exploded at the Führer's HQ in Rastenburg. Among the hundreds of Brandenburgers in training or convalescing in Berlin, two officers of the division belonging to the circle of conspirators put together the strength of a battalion that they kept on alert for the whole day. How could it be avoided that Adolf Hitler placed less and less trust in the Wehrmacht?

The order to regroup the Brandenburg units committed in the Balkans on Belgrade was signed on the 8th of September. From then on the division was simply transformed into a conventional tactical unit. On that date, it had approximately 14,000 officers, NCOs and men, only 900 of whom spoke a foreign language. Five days later the fateful order was signed. The Brandenburg Division had to become a *Panzergrenadier* division, an ordinary motorised infantry formation.

Chapter XVII

The Brandenburg Division
dies on the Neisse
(1944-1945)

The order of the 13th September 1944 from the Wehrmacht Operations Staff had to be carried out by a reorganization staff set up in Baden, the former home base of the Brandenburg Regiment's II Battalion and later the 2nd Regiment of the division. But, at that date, the units were fighting some tough retreating actions in the Balkans.

The 1st Regiment's I Battalion, under Lieutenant Hebeler, moved towards Ub against the masses of Tito's partisans. III Battalion was at Mokri Lug, south-east of Belgrade, and had to cut in front of the partisans coming from the west. II Battalion under Major Pinkert was fighting at the confluence of the Theiss River and the Danube.

The 2nd Regiment's I Battalion was moving towards the Bulgarian border near Negotin, supported at the south by II Battalion. It then had to cross the Danube to the north in order to protect the navigation on the river, as Canaris' Brandenburgers had done in 1940-1941.

The 3rd Regiment was still in Italy. Its II Battalion was north of Turin, but its I Battalion was to be the first to reach Vienna for the planned reorganisation.

The 4th Regiment, now commanded by Captain Kriegsheim, could only muster two battalions, the II having been amalgamated with the I. It was north of Belgrade. III Battalion was to be decimated during ferocious combat in the north of Rumania.

The last troops of the Parachute Battalion were seeking to escape capture in Transylvania.

Captain von Leipzig's *Küstenjäger* Battalion was continuing tirelessly with its mopping-up operations in the islands of the Adriatic.

On the 27th of September 1944, General Kühlwein set up his CP in Belgrade. His division was now reduced to a *Kampfgruppe* which bore his name and the Soviet Army was advancing in the direction of the town. The Reorganisation Staff which had to carry out the transformation of the division was under Captain Witauscheck, the *IIb* [1] of the division. But he had a near impossible task.

At the beginning of October, the Brandenburgers were fighting against the Russians on a position of the Theiss River. Rumanian and Hungarian Armies were now joining up with the Russians. On the 29th of October, the remainder of the 2nd Regiment under Lieutenant-Colonel Oesterwitz escaped encirclement near Belgrade with less than 800 men. On the 4th of November, General Kühlwein passed his command to Colonel Hermann Schulte-Heuthaus. In mid-November, the divisional *Kampfgruppe* was on the Hungarian-Croatian border, near Esseg, and suffered onslaughts by Soviet troops attacking from the southern bank of the Danube. At the end of the month, it was brought back to a new line of resistance and the 2nd Regimen's III Battalion held the Apatin bridgehead to enable the retreat of German forces.

On the 27th of November, the division was transported back to the south of Hungary. Only a battle group formed from the remainder of the 2nd Regiment was held on the front line. At the beginning of December, the last units of the division withdrew to the south of Balaton Lake then towards Vienna, in order to be integrated into the

1. Adjutant of the General commanding the division concerned with matters of promotions, awarding of medals, etc.

Grossdeutschland Armoured Corps, which regrouped the elite divisions of the Army. The Brandenburgers were then transported to East Prussia, to the camp at Mauerwald, near Angerburg. The new *Panzergrenadier-Division* could at last be formed. It had to line up two light infantry regiments and the usual divisional units. However, the coastal raiders and II Battalion, 3rd Regiment were not a part of its table of organization. All Brandenburgers had a choice: either to join the new division, or to take up service within the *SS-Jagdverbände* under *SS-Obersturmbannführer* Otto Skorzeny who required the several hundred specialists still on the strength of the 'Brandenburg'.

Scarcely 350 men were to don the uniform of the Waffen-SS, the others remained faithful to their unit. The veterans were bitter, the new recruits disappointed.

On the 12th of January 1945, the Russians launched a new major offensive against the German front, now back in Poland and reduced to a thin cordon of troops. Twenty-five armies and a mass of 300 divisions threatened to submerge everything. Like several other formations, the Brandenburg *Panzergrenadier-Division* was hurriedly transported towards the lines, in the Army Group Centre zone of action, with Litzmannstadt, Lodz for the Polish, as an assembly point.

When the train transporting the 6th and 7th Companies of the 1st Light Infantry Regiment arrived at Kutno, on the Warsaw-Posen line, both small units received the order to occupy positions at the east of the town immediately. Two companies, in other words precisely two officers, thirty NCOs and 350 light infantrymen!

Night was falling on the foxholes dug into the frozen earth where the men buried themselves up to their chests. Daylight did not reveal the enemy advanced guard, only the lamentable columns of refugees congesting the roads, joined by soldiers of the Wehrmacht, whose units had disintegrated. The cold was biting and the ice had frozen lakes and rivers.

At nightfall, the men had a hot meal. At 9 p.m. the first Soviet tanks emerged, disturbing the night with their grinding tracks and their tongues of fire. Until 2.30 a.m., the Brandenburgers repelled three tank attacks. Each time, the tanks at the head were destroyed by the *Panzerfaust* or set on fire by grenades in close combat, and the ones behind retreated. Sheltered from the smoking wrecks, the Soviet infantry now rushed to the attack. Lieutenant Erich Röseke, commander of the 6th Company, had the windmill he was using as an observation post set on fire in order to light up the battle field. The enemy was repelled.

At 7.30 a.m., the order to withdraw reached the unit, at the very moment when Ivan was attacking again.

Röseke consulted his comrade Geisenberger, commander of the other company.

"What damned stupidity to make us lose touch now daylight is approaching, when the manoeuvre could be so easy at night!"

But anything can be done with a well trained and disciplined unit. Covered by cross fire from the machine-guns, the withdrawal was carried out without losses. At Kutno, some bad news was awaiting the light infantrymen. They had to march without delay towards the west to avoid being surrounded by Russian armoured vans, which had penetrated deep within the German defence deployment and were turning off to link up.

The two companies had scarcely started on their way when they saw, 800 metres to the north, a column of tanks which threatened to block the road a little further on. The unit left the road and headed south east, across some fields. Discipline still worked wonders. The column went off diagonally just as if it were an exercise. It arrived at a large farm before dusk and set up there in order to spend the night. The *Jägers* had a hot meal, the last for a long time.

A study of the map showed Röseke and Geisenberger that they were very near the Warsaw-Posen line. Wasn't avoiding the roads and following the railway track the best way of escaping the Russian tanks? The bridge over the Vistula was thirty kilometres away. They had to reach it before it was destroyed.

Walking on a railway track is exhausting. If you don't take the narrow strip of ballast either side of the rails, then your stride must be the same length as the distance between the sleepers. Snow covered everything. The men stumbled, fell, swore, but carried on. Around 1 a.m., they ran right into the ruins of the metal bridge which made a simple waterway into an apparently insurmountable obstacle. Only at dawn of the 21st of January did the column find a makeshift way of crossing it. They arrived at last at the Warthe River, along which a line of German resistance, or what was supposed to be one, had been established. The Russians were reported everywhere. The men, who had not slept in three days, could no longer stand up. There was no sign of supplies of ammunition or rations. On their own, the two companies tried to escape using different ways. Lieutenant Geisenberger was killed. Lieutenant Röseke suffered a chest wound. He was injured a second time entering a house in order to rest. His men carried him off in a tent quarter. As they were running away, they had the unpleasant impression that they were being shot at like rabbits. When they stopped in a wood, in front of a forest ranger's house, there were only a dozen left. It was 1 o'clock in the morning. The Polish man was helpful and helped them to dress the lieutenant's wounds, he soon fell asleep. They all copied him. They decided to leave again at 3 a.m., because the large open space which was awaiting them ahead had to be crossed under cover of darkness.

The 25th of January started with an arduous march in the deep snow, with more and more frequent stops proving necessary to enable the men to get some strength back. Each time, starting off again became more difficult. But it was enough to say "Do you want to get nabbed by the Russkis?" to the exhausted rifleman for him to get up again, pushed on by the resilience of some vital instinct. Everyone knew that the Soviet patrols did not burden themselves with prisoners.

Despite the enormous effort that the Brandenburgers made, they could not reach the edge of the forest before daylight. On their left, right against the forest, they discovered a large farm. It attracted them like a magnet. To sleep in warm straw! To eat bacon soup!

Just in time they spotted a Russian soldier coming out carrying a bucket. Röseke searched the landscape with his binoculars. The border of a second forest, beyond the open space, was visible on the horizon. He gave orders for his troop to split up into two-man groups, 100 to 200 metres apart. The *Jägers* crossed many cart tracks, several frozen streams and a single railway track, without anyone noticing them when, suddenly, they saw two civilian cyclists draw nearer, stop and alight. After exchanging a few words, they got back on their bicycles and went towards the nearest village, whose rooftops could be seen in the distance.

"Those bastards are going to denounce us to the Russians, it'd be best to shoot them down," said a rifleman. *"Herr Oberleutnant,* I am a marksman. Can I do it?"

"Clever Dick", replied Röseke. "That's the sort of thing that will bring all the Russians down on our backs."

"It's better to get away as fast as we can!"

They then did something that they never thought they were capable of: they ran, even the lieutenant with his bandages. Just when they reached the edge of the woods, a troop of horsemen leaving the village galloped in hot pursuit. Unfortunately, the wood was not dense, the trees were sparse and there were no bushes to slow the horses down, but the trees nonetheless stopped them from staying together. The Russian horsemen fired at random without dismounting. The Brandenburgers split up and opened, in return, well-aimed fire. The Russians fell, horses collapsed, but the others pushed their horses on and an encircling movement was taking shape.

"We are done for..."

"No, we are saved! Look in front of you instead of whining," shouted Röseke.

Beyond a clearing, which they crossed briskly without hearing any bullets whistle past their ears, the wood began to change its appearance. It was overgrown with shrubs and thorny bushes, which formed an impassable barrier for the horses. The Brandenburgers threw themselves down, tearing their clothes and could at last allow themselves to flop onto the ground and get their breath back. Three men were missing.

Two hours later, they started off again through the thick undergrowth. Suddenly, they could make out the sound of engines. Very near, they saw a road crossing the forest and lay down on the ground. They didn't do it quickly enough. The lookouts positioned on the footboards of two Russian trucks packed with soldiers had seen them. They jumped to the ground and entered the forest in open order. The chase to the Germans started again. Once more, the bushes saved them. They counted up: three more missing. Along with the first three, nothing more was ever heard of them.

They had to set off again, intensifying their caution and spending as much time listening as walking. In the afternoon, they reached an area of land under cultivation studded with several farms. They approached the first one, weapon in hand. The lieutenant was pleasantly surprised to discover that he could still seize his pistol with his right hand and raise it as high as his hip. The farmer was a German from Poland. He was sorry not to be able to help his compatriots, as he had put all his belongings in two waggons and was preparing to flee, fearful of being attacked by his Polish neighbours. The Brandenburgers left again. The Polish men at the next farm had seen them and unleashed their dogs in pursuit.

By the evening of the 25th of January, they had been walking for five days and had not slept more than two or three hours at a stretch, on just three or four occasions, walking in snow all the time, with just one meal a day if they were lucky. Lieutenant Röseke was genuinely surprised to still be upright and to be able to make such an effort with two wounds which were only just starting to heal up.

A cottage inspired confidence in them and they entered it. Their appearance alone was enough to frighten anyone. Two women, the mother and the grandmother of an infant, welcomed them in a friendly manner however. They cooked a soup in the fireplace and gave them some bread and milk. Röseke was even invited to sleep in a bed. A *Jäger* put a compress on his burning forehead. He went to sleep. Two hours went by. It was time to set off again.

Shivering with cold and fatigue, the small troop crossed a never-ending succession of fields, woods, streams and groves. At the first light of day on the 26th of January, the fugitives found themselves in front of a village that the road they were following went right through. Here and there, a watch-dog barked. They did not have the courage to make a detour and went in between the low houses which bordered the road.

An abrupt *"Stoi"* stopped them and a Russian sentry emerged from the dark, his rifle aimed at them. Behind the lieutenant, a Brandenburger had lowered his weapon. A shot rang out, the Russian fell and they left the village in haste. But, behind them, nobody moved. It must be that the Russians no longer paid attention to shots fired by excessively nervous sentries, they concluded.

At 7 a.m., they were on the banks of the Warthe. It was completely covered in ice, but crossing it was not easy. Röseke thought they were to the south east of Posen. On the other bank, there was a house that seemed likely to welcome them. One of the *Jägers* had already grabbed the door handle when snatches of a song coming from the inside reached their ears. They beat a hasty retreat. It was Russian. Further on, they passed two fearful women, who said that they were afraid of the Russians and steered clear of them.

"It's not easy, they are everywhere around here."

All of a sudden, from behind, a voice called out to them in Polish. They were young armed civilians. *Oberschütze* Kruch was the best shot of the group: he fired several bullets over the heads of the young people, who immediately took to their heels.

They then entered a quiet forest. At midday, they all went into a house situated on the edge of the forest, determined to eat something and rest without concerning themselves with its occupants. They were two women with a brood of children. The men were given food. For the first time since Kutno, they took off their shoes. Their socks were nothing more than foul smelling rags.

Around 4 p.m., a sentry announced that several farmers' waggons were approaching on the path which led directly to their refuge. They were still a kilometre away. An examination with the binoculars revealed that they were Russians.

The Brandenburgers left the welcoming house in a mad rush, holding their ankle boots which their swollen feet no longer fitted.

Some shots rang out in their direction. The forest and the night shrouded them once more. They came across a road which proved difficult to cross as there were so many Russian vehicles blocking it. On the other side, they came upon another house in the forest which meant they could shelter from the snow. The good man who inhabited it shared out the bread he had. Röseke swapped his pocket knife for a pair of good socks. But the son of the household did not have an honest expression and, when he wanted to leave, the Brandenburgers prevented him from doing so. The man on guard woke the officer up several hours later: the young man had managed to escape his attention and fled.

Röseke did not want to risk staying there. His unit went in the opposite direction to the forest, which was buzzing with rumours. The snow was falling so thickly that they could not see beyond a metre. A barbed wire entanglement stopped them. They tried to find a way through.

"Be careful of the mines! There are certainly some here if it's a position which has been organised by our forces. We have to pass exactly where we have already started to go."

Without wirecutters, it was a disastrous experience for their clothes which were already in a sorry state. Beyond the barbed wire there were trenches to be crossed. There was no doubt this was an *Ostwall* segment as the organization was facing east. This deserted position clearly showed the inability of the Wehrmacht to repel the invasion. The Brandenburgers felt it like an open wound in the flanks of the Fatherland.

Once more on the hard surface of a road, Röseke suffered from the injury on the sole of his foot and had to walk by placing his foot on the side or by jumping. Faces were marked by the biting icy wind and their gums were swollen because of having to suck snow.

Suddenly, they all threw themselves on the ground. A searchlight had lit up in front of them and had caught the three light infantrymen at the front in its beam. They recognised an armoured car, probably stopped on the road in a surveillance position. The simple sound of walking and voices had given the Germans away.

The lieutenant knew that he was invisible from the vehicle blinded by its own light. He took hold of his last stick hand grenade, that he had kept stuck in his belt since Kutno, unscrewed the cap with his numb fingers, leapt forward, pulled out the porcelain bead, threw the grenade in the hatch of the armoured car, flattened himself on the ground, his face buried in the snow. The explosion was followed by total darkness. The Brandenburgers hurried away without wanting to know more.

When they stopped to get their breath back, there was a *Jäger* missing, Richard. It was not possible that he had been killed or injured, because no shots had been fired. As he had no compass, to abandon him would be to condemn him.

The Brandenburgers did not abandon a comrade. Röseke deployed his small numbers in a extended order, each one staying within earshot of his neighbour, to give Richard the maximum opportunity of finding them again. After two hours of patience their lost comrade finally showed up. The group got back together again and went on their way.

Richard's report was reassuring. Some other Soviet AFVs were following. Their crews had taken care of the injured, picking up the dead and had withdrawn without initiating any kind of pursuit. As he was hidden very near, Richard had had to wait for their departure before setting off on his way.

Röseke's troop kept his course on the road to advance more quickly. At dawn, they left it only to come across a wide antitank ditch full up to its edges with soft snow, that the men had great difficulty crossing. It was now broad daylight. Röseke pointed his binoculars towards the new village that spread out before their eyes. It was swarming with Soviets. The only way left for them was to hide in a small neighbouring wood and wait for nightfall.

Around 10 a.m., a squadron of planes appeared and dived onto the village releasing their bombs. They bore black crosses! Their joy was short-lived. The planes had scarcely vanished in the sky when Russian tanks which had escaped the destruction of their battalion stationed in the village emerged to seek refuge in the neighbouring woods. Four of them were heading directly towards the Brandenburgers. Hurriedly, the Germans covered the little fire they were huddled around with snow and hid under the brushwood. The Russian tanks stayed near the edge of the wood. From their hiding place the small group could hear the crews talking. For fear of being discovered, they pushed some snow in front of them to form a little wall which hid them completely from view. They spent the whole day crouched down in the snow, shivering. At dawn, the tanks went back to the warm shelter of the village. For many hours, Röseke tried to comfort the youngest of his men, Jonny, who had run out of strength and whose will was broken.

"Let me die here, *Herr Oberleutnant*. I can no longer walk. I will only hamper you. I will give up..."

Röseke had to force him to stay and, when they set off once more on their harrowing march, he had to be held up by two comrades.

Two hours of staggering convinced them they could go no further. They entered the first house they came across on the edge of the road. The occupants received them with pity and fed them as best they could. Without asking for anything more, the Brandenburgers lay down on the mud floor. There was no sentry. Everybody had fallen into a sleep of animal-like intensity, when the lieutenant felt himself being grabbed by the shoulder. It was the old man: "The Russians!" he whispered.

Röseke had no idea if he had been asleep for one hour or four. He half opened the main door and saw the endless column of Russian requisitioned waggons streaming past on the road. Escape remained possible in one direction only, the one they had come from. The Germans, now awake, held a meeting and chose to wait. But the unexpected happened. One waggon separated from the others and stopped in front of the house. There were knocks on the door and noisy shouting. The old man was terrified; his wife, who knew what to expect, moaned and cried.

"Hide as best you can!" the lieutenant ordered. The men carried this out but his injuries prevented Röseke from doing the same. He remained standing in the furthest recess from the main room, ready to grab his two pistols. He made a sign to the old man, who opened the door.

From outside, the full moon made the inside of the dwelling appear even darker. The Russians shouted for someone to light a lamp. The old man did as he was told, wasting match after match as his hands were shaking so much. His wife then went to the cupboard to get some food for the Russians who said they were famished.

Röseke thought it inevitable that he would eventually be discovered, now that there was a little light in the room. He hoped not to be recognised. His white, double-breasted winter combat jacket concealed his field blouse well. He had taken off his *Feldmütze*. But he suddenly realised that the binoculars hanging round his neck were going to give him away and thought carefully about the movements that he had to carry out in order to shoot first if one of the Russians threatened him. A real problem with his injured right arm. He settled for hoping that his men, on their side, would shoot the other two Soviets before they opened fire on him.

One of them, a lance-corporal, spoke to him. He only understood the word 'soldier'. The answer came to him spontaneously:

"*Da, da. Polski soldat! Partisan!*"

"*Karosh, tovaritch,*" replied Ivan, "*idi souda, koushat!*"

A gesture in the direction of the table made him understand that he was invited to share the dinner. With his good arm, he let his pistol slip into his pocket, but without letting go of the grip, and sat down next to the lance-corporal. The word *'polski partisan'* flew around the table, while the Brandenburger endlessly filled his mouth with bread so as to only have to reply with a mixture of grunts and other inarticulate sounds. Full up, the Russians took their leave. Röseke stifled a cry of pain when they warmly shook his hand. Soon after, the crack of a whip and the grinding of an axle was heard outside. On the road, the waggons continued to stream past.

It had been a close call. Rather than repeating such an experience, the Germans preferred to leave the place. Their walk by compass lasted the remainder of the night, until dawn on Sunday the 28th of

January, when they arrived in front of a large farm. An old man was there, with a spade on his shoulder. In German they sought some information from him. The man replied correctly, but with a revealing accent: they were not yet in German territory. He declared that the Russians had come the day before, had requisitioned some straw and some potatoes, then left again. The lieutenant thought that the way was clear. He took Richard with him and entered the house.

There he found a Russian officer, sitting between two women, just about to take a sip of tea. The amazement was reciprocal. The two enemies immediately identified each other, as this time Röseke was wearing the Wehrmacht standard field-cap. The Russian dropped his cup and leapt up. But before he had the time to grab his revolver from his belt, Richard fired. He fell back, knocking over his chair. The Germans got away running through the courtyard where there were also some Russians hurrying through, the majority of which were fortunately unarmed. At the crossroads there was a sentry, near an unhitched waggon, against which he had placed his rifle. The Russian shouted "*Stoi! Stoi!*". The lieutenant faced him, aimed and fired. But there was no shot. The magazine of his pistol had fallen during the chase. The surprise of the sentry was such that he did not realise what was happening and timidly raised his arm, while the German retreated continuing to threaten him with his empty weapon, then turned on his heels and took off. Before the sentry could pick up his rifle, work the bolt, aim and fire, Röseke was far away.

The Brandenburgers were separated once again. The lieutenant only had Richard and Jonny with him, who from then on no longer wished to give up.

The three others had gone on ahead. The sound of galloping now reached them from a farm very nearby. A trench where a stream flowed offered an acceptable hiding place. They jumped in, and fell into the arms of their three comrades who had sought refuge there before them. A troop of horsemen passed ten metres away from them at a great gallop. They set off again bearing towards the south-east.

A village was waking up to the sound of bugle call. They went round it. One of the *Jägers* listened out.

"*Herr Oberleutnant*, I can hear the guns."

They were all excited. The officer calmed them down.

"Keep a cool head, boys! The front is over there, that's for sure, but how far away? And then how are we going to cross over the lines? In civilian clothing would be best. But where are we going to get the clothes from? Even if we do find them, look at you! Our appearance will give us away."

Indeed, they were not very handsome to look at. They were all suffering from chills and coughs. Their hands were deformed and their lips were chapped. They hobbled along and their ten-day old beards scarcely hid the hollows of their cheeks. Their over-bright eyes threw out expressions betraying their suffering and anguish in an almost palpable way.

The officer, even though he showed the strongest will, was of all of them the most affected. He suffered physically as much as his men and, in addition had several wounds which had started to run again. What faith could sustain him, he who knew that the German Army amounted to a pitiful gathering of skeleton-like divisions, and that it had to call on children and old people to stop the Soviet hoards?

Röseke knew however that nothing could break his will to fight until his last breath. Patriotism? Pride?

In the evening they tried to get themselves inside a haystack. It was packed so tight that they couldn't even dig out small holes with their knives deep enough to shelter themselves completely. When daylight came they left, stiff and cold. They were so weary that they didn't even take the trouble to hide. A Russian column passed 400 metres in front of them. Without having given themselves the cue, they gave large friendly waves. The lieutenant was inwardly struck with amazement that the training of the Brandenburgers had conditioned their reflexes so strongly. The Russians, believing them to be partisans, responded in the same way.

Yet more woods. They hoped to find a forester's house, by following a forest track. They soon saw a pointed roof before them. They had the patience and the courage to observe it for one hour. What amounted to an eternity for those dying of hunger and cold. Not having seen anything suspicious, they went to knock on the door. The forest-guard let them in. The map on the wall showed them that they were 40 kilometres from the 1939 border of the Reich, at Obra-Bruch. The front had for the moment come to a standstill, slightly forward, in Posnan Polish territory. But no sounds of battle could be heard.

"I don't understand it," said the forest-guard. "Every day there are wounded brought back here."

"No," retorted the officer. "Sound is made up of waves. They bounce off undulations on the ground, forming pockets of silence. We can't hear the guns here, yet they can be heard fifty kilometres further away."

Late afternoon they were received in a new house where they were generously offered some soup, bread, coffee and even some cigarettes. At 1900 hours, they set off again, in an almost joyous frame of mind in spite of their misery, at the thought of having reached so near to their lines in spite of all odds.

Well sheltered by the copses, they lit a small fire and grouped around it, stretching their hands or their bare feet towards its warmth. Two silhouettes stood out against the night, lit up by the shimmering flames. They were two Germans, a customs officer, who was still in uniform, and a civilian. They asked permission to join up with the group to "pass to the other side."

On Monday morning, mislead by what seemed to be a short cut, they lost their way. When, around midday, they eventually found the right direction at the edge of the forest, they had to stop, beaten by fatigue and hunger. The two newcomers sat on one side. They got some provisions out of their bags and started to eat. *Oberschütze* Kruch kindly suggested to them that they share their food with the soldiers. They refused and started to smoke. Kruch got angry. He put his submachine-gun to his hip: "Give me the *Verpflegung!*"

Terrified, both men got up and fled.

The Brandenburgers crossed yet another wood. This time, they could clearly hear a burst of MG 42. Having reached open country, they saw a village. Shells hissed over their heads and swooped down on the houses transformed into flames. Behind them, only a few hundred metres away, they heard infantry orders in Russian.

"No cock ups, men" said the lieutenant. "We are between the lines. Follow my orders to the letter."

A burst of howitzer fire swept down upon the edge of the forest just when the first line of Russian riflemen came into view. Röseke and his men just had the time to throw themselves into a small hollow. Shell splinters and machine-gun bullets roared over their bowed heads. The assailants surged back, the firing stopped. Lieutenant Erich Röseke turned towards his men:

"This time boys, there are only Germans in front of us. We six, we have crossed the Russian lines. Nobody will believe us, but what does it matter?"

The village was called Schwenten. The old colonel in charge of the defensive sector cried out when he saw them:

"Where have these cripples come from? What a dress, *mein Gott!*"

"6th Company, II Battalion, 1st Brandenburg Light Infantry Regiment, *Herr Oberst*, or what's left of it. Lieutenant Röseke, company commander.»

"I need some men. Pick up some weapons if you haven't got any, we are not short of them. And go and take up position at the outposts, there where you came from."

Röseke shook his head.

"*Herr Oberst*, we have come from Kutno by foot, forced to walk for eleven days, across enemy lines. We are totally finished. As well as that, I am suffering from several wounds which have not yet been treated."

The colonel exploded: "*Sakrament!* We are fighting here, and you are talking to me about a rest? I gave you an order. Carry it out!"

The Brandenburgers, demoralised, moved away. The colonel's adjutant caught up with them and strongly advised them to go back to the rear as quickly as possible.

On the 30th of January, the group was admitted to the field hospital at Sagan, where frostbite and injuries were at last treated.

On the 1st of February, Lieutenant Röseke left the hospital surreptitiously and on his tottering legs turned into a road which indicated the direction of Glogau. He boarded a truck. From there, the *Feldgendarmerie* put him into a car which dropped him off at the CP of his battalion.

The officer in command of the remnants of the battalion was Lieutenant Friedrichsmeyer.

"You're back and strong enough to carry on? I have enough to occupy you."

"That's all I ask."

From mid-January to mid-February 1945, the main body of the Brandenburg *Panzergrenadier-Division* fought in the Warthegau, zone of action of Army Group Centre.

In March it held a position on the Neisse River.

On the 16th of April, when the massive Russian offensive on the Oder and the Neisse was launched, the division was north of Görlitz. The 2nd Light Infantry Regiment was almost entirely destroyed but managed to slow down the Soviet forces in its sector.

On the 18th of April, the remainder of the division was surrounded south of Nieske. But the Brandenburgers succeeded in breaking through after some bloody fighting and regrouped in Saxony, at Löbau. From then on, they retreated without stopping.

On the 28th of April, the division was near Bautzen, where it received the order to head for the Army Group South area of operations. Some units started on their way while others still fought.

On the 29th, the first companies arrived in Moravia. At the beginning of May, the units were once again committed against the Russian Army and tried to set up a rearward position between Olmütz and Bistra. The surrender of Germany was signed that very day. Colonel Schulte-Heuthaus gave the order to all Brandenburgers to break through towards the west. The movement began on the 9th of May. But communications no longer existed. One after the other the units were captured by the Russians, when they were not decimated in ambushes held by the Czechs.

At Vlaschim, the Brandenburgers were thrown out of a train and massacred by a population hungry for revenge.

For a great many other Brandenburgers, the old reflexes of the years of victory came into play again. They managed to reach the American lines disguised as Sudeten refugees.

Those who remained Russian prisoners were to be treated as war criminals.

A tragic destiny for these volunteers who had come from every geographical and even political scope, united under the folds of the white flag with the red eagle of Brandenburg, cradle of Prussia and Germany. A passionate, burning, devouring love of this Germany alone had brought them to deliberately take risks that would not normally be requested of an ordinary unit. Did they transgress the laws and customs of war? The outcome of the second world conflict was going to confirm what the first had set down as a common principle: there is only one law for those who make war, to be victorious.

APPENDIXES

APPENDIXES

APPENDIX I

THE ORGANISATION
OF THE ABWEHR

The espionage and counter-espionage agency of the Reichswehr, which became the Wehrmacht in 1935, was commonly referred to as *Abwehr* (defence, parrying). But its official name was *Abwehrabteilung/Reichskriegsministerium* (*Abwehr* Branch in the War Department) until 1938, *Amtsgruppe Auslandnachrichten und Abwehr* (Foreign Intelligence and *Abwehr* Group) in 1938-1939 and *Amt Ausland/Abwehr des OKW* (OKW Office for Foreign and Counter-Intelligence) from 1939 to 1944.

The first *Abwehr* was headed by General von Bredow until 1932. He passed his command to Captain Patzig, who was himself replaced by Admiral Canaris on the 1st of January 1935.

From 1938, the year when the *Oberkommando der Wehrmacht* replaced the War Department, until February of 1944, the OKW Office for Foreign and Counter-Intelligence was divided into five departments:

'Foreign' Department (*Abteilung*, then *Amtsgruppe Ausland*).

Head: Rear Admiral (promoted Vice Admiral) Leopold Bürkner.

Purpose: Liaison between the OKW and the Foreign Office. Worked in collaboration with the *Abwehr* II in order to prepare several operations assigned to the Brandenburg units.

Abteilung I (*Abwehr* I): intelligence.

Head: Colonel Hans Piekenbrock (1938-1943), then Colonel Georg Hansen (1943-1944).

Purpose: Gather intelligence and use it against the enemy with a view to the pursuit of conflict on military, political and economic levels, in peace time as well as in war time. Used both military personnel and paid or voluntary agents.

Abteilung II (*Abwehr* II): diversion and sabotage.

Head: General Staff Major (promoted to Lieutenant-Colonel then Colonel) Helmut Groscurth (1938-1939), then Lieutenant-Colonel (promoted Colonel, then Major- General) Erwin Lahousen, Edler von Vivremont (1939-1943), then Colonel Wessel von Freytag-Loringhoven (1943-1944).

Purpose: Thorough and systematic reconnaissance of enemy capabilities and preparation of the destruction of its military means. This *Abwehr* department was the largest. The Brandenburg units were assigned to this department until 1943.

Abteilung III (*Abwehr* III): counter-espionage and counter-intelligence.

Head: Colonel Franz-Eccard von Bentivegni (1938-1944).

Purpose: Thwart the action of enemy intelligence services in Germany and in occupied territories. Collaborated closely with the RSHA (Reich's Main Security Office, to which the SD, Gestapo and the Criminal Police were attached).

Central Department:

Head: Colonel (promoted Major-General) Hans Oster (1939-1944).

Purpose: administration, finance and legal matters.

Following a decision by the Commander-in-Chief of the Wehrmacht (Adolf Hitler) on the 18th of February 1944 aiming to create a unified intelligence service in Germany, the *Abwehr* was *de facto* reduced to nothing. Departments I and II, brought together in a *Amt Mil.* under Colonel G. Hansen, were attached to the Reich's Main Security Office led by *SS-Obergruppenführer Kaltenbrunner*; the 'Foreign' Department and the Central Department were disbanded; only Department III was conserved and constituted a *Truppenabwehr* under Colonel Martini, integrated into the Wehrmacht Operations Staff (General Jodl) and whose role was confined to counter-espionage within military units.

APPENDIX II

CHRONOLOGICAL AND HISTORICAL SUMMARY

During the 1914-1918 war, the Kaiser's intelligence services turned to Germans living abroad and speaking one or more foreign languages well, to carry out several isolated missions.

After 1923, within different HQs and Reichswehr schools, notably at Munster and Kassel, the 'little war' was studied closely and small combat detachments with the purpose of waging it were even set up, named *Einsatzkommandos*. From 1935, the *Wehrmacht* having replaced the Reichswehr, officers from the Silesian station of the intelligence service of the Army, the *Abwehr*, actively pursued this type of study. In Berlin also, officers such as Lieutenant-Colonel von Lahousen, future head of *Abwehr II*, or General von Witzleben, commander of the III Military District, started to consider the creation of fighting formations depending directly on the *Abwehr*, which, furthermore, they anticipated using as part of a putsch against the national socialist regime.

Industrieschutz Oberschlesien

In 1919-1920, after the occupation of the industrial areas of Upper Silesia by the Polish, the self-defence movement of the Germans of this region raised a free corps named 'Defence of the Industries of Upper Silesia' (*Industrieschutz Oberschlesien*) composed of volunteers who spoke Polish well. The task of these men was to protect industrial infrastructure and channels of communication. The matter of the German-Polish border was provisionally settled, but the *Industrieschutz* was not officially disbanded.

After 1935, the *Abwehr* at Breslau assembled the former members of the free corps with a view to a possible conflict between Germany and Poland. The German blast-furnace workers and miners of the new *Industrieschutz* were to infiltrate enemy territory before the bulk of German forces and prevent destruction of the industrial plants.

The Free Corps of the Sudeten Germans

From 1936, Konrad Heinlein's German Sudetenland Party set up a highly disciplined 'voluntary protection service'. As the Government of Prague had ordered general mobilisation, the volunteers of this service were eligible for call-up as Czech citizens. Consequently, Heinlein's party had them cross the border secretly in order to regroup them in a camp in Germany. **In August,** the *Abwehr* at Dresden instigated the creation of a Free Corps of Sudeten Germans (*Sudetendeutschen Freikorps*) in Germany with the purpose of welcoming all Sudeten Germans with military training in the Czech Army. The exodus of Sudeten Germans was organised and Germany lined her border with reception camps that were not only inspected by officers of the *Abwehr*, but also by SA, SS, Reich Labour Service officers and representatives of large industrial companies looking for specialists. When it was finally formed, the free corps initially had no clearly defined task and was merely responsible for order among the refugees. But, in September, it was assigned its first missions in the Sudetenland. Other men were sent to an *Abwehr* school.

In October, at the time of the annexation of the Sudetenland, several teams of the free corps were successfully deployed forward of German forces. But the Freikorps was not yet attached to the *Abwehr* which wanted to see it pass completely under its control. **In November,** it was disbanded and a number of its members joined the SA of the Sudetenland ; those who had been trained by the *Abwehr* were taken on the strength of the IV Military District and remained at the disposal of the espionage service of the Wehrmacht.

August 1939

The recalled volunteers of the *Industrieschutz Oberschlesien* were assembled at the camp at Bihacz. In addition, the SA of the Sudetenland freed a certain number of former elements of the Heinlein Free Corps brought together at the Bruck camp, in Austria. In fact, the *Abwehr* stations at Breslau and Vienna were actively preparing the approaching Poland campaign. **On the 10th of August,** 80 men left the Bruck camp for Bohemia-Moravia.

The *Abwehr* station at Königsberg, in East Prussia, formed several combat detachments with the same aim.

The Poland Campaign

With a view to carrying out different actions on the German-Polish border, the *Abwehr* station at Breslau formed a *Kampfverband* (combat unit) that was given the name of one of the officers that commanded it: Ebbinghaus. This unit was itself subdivided into small *K-Trupps* where a great number of former volunteers of the Heinlein Free Corps and the *Industrieschutz* of Upper Silesia were to be found, along with some *Volksdeutschen* (ethnic Germans) from Poland. The *K-Trupps* fulfilled a certain number of missions, with a fair amount of success, including:

- Second lieutenant Herzner's special unit's occupation of the Jablunka Pass on the Slovakian-Polish border, to the south of Cracow, and their holding of it until the arrival of the 7th German Infantry Division assembled at Sillein. The operation began **in the night of the 25th and 26th of August**, the date initially planned for the offensive. Herzner fulfilled his mission but had to turn back when daylight arrived, as no other unit had crossed the border! In fact, the beginning of operations had been postponed for several days.
- **On the 1st of September,** the *K-Trupp* of Lieutenant Grabert seized the important marshalling yard at Katowice.

Birth of the first units

On the 15th of September 1939, Captain Putz, head of the *Abwehr II* in Vienna, created a B*au-Lehr-Kompanie zbV* (Special Purpose Training Construction Engineer Company) at the Bruck camp, with the former Free Corps of the Sudeten Germans assembled there in August, reinforced with new volunteers. The company was commanded by Reserve Captain Verbeek, who was soon replaced by his assistant unit commander, Lieutenant Dr. Kniesche. This company was sent rapidly to Sliac, in Slovakia, to the north-east of Bratislava. Arriving in civilian clothing, the 250 men of the unit put on Slovakian uniforms with an armband bearing the inscription *Deutsche Kompanie* (German Company). The training given at Sliac was for the destruction of bridges. Other new Sudeten Germans were soon taken on into the unit.

At the end of September, another unit of saboteurs was assembled at Brandenburg-an-der-Havel, near Berlin, with the expectation of them being used on the Western Front. This company, 320 men strong, was commanded by Captain Dr. von Hippel and made up of elements of the *Abwehr*, including many reserve officers and former Heinlein Free Corps members.

- **1st of October 1939:** the training company at Sliac officially became the *Deutsche Kompanie zbV*.
- **Early October:** Captain von Hippel's company was barracked in the *Generalfeldzeumeister-Kaserne* in Brandenburg. Sixty men from the *Deutsche Kompanie* were withdrawn from their unit by the *Abwehr III* in Vienna in anticipation of their use in Rumania.
- **25th of October 1939:** the unit barracked in Brandenburg officially became the *Bau-Lehr-Kompanie zbV 800*.
- **1st of November 1939:** the Sliac company became the *1. /Bau-Lehr-Kompanie zbV 800*, from then on alloted as a component to von Hippel's company in Brandenburg.

- **11th of November 1939:** a part of officer personnel from the Sliac company left for Brandenburg to form the *2. /Bau-Lehr-Kompanie zbV 800.*

In November, the *Abwehr* started to assemble a detachment under Captain Rudloff at Münstereifel, near Cologne, once again in anticipation of the campaign in the West. The Sliac company reached Innermanzig, near Vienna, and donned the German uniform. At the end of the month, the equivalent of three companies constituted the *zbV 800* unit. In Brandenburg, von Hippel's company, strengthened by *Volksdeutschen* from Rumania and the Baltic States, was essentially used as a reception unit for the newcomers. At Innermanzig, the *1. /Bau-Lehr-Kp.* served as a transit company and sent the majority of the volunteers, especially the South Tyroleans, to Brandenburg

THE BAU-LEHR-BATTALION ZBV 800

- **15th of December 1939:** at Münstereifel, Captain Rudloff's unit became the *3./Bau-Lehr-Battalion zbV 800.* In Brandenburg, the *Bau-Lehr-Bataillon zbV 800* was officially created, commanded by Captain von Hippel. A headquarters company was organised there.
  The custom of nicknaming the new Special Purpose Battalion 'Brandenburg' and its personnel 'Brandenburgers' soon became the rule.
- **At the end of January 1940,** *Feldwebel Kürschner,* of the HQ Company, received the order to form a Stosstrupp intended to seize the bridges over the Juliana Canal, in the Netherlands, during the next campaign. His unit became *Bau-Lehr-Zug zbV* (Special Purpose Training Construction Engineer Platoon).
- **22nd of February 1940:** a 4th Company was created in Brandenburg with some troops from the 2nd, mainly from the *Trupp* of Leutnant Herzner which had occupied the Jablunka Pass the previous August; two platoons were formed and sent to their staging positions: the 1st under Second lieutenant Witzel in the Reichswald, subordinated to the XXVI Army Corps, the 2nd under Second Lieutenant Siegfried Grabert at Arsbeck, subordinated to the XI Army Corps.
- **In February and March,** some Upper Silesians were taken to Oranienburg, north of Berlin, by *Feldwebel* Böhme, for airborne training.
- **In March,** the Eggers Platoon, 2nd Company was sent to Saint-Thomas in anticipation of an committing in the territory of the Grand Duchy of Luxemburg and went into position along the fortified line of Westwall; some other troops reached Trier with Lieutenant Schöller.
- **11th of March 1940:** the non detached units of the *Bau-Lehr-Kompanie zbV 800* strictly speaking became the Battalion's Staff.
- **At the end of March** a preparatory *Kommandostelle* was set up in Berlin corresponding to a regimental operations staff for Brandenburg type units. Major Kewisch, who ran it, organised an *Einsatzstab* (advanced staff).

The Scandinavian Campaign

In April a *Nordzug* (North Platoon) was created in Brandenburg, with the actual strength of a company, in anticipation of operations in Norway. It consisted of a platoon of Polish speaking Upper Silesians, a platoon of English speaking Germans from the Palestine, some South Tyroleans and some Sudeten Germans.

- **20th April 1940:** the *Nordzug* left Brandenburg by train for Oslo to be put at the disposal of the *Einsatzstab* which had reached Norway; its mission was to destroy radio and telephone systems ahead of German forces, then cut the supply lines of landed British forces.
- **1st May 1940:** a troop from the *Nordzug* was transported by plane to Trondheim, in the north of the country, to open the way for the 181st Infantry Division marching to Namsos; Second Lieutenant Benesch's platoon preceded the 2nd Mountain Division.

Norway capitulated on the **12th of June** and the *Nordzug*, reunited at Oslo, left the country on the **20th of June.**

May-June 1940

All units that had been getting ready for months came into action the same day as the German offensive, **the 10th of May:**
- In Luxemburg, Lieutenant Schöller's combat team, wearing civilian clothing, crossed the Suire ahead of the *1st Panzerdivision* and *Feldwebel* Eggers' team (2nd Company) seized the bridges over the Our.
- Between Elsenborn and Saint-Vith, on the fortified Belgian line, units of the 3rd Company seized 19 targets out of the 24 which had been assigned to them (Born railway bridge, Saint-Vith bridge, etc.); the company got back to Münstereifel the same evening, then was sent to Düren where III Battalion of the new regiment was getting organised.
- The *Westzug* under Second Lieutenant Kürschner, wearing Dutch uniforms, took four bridges over the Juliana Canal intact to allow the 7th Infantry Division pass (Berg, Obbicht, Stein and Urmond).
- The 1st Platoon of the 4th Company, commanded by Lieutenant Walther, seized three bridges over the Meuse at Gennep to allow von Hubicki's 9th *Panzerdivision* to pass.
- The 2nd Platoon of the 4th Company (Second Lieutenant Grabert) only succeeded in taking one bridge intact out of the four that had been assigned to it (Maaseyck bridge on the Juliana Canal and both bridges at Roermond, over the Meuse, fell).
- A team dressed in civilian clothing occupied one bridge over the Albert Canal, to the east of the forts at Eben-Emael.

During the operations that followed, the only outstanding action was that of Second Lieutenant Grabert's platoon, in which the destruction of the locks at

Nieuport was averted, which would have caused the flooding of the Belgian lowlands.

THE LEHR-REGIMENT BRANDENBURG ZBV 800

Between May and December 1940, the *zbV 800* Battalion was raised to the level of a regiment with three battalions.

This development of the unit reflected the increase of missions entrusted to the Brandenburgers. It also had the aim of regrouping all the fighting units of the *Abwehr* under a unified command.

Created **on the 15th of May 1940,** the *Lehr-Regiment Brandenburg zbV 800* was split up between different garrisons:
- Berlin (Staff, Liaison Staff, signals),
- Brandenburg (I Battalion, intended for use overseas),
- Baden-Unterwaltersdorf, in ex-Austria (II Battalion, intended for use in eastern and south-eastern Europe),
- Aachen, later Düren, in Rhineland (III Battalion, intended for use in western, northern and southern Europe).

The setting up of new units was held up by the preparation of two large-scale operations, 'Seelöwe' (landing in Great Britain) and 'Felix' (seizure of Gibraltar).

Operation Seelöwe

The new I and III Battalions, at that time in full training, were placed on alert **after July.** I Battalion was subordinated to the 16th Army (CP at Nieuport), III to the 6th Army (CP north of Caen). Troops from both battalions were to train for the landing operations at Helgoland. It was planned that a detachment of one hundred Brandenburgers would land as an advanced guard of the 9th Army. The men were to wear British uniforms. The operation was finally suspended **on the 12th of October 1940** and cancelled definitively **in January 1941.**

Operation Felix

Captain Rudloff, commander of III Battalion, met up with Admiral Canaris and Colonel Piekenbrock in Madrid in July to prepare the operation, the plan of which was approved by Hitler **on the 24th of August.** A detachment from III Battalion had to be taken to Algeciras by truck, in civilian clothing ; the operation required the use of the 51st Engineer Battalion — which had contributed to the capture of the forts at Eben-Emael — and a heavy artillery battalion having to support the troops from the Spanish coast.

Because reluctance on the part of the Spanish government, the operation was temporarily suspended **on the 10th of December** (it was not definitively abandoned until June 1943). The Brandenburg units involved were however maintained on their staging areas until January 1941.

The month of September 1940 marked the outcome of a crisis that had begun within the regiment from its creation. It brought Major Kewisch, regimental commander, into conflict with von Hippel, 'historical' leader of the unit, at that time in command of I Battalion. The former was anxious to preserve his men by submitting them to a training programme as tough as possible and to be maintained in a strictly hierarchical position in relation to the *Abwehr*. The latter wanted much less confined limits for his volunteers. Within an interval of a few weeks, both were to lose their command in order to put an end to a situation of conflict which went as far as affecting the NCOs and men.

The month of September also marked the arrival of elements of the 5th Company in Rumania, part in Ploesti, part on the Danube.

The intervention of the Brandenburgers in Rumania

Since before the war, contacts had been made between the *Abwehr* and Colonel Morusov, commander of the *Siguranza* (Rumanian Security Police) regarding measures to take in case of a conflict. The Allies sabotaging the Ploesti oil sources and holding up the shipping on the Danube was indeed something to fear.

From October 1939, the *Abwehr III* detached 60 men from the company garrisoned at Sliac to send them to Rumania. These men crossed the border in small groups from December and successfully carried out different missions (notably within the Astra Romana, the largest Rumanian oil company) with the aim of thwarting sabotage attemps by the British agents.

The first Wehrmacht military instructors for the Rumanian Army arrived in Rumania at the end of October 1940. In November, the Brandenburgers of the 5th Company were reinforced by those of the 6th (Lieutenant Meissner) who set up in Ploesti.

The completion of the setting up of the regiment

During the following months units returned to their respective home bases, other companies left, new regimental units were created and the Balkans campaign was in preparation.

In December 1940 the setting up of three battalions of the regiment was completed, although the 4th and 12th Companies had only just been created. Basic and advanced training was far from being completed.

The last troops to be detached from operations 'Seelöwe' (Kürschner Company) and 'Felix' got back to their garrisons **in January and March 1941** respectively. **In January,** the Signals Company was created.

April was to see the creation of the following other units :
- 13th 'Special' Company at Brandenburg,
- 14th (Replacement) Company at Düren,
- Trommsdorf Company (future 15th) at the camp at Zossen,
- 16th 'Light' Company at Düren,
- 17th 'Special' Company at Baden-Unterwaltersdorf,
- *Lehr-und Ausbildungskompanie* (Training and Instruction Company) at Meseritz.

The Balkans Campaign (April 1941)

During **the first months of 1941**, only II Battalion was available, although the 6th Company and a part of the 5th were still maintained in Rumania.

In March, the 8th Company was sent to the southern Carpathian Mountains to prepare themselves, then were sent to Bulgaria where its troops took provided security for major plants, either in civilian clothing or in Bulgarian Army uniform.

During the starting up of operations **on the 6th of April,** the units of II Battalion fulfilled several missions forward of German forces:
- troops of the 5th and 7th Companies took part in the crossing of the Danube with assault boats near Orsova (Yugoslavian border);
- a combat team of the 8th Company wearing Yugoslavian uniforms took the bridges over the Vardar, near Axioupolis, after a short action against British forces, and opened the way for the 2nd *Panzerdivision*;
- several other teams of Brandenburgers secured targets of lesser importance: the Kulma border bridge, bridges at Akrdinmion, Strumica, Gallikos, etc.

The units of the battalion also distinguished themselves during the campaign. Troops from the 5th Company made up a reinforced detachment which advanced **from the 12th of April** in Croatia, in the direction of Karlovac, and reached Fiume in front of the German Army, connecting with Italian forces.

On the 21st of April, a detachment of the battalion landed in the island of Euboea (Gulf of Volos), three days before the main body of German forces, so as to occupy the port of Chalkis. The operation was aimed at disorganising British defences which were being set up on the island.

Units of II Battalion got back to their garrison **in May**, except the 6th Company which remained at Ploesti. The Balkans campaign had been a complete success for the Brandenburgers and went some way to establishing their reputation.

Operation Barbarossa

Practically the entire Brandenburg Regiment took part in the offensive **of June 1941** against the USSR. However, each of the battalions could only muster three ready companies out of four. In May, these companies reached their starting positions. They were to be committed separately to support each of the three army groups.

I Battalion

Subordinated to Amy Group South, I Battalion transferred to the High Tatra, at Zakopane, at the same time as a battalion of Ukrainian volunteers named 'Nachtigall'. The Staff, the 2nd and 4th Companies were subordinated to the 17th Army, the 3rd Company to the III Armoured Corps (6th Army) that left from Hrubieszow (south-east of Lublin).

On the 22nd of June the 2nd Company seized a railway bridge over the San River ahead of Bucow, then reached Lemberg (Lvov) **on the 30th. In July,** it continued to advance ahead of the German units to stop at Vinnitsa on the 22nd, having lost 28 men, killed in the attack of Ljudowka **on the 18th of July.**

The 3rd Company seized two bridges over the Bug, at Piadytnie, **on the 22nd of June** and formed a bridgehead for the III Armoured Corps. It went on to form a second over the Styr River in July, and took new bridges over the Dnepr in August before coming back to Brandenburg at the end of the month, the last of the battalion to return.

The 4th Company took part in the capture of Lemberg with a battle group of the 1st Mountain Division. **On the 25th of June** its parachute platoon (Second Lieutenant Lütke), completely independent, jumped to take two railway bridges on the Lida-Molodechno line (Operation 'Bogdanov'), thus inaugurating a new form of combat for the Brandenburgers.

The Nachtigall Battalion had been formed during the previous winter with Ukrainian volunteers from the Lemberg and Przemysl regions, raised by the *Abwehr II* and provided by the OUN under Melnik. Its military commander was Lieutenant Herzner, its political advisor was Captain Oberländer. The establishment of a Ukranian Free State proclaimed by Ukranian officers from the battalion **on the 30th of June** over Lemberg radio, associated with the beginnings of a mutiny, caused the disbandment of the unit.

II Battalion

The three ready companies of II Battalion were subordinated to the Army Groups North and South.

By seizing the bridges over the Dnepr at Mogilev and Ataki, the 6th Company opened the way for the 22nd Infantry Division (11th Army). Afterwards committed in Perekop, Sevastopol and Kerch, it was not destined to leave the Eastern Front **before the summer of 1942.**

The 7th Company, with the responsibility of seizing the bridges on the Jura River ahead of Schaulen to open the way for the the 18th Army's I Corps, could not fulfil its mission. It did however take the bridges on the Dvina near Riga. Increasingly employed as an ordinary infantry unit, it was to be repatriated in August.

The 8th Company cleared the way for the *Panzergruppe Hoepner* (1st and 8th *Panzerdivisionen*). Lieutenant Knaak's team seized the bridges of the Dvina River opposite Dunaburg **on the 26th of June.** Another team occupied the bridges of

Josvainai on the 23rd. *Feldwebel* Werner's team took some other bridges over the Dvina, west of Jacobstadt, **on the 28th of June.** At the end of July, a detachment of the company stopped 80 km from Leningrad.

III Battalion

The 9th Company did not reach the Eastern Front **until September,** in the Wokololamsk sector. It cleared the way for the SS Reich Division until the German offensive started to falter. In December, the company was sent to the Borrozhetshe sector to secure the flank of the LI Army Corps' HQ. It was not to leave the Eastern Front **until the summer of 1942.**

The 10th Company seized eight bridges **on the 22nd of June** in Army Group Centre's area of operations: north of Augustovo, at Siolko, Holynka, south west of Lipsk. It was to get back to Düren in October.

The 12th Company took a bridge on the Bug River **on the 22nd of June,** then other infrastructure works in July on the same river to open the way for Guderian's armoured columns. It returned to Düren in August.

Amongst the regimental units, only the 16th Company came into action in the East in the course of Operation Barbarossa, to take part in a combined operation aimed at the capture of the island of Ösel (Gulf of Riga) **on the 14th and 15th of September.**

In the Autumn of 1941, all the units committed in the East during the summer had returned to their barracks, with the exception of the 6th and 9th Companies. From this campaign, it emerged that the Brandenburg units were essentially instruments of mobile warfare, which in any case seemed obvious from 1940. The best use for these troops was as a company operating in support of an armoured or motorised unit. Colonel von Haehling drew up new rules aimed at obtaining an increase in the combat value of his unit.

The Winter of 1941-1942 was marked by a certain movement among the regimental units.

The 13th Company, having become 'tropical' **in mid-May 1941,** left Brandenburg **in the Autumn.** Half of it set up in Tripoli (Libya), under the direct orders of the *Panzergruppe Afrika* Staff, the other half in Naples to receive the wounded and sick. **At the end of 1941 and the beginning of 1942,** Lieutenant von Koenen's men fulfilled different missions in 'Brandenburger' style in aid of the *Panzergruppe* which was to become *Panzerarmee Afrika.*

The 15th Company also left Germany **at the end of 1941** to be subordinated to the Mountain Army Corps under General Dietl in Finland.

The 16th Company was disbanded **in January 1942** to reconstitute the 11th, subordinated in July 1941 to the *Sonderstab Felmy* which had to be dispatched to the Near-East.

In February 1942, a 'Light Engineer Company' was created at Swinemünde in Pomerania, equipped with *Sturmboote* (assault boats) and destined to carry out surprise landing operations in the enemy's rear.

Summer 1942

Both companies kept on the Eastern Front since the summer of 1941, the 6th and the 9th, were repatriated in June and August 1942. The first had fought hard in the Crimea. It was assigned to the *Ob-West* in France. The second had fought against partisans between Vyazma, Rzhev and Smolensk.

At the beginning of the Summer, all the other units were put on alert at Brandenburg, Baden and Düren. Almost the entire regiment was sent to the army groups deployed in the Ukraine.

I Battalion

The companies of I Battalion were sent to the Army Group A (except the 1st, subordinated to the Army Group B). In theory still used in support of armoured units, they did not however participate in lengthily prepared operations, remaining simply at the disposal of the formations' staffs.

The 1st Company crossed the Don on the 2nd of August with the 14th *Panzerdivision*. Later subordinated to the 24th *Panzerdivision*, it took part in fighting in the Don Bend. Finally accompanying the 29th Motorised Infantry Division on the Volga south of Stalingrad, it was repatriated to Freiburg in October.

The 2nd Company left Kursk on the 1st of July, subordinated to the XL Armoured Corps (4th Army); then subordinated to the 13th *Panzerdivision*, it fought by the Nogay Steppe. In October, then subordinated to the III Armoured Corps west of the Terek Bend, it took part in the great attacks against Nalchik.

The 3rd Company was successively subordinated to the 3rd *Panzerdivision* and to the XL Armoured Corps. It performed several missions in Russian uniform. These included Millerovo, the Konstantinovskaya bridgehead, Proletarskaya, the Lenin Canal, the Isherskaya bridgehead, and in October the Mozdok bridgehead.

The 4th (Parachute) Company was put on alert in October to jump on the Ordzhonikidze-Tiflis route.

II Battalion

II Battalion grouped in the Nikolayev region around the 10th of July 1942.

The 5th Company was subordinated to the III Armoured Corps and entered Maykop on the 12th of August. In September, it was integrated into a battle group of the 13th *Panzerdivision* and seized two bridges on the Terek west of Arik. It then went by Gnablenburg, Planowskaya, Elkhotovo, Argudan, Nalchik. In November, it took part in Operation 'Darg Koch' leading to the seizure of four bridges at Ardon, which ended in a bloody failure.

The 7th Company was subordinated to the SS Wiking Division (LVII Armoured Corps); it came into action in the Beloreshenskaya region **in August.**

The 8th Company endured heavy losses **on the 25th of July** when it attempted to take several bridges on the Don delta north of Bataisk (Captain Grabert, the legendary Brandenburger, was killed there). In early August, it secured some bridges at Maykop, on the Belaya River, to enable the 13th *Panzerdivision* to pass through, before being subordinated to the 23rd *Panzerdivision* on the Terek for some time. It fought some tough battles at Glücksburg, Samankul, Giselj and Chikola **in November.**

III Battalion

The 10th Company left Rovenki (south of Voronezh), subordinated to the 17th Army's V Corps, for the direction of Novorossiysk.

The 11th Company, recently reformed, reached Armavir **on the 8th of August** then reached the Terek. **In October,** it was subordinated to the III Armoured Corps in the Caucasus. **At the end of that same month,** it was on the Terek.

The 12th Company fought the partisans in the Army Group Centre's line of communications area, in the region of Dorogobush, Smolensk and Vyazma, **until Spring of 1943.**

Among the regimental units, only the Light Engineer Company was committed on the Eastern Front **in 1942.** Transported to the Crimea in August, it helped to destroy several targets in the Taman Peninsula (Cape Pekly positions, observation ship Gornjak). The company was to remain in Anapa **until December.**

The Trommsdorf Company in Finland

The 15th Company took part in Operation 'Lutto' in March-April 1942, which consisted of infiltrating the rear of the Russians in order to reach the large supply dump at Ristikent south-west of Murmansk. It was a failure. In August, it carried out a new in-depth raid to cut the Murmansk-Leningrad railway line. It did not leave Finland until December.

African theatre of operations

In addition to Operation 'Salaam' which the Brandenburgers took part in, the most remarkable operation carried out in 1942 by von Koenen's company was to be cutting Allied supply lines between the Gulf of Guinea and the Red Sea ports. However, it failed **(July 1942).**

In the autumn of 1942, the Tropical Company was increased to a battalion strength because of the addition of new units: the 9th Company and the 1st Platoon of the Coastal Raider Company. Having become the 5th Company of the battalion, the latter carried out security missions along the Tunisian coast **until the end of the year.**

The first operation of the new battalion (**26th of December**), which consisted of destroying two railway bridges north-east of Kasserine and at Sidi bou Bakr (Oran-Algiers line), was a partial failure. A similar operation was executed successfully **in January 1943** against the Wadi el Melah, on the Tozeur-Sfax line.

In January 1943 again, the 5th Company pulled off a very fortuitous coup using captured radio equipment, to get a British team to land, which they then captured. The coastal raiders, who had received some new Sturmboote in February, continued to observe the coast.

In April, the main part of the Tropical Battalion was subordinated to the Von Manteuffel Division and fought as ordinary infantry. It nonetheless succeeded in reaching Italy at the time of the surrender by the means of small light craft.

THE SONDERVERBAND BRANDENBURG

At the end of 1942, the bulk of the Brandenburg Regiment was committed on the Eastern Front to ferocious fighting. The *Abwehr* seemed to take no further interest in them and the dependence on the units to which its troops were subordinated grew proportionately. But these formations used the Brandenburg units in a disorganised manner and unrelated to the type of missions for which they had been trained. They did little to replenish men and equipment in the units.

This distressing situation reflected the crisis that the *Abwehr* was going through, split by internal quarrels and more and more subject to the rivalry from the SD whose Office VI went as far as setting up a *Lehrbataillon zbV Oranienburg* whose use had remarkably much in common with that of the Brandenburg Regiment.

All this necessarily resulted in the use and the subordination of the regiment to be called into question. The OKW decided to raise it to the level of a division, placed under the Wehrmacht Operations Staff (General Jodl), and no longer of the *Abwehr II.*

During a transitional period which was to last four months, the existing units were transformed into *Sonderverbände* (special units). The Brandenburg *Sonderverband* was officially created **on the 1st of January 1943.** Its staff took the number 800, I Battalion the No. 801, II No. 802 and III No. 803. A *Sonderverband 804* was formed from new elements. These new units had to give rise to regiments that would, **in April,** make up the new division.

On the Eastern Front, the Brandenburg units were caught in the Elchotowo bottleneck **in December. On the 31st of that month** came the order to withdraw, directed at all the German forces from the eastern Caucasus as far as the lower course of the Don. **At the end of March,** the front stabilised north of Taganrog and all Brandenburger units were brought back to Germany, including those which were still committed in the Army Group A area of operations.

After December, I Battalion was reduced to *Kampfgruppe Walther* and fought on the Terek, at Aleksandrovsk then in the Rostov region. Its units finally left the front **on the 4th of April** for Freiburg where the new 1st Regiment was being organised. Its I Battalion had already been created and sent off to the Eastern Front, in the lines of communications area of the Army Group North, to fight against partisans.

II Battalion was reduced to *Kampfgruppe Horlbeck* to which the 11th Company was attached as well. It endured tough fighting in the snow north-west of Ardon, then struggled to hold the north route open which would allow the German units to retreat. The unit, which became *Kampfgruppe Weithoener* **in January,** withdrew fighting through Armavir, Kalhibolotskaya and Krapathin, and was the last to cross the frozen Don delta. After some final battles on the Mius River, the unit reached Germany **at the beginning of April** and was quartered at Oberwaltersdorf and Neuhaus (the 7th Company was already barracked south of Vienna).

II Battalion, *Sonderverband 803* had been created **in December 1942** from the former 6th Company back from France. Sent back to France, it deployed along the Spanish border.

In April, two companies from former III Battalion came back to Düren (the 10th coming from the Crimea and the 11th until then integrated in the *Kampfgruppe Weithoener*). The 12th was temporarily left in the central sector of the Eastern Front.

THE BRANDENBURG DIVISION

The new division, naturally formed from unusual wartime organisation and equipment tables, was comprised of a divisional staff, four light infantry regiments each with three battalions, a signals battalion, a tropical battalion and a coastal raider battalion (*Küstenjäger-Abteilung*).

To these field units was added a training regiment and a battalion of Russian volunteers christened 'Alexander'. The new commander of the division, Colonel Alexander von Pfuhlstein, took up his duties **in February 1943.**

The setting up of the division was naturally connected to the return of the units committed on the faraway fronts. Among the divisional units, the *Küstenjäger-Abteilung* was the first to be constituted (from January to March) thanks to the contribution of new volunteers from the Kriegsmarine or Germans from overseas. The Tropical Battalion was finally integrated with the 4th Regiment.

The month of April 1943 marked the return of the majority of the *Sonderverbände 801, 802* and *803* to German home bases (except the I./801 which was kept in White Russia).

Units from the 3rd Regiment (Staff and III Battalion) were immediately sent to the Eastern Front, south of Karachev (north sector).

But the sights of the OKW were moving towards south-eastern Europe as far as the use of the division was concerned. The rumour that the Allies were to attempt a landing in Greece or Yugoslavia was spreading and the formations of partisans were being strengthened in these areas. In actual fact combat against the partisans was from then on to be the customary duty of the Brandenburgers.

The 4th Regiment left Brandenburg **from the 17th of April.** It was stationed in

Sjenica (Yugoslavia), subordinated to the 1st Mountain Division. The 1st Regiment's II Battalion joined them there **in May. In June,** it was the turn of the 1st Regiment's Staff to join the Eastern Front (Orlino marsh); whereas the 4th Regiment detached its I Battalion to the Peloponnesus. **In July,** the 2nd Regiment left Baden for the Ptolemais region, in Greece (except II Battalion). The III./I reached Greece in turn, while in Russia the I./1 detached some units to Orodesh (the Pustoshka region, lines of communications area of Army Group North). The 3rd Regiment, whose I Battalion had just arrived, relieved the I./1 in the Pustoshka sector. The latter were to struggle for a certain time against gangs of partisans at the rear of the army group under the concealed name of *Jägerregiment 200.*

As part of Operation 'Zitadelle', the III./3 and units of the Alexander Battalion had to seize several bridges near Kursk, but the operation was cancelled on account of the German attack.

The Coastal Raider Battalion was to set up on the Dalmatian coast (Fiume, Brindisi and Sesto Calende).

On the 5th of August, the I./1, very weakened by its stay on the Eastern Front, reached Baden to make up men and equipment. The II./3 left the Spanish border for the Riviera, with the mission to carry out, from September, the disarming of the Italian forces.

The month of September 1943 was marked by several new movements of units. The I./1 reached Greece (the Levadia region) to watch over the Thermopylae Pass, while the main body of the regiment stood in the region of Aliartos in order to protect the Athens route (the Gulfs of Corinth or Euboea would have indeed been suitable for an Allied landing.) The 2nd Regiment was spread between Greece (I./2 and III./2 east of Korcë) and Albania (II./2 at Tirana). On the Eastern Front, the III./3 suffered heavy losses fighting on the front line against the Red Army. In the region of Sarajevo (Bosnia-Herzegovina), the 4th Regiment carried out the disarming of Italian forces, as the II./3 in France; the regiment's 15th (Parachute) Company was transported to Kralpevo. The Coastal Raider Battalion also made a movement towards Sibenik, Athens and Sardinia.

In October, the *Küstenjäger-Abteilung's* 1st Company contributed to the capture of the island of Cos (Dodecanese), occupied by Anglo-Italian forces (Operation 'Eisbär). While the I./3 continued to fight some tough battles in Russia, the III./3 was sent to rest south-east of Minsk: it numbered no more than 360 men; for its part, the II./3 was transported in the Abruzzi. The I./4 left the zone of action of the 1st Regiment to reach Sarajevo; now complete, the 4th Regiment was specialised in the anti-partisan struggle in contact with the Chetniks and the Croatian population (the Kirschner Unit, formed from elements of the I./4 familiar with the mountains and its near-eastern languages with a view to operations in Kurdistan, was finally committed in Yugoslavia in the Banja Luka sector, in Bosnia-Herzegovina; it was joined by the Böckl Unit made up of Bosniacs). The 15th Parachute Company, 4th Regiment took part in the capture of the Levita and Stampalia islands, which were also occupied by Anglo-Italian forces. The 16./4 left Sardinia to reach the regiment in Yugoslavia.

The month of November was especially marked by Operation 'Leopard', which was the capture of the island of Leros, a key position in the Dodecanese; the *Küstenjäger-Abteilung*'s 1st Company, the 15./4 Para Company and some troops of the III./1 took part (the island was solidly defended by almost 9,000 British and Italian soldiers and the resistance gave in when Lieutenant Wandrey captured the British General Tillney). The island of Samos was captured by units of the 1st Regiment. The 2nd Regiment was transported to Montenegro. The II./3 reached the sector of Ovindili in order to be transformed into a mobile unit intended to chase partisans and Italian Badoglio forces. On the 2nd of December, the 2nd Regiment took part in Operation 'Kügelblitz' in the Lim Valley (central Bosnia), directed on the town of Prijepolje; the Brandenburgers captured 2,000 prisoners but sometimes found themselves threatened during the course of the mopping up operations that followed.

Until January, two battalions of the 1st Regiment were to ensure the protection of the Thermopylae Pass (I./1 to the south, observing the coastal zone of the Gulf of Euboea, and III./1 to the north, in the Lamia sector). The 4th Regiment continued to ensure the protection of major routes. The Coastal Raider Battalion was reorganised north of the Dalmatian islands.

1944

In the night of the 31st of December, Banja Luka was attacked by ten Titist brigades. The 4th Regiment was extricated from a critical situation just in time. The partisans were also very active in the 1st Regiment sector. On the Eastern Front, units of the 3rd Regiment were transported to the east of Pinsk (Minsk sector). **In February,** the 1st Regiment left Greece in order to assemble at Dakovica (Kosovo) and act as a reserve unit in the event of an Allied landing on the Dalmatian coast, while controlling the partisans in Bosnia.

At this period of the war, Hitler decided to set up a unified intelligence service in the military field. He made Reichsführer SS Himmler responsible for this task, which inevitably resulted in the services of the *Abwehr* being subordinated to the RSHA (SD and Security Police).

Between the 11th and the 20th of March, some units belonging to the 1st, 2nd and 4th Regiments took part in Operation 'Margarethe I' which was aimed at occupying Budapest and disarming the Honvéd; the Brandenburgers were part of the south group coming from Montenegro and Serbia. The Brandenburger Parachute Battalion which had only just been formed at Stendal from the 15th Company, 4th Regiment also played a part. In northern Dalmatia, the III./1 was fighting endless ambush type actions in the middle of an inextricable local political situation and achieved minimal success with some heavy losses.

On the other hand, relative calm reigned in the zone of action of the 2nd

Regiment. However, Titist partisans were growing in strength and Tito seemed to want to break through towards Serbia and cut the Belgrade-Salonika line, vital for the South-Eastern Front.

The spring of 1944 was accompanied by a new factor concerning the use of the Brandenburg units. The question of their subordination, which, from the origins of the unit, had been at the heart of discussions, resulted in the departure of Major-General von Pfuhlstein on the 15th of April, as Jodl wanted to avoid an open conflict between the general and the Chief of Staff of the Army. He was replaced by Lieutenant-General Kühlwein.

On the 27th of May the new commander of the division sent a memo to the Wehrmacht Operations Staff. Bringing to mind the fact that the Brandenburg units had been created for the war of movement, he highlighted their inability to adapt to the form of war imposed on them since the Wehrmacht had been retreating. In practice, the Brandenburgers were used as a stopgap. He proposed therefore that, if the fight against the partisans that his men had undertaken for a year had to fall to them on a permanent basis, there be created parallel to the existing regiments, *Streifkorps*, patrol corps specialised in guerrilla warfare and subordinated to the Brandenburg Division alone. The Wehrmacht Operations Staff gave its approval.

In May 1944, Operation 'Rösselsprung' was launched. It had been carefully prepared since the previous winter by the 2nd Armoured Army Staff. This operation carried out by air and land consisted of surrounding Tito's CP at Drvar. The volunteers of the Benesch Unit were brought to Drvar in gliders following after the SS Parachute Battalion. Troops of the 1st Regiment attacked near Grahowo but although Drvar was captured, Tito escaped. There were heavy losses, mostly in the II./1 (the partisans drew up six divisions in the sector).

On the 30th of May, the I./3 left the Eastern Front for Italy where the 3rd Regiment was gathering in the region of Trent (except the II./3 still detached in the south). The I./3 was rapidly committed against the partisans in Slovenia, between Udine, Gorizia and Fiume.

In June, the Parachute Battalion once again left its garrison at Stendal in anticipation of Operation 'Tanne' with the objective of occupying the island of Aaland by means of a combined attack, following the yielding of the Finnish Army. This operation never took place. Meanwhile, the *Küstenjäger-Abteilung* was reorganised. From July to November, it carried out numerous operations in the Adriatic against the islands occupied by the partisans.

The month of July saw the strengthening of the units of Yugoslavian partisans, who were getting better and better support from the Allies. On the other hand, for the Brandenburg Division, any bringing up of units to strength was becoming impossible.

The order to set up patrol corps proposed by general Kühlwein was signed on the 14th of July. The first of its type, a *Streifkorps Südfrankreich*, was formed by the 3rd

Regiment. Each *Streifkorps* was subdivided into *Einsatzgruppen* of 2 officers and 36 men. Groups *Slowakei*, *Baltikum* and *Rümanien/Siebenbürgen* were also formed in that way to constitute a *Streifkorps Karpaten*.

In August the II./4 Battalion was disbanded and its units integrated in the I./4. Some Brandenburgers took part in Operation 'Rübezal' which aimed to prevent Tito going to Serbia; the 2nd Regiment operated in the Tara region. The III./3 protected the German convoys on the French-Italian border.

Following the reversal by Rumania **on the 23rd of August**, the Commander-in-Chief Southeast formed a deployment group with the 4th Regiment and two companies of the Parachute Battalion. The latter occupied the aerodrome at Otopeni, north of Bucharest.

In September, faced with the threat created in the north by the Soviet offensive launched on the 20th of August, the German High Command ordered the withdrawal of all forces in the Balkans. **Between September and November,** battalions of the 1st, 2nd, and 4th Regiments were committed in a series of delaying combats around Belgrade, then on the Danube. Some of them suffered particularly high casualties, such as the III./4 in the north of Rumania or the I./4 in Belgrade. At the end of November, the bulk of remaining units of the division assembled in Hungary, west of Pécs.

Meanwhile, **on the 8th of September**, the Wehrmacht Operations Staff had signed a reorganisation order for the unit to become a motorised *Jägerdivision* (light infantry formation).

The logical outcome of previous events has to be seen in this decision.

The RSHA had replaced the old Brandenburg Regiment with SS commando units under SS-Ostubaf. Skorzeny. Besides this, Hitler's distrust was heightened after the assassination attempt of **the 20th of July** when, in Berlin, several Brandenburger officers became implicated with the plotters. Finally, **in the Summer of 1944,** the Brandenburg Division had, out of a total strength of around 14,000 men, no more than 900 volunteers speaking one or more foreign languages.

THE PANZERGRENADIER-DIVISION BRANDENBURG

On the 13th of September, a new order from the Wehrmacht Operations Staff transformed the division into a *Panzergrenadier* formation, a motorised infantry division with two regiments of three battalions and several divisional units (artillery regiment, antitank battalion, reconnaissance battalion, engineer battalion, Flak battalion, etc.). The 'veterans' were hardly satisfied with this solution which put a definitive term to the specificity of their unit. But scarcely more than 300 of them joined Skorzeny's *SS-Jagdverbände*.

Several months were required to set up the new division, a task assigned to a reorganisation staff in Baden, while the main body of the unit was committed in the Balkans. Only the 3rd Regiment could be withdrawn from Italy, not without some difficulty due to Marshal Kesselring who wished to preserve the Brandenburg units. Neither the Coastal Raider Battalion, nor the Parachute Battalion were to form part of the new division.

It was not before **mid-December 1944** that the different divisional units were all assembled at the Mauerwald camp, in East Prussia.

The last actions

The Brandenburgers were, **from January,** put into combat in Warthegau and fought at Kutno, Litzmannstadt, Szaskowice, Jauschwitz, then withdrew to Lower Silesia in February. **In March-April,** the division engaged the enemy on the Neisse River. During the great Soviet offensive of **the 16th of April,** the 2nd Regiment was virtually wiped out in the sub-sector of Rothenburg-Penzig and the bulk of the division was surrounded near Gross-Radisch, south of Niesky. **On the 18th,** the units succeeded in breaking through to Löbau, in Saxony.

The division was transported to the Sudetenland **at the end of the month** and subordinated to Army Group South. It fought some tough defensive actions in the Olmütz region and Bistra **at the beginning of May.** After the surrender was signed, the Brandenburgers were ordered to break through to the West.

APPENDIX III

PLANNING AND CARRYING OUT
OF A BRANDENBURG UNIT OPERATION
(1939-1942)

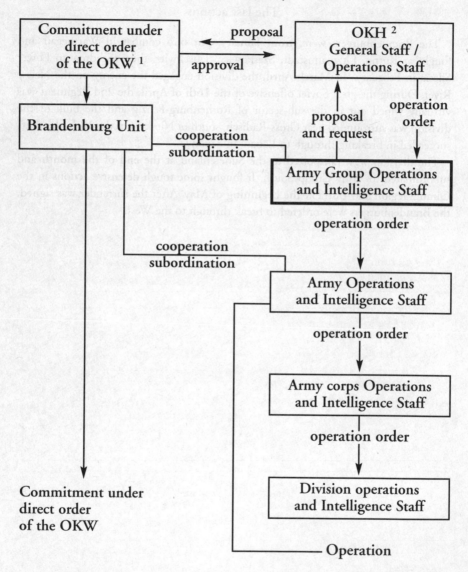

1. *Oberkommando der Wehrmacht* = High Command of the Armed Forces (Army, Navy and Air Force).

2. *Oberkommando des Heeres* = High Command of the Army.

ORDER OF BATTLE OF THE BRANDENBURG BAU-LEHR-BATTALION zbV 800
(December 1939 to May 1940)

Staff (created 11th of March 1940 from the *Bau-Lehr-Kompanie zbV 800).*
Commander: Captain Dr. von Hippel.
Adjutant: Second Lieutenant Johannes.

Bau-Lehr-Kompanie zbV 800 (disbanded in March 1940).

HQ Company.
Commander: Lieutenant Kotschke.

1st Bau-Lehr-Kompanie (ex-*Deutsche Kompanie).*
Commander: Lieutenant Dr. Kniesche.
Raised from: Germans from Sudetenland, Slovakia, Poland and overseas.

2nd Bau-Lehr-Kompanie (created November 1939).
Commander: Captain Fabian, then Captain Dr. Hartmann.
Raised from: Germans from Germany, Rumania, the Baltic States and Palestine.

3rd Bau-Lehr-Kompanie (created 15th December 1939).
Commander: Captain Rudloff.
Raised from: Germans from Sudetenland and Rumania.

4th Bau-Lehr-Kompanie (created 22nd February 1940).
Commander: Lieutenant Walther.
Raised from: Primarily Germans from Sudetenland and Upper Silesia.

ORDER OF BATTLE OF THE BRANDENBURG LEHR-REGIMENT zbV 800
(May 1940 to December 1942)

Staff (Berlin).
Commander: Major Kewisch, then Major von Aulock, then Lieutenant-Colonel (promoted Colonel) Haehling von Lanzenhauer.
Adjutant: Lieutenant Zülch.
Ia (operations): Lieutenant H. Pinkert, then Lieutenant Wülbers.
Ic (intelligence): Lieutenant H. Pinkert.

I Battalion (Brandenburg/Havel).
Commander: Captain (promoted Major) Dr. von Hippel, then Lieutenant Walther, then Major Heinz, then Captain (promoted Major) Walther.
Adjutant: Second Lieutenant Johannes, then Lieutenant Gerlach.

HQ Company (created in June 1940 by changing the appellation of the Brandenburg Battalion's HQ Company; disbanded in May 1941).
Commander: Second Lieutenant Johannes.

1st Company (created in May 1940 from the 1st Platoon, 4th company of the Brandenburg Battalion; re-created in August 1940 from the Battalion's HQ Company; disbanded in May 1941; re-created in December 1941 by changing the number of the 17th 'Special Company').
Commander: *Oberfeldwebel* Babuke, then Captain Vatter, then Captain Babuke, then Second Lieutenant Schulte.

2nd Company (created in June 1940 from the Brandenburg Battalion's Staff).
Commander: Lieutenant Walther, then Captain Dr. Hartmann, then Lieutenant G. Pinkert.

3rd Company (created in August 1940 from the 1st Company).
Commander: Lieutenant Weiner, then Lieutenant John, then Second Lieutenant Weithoener, then Captain John.

4th Company (created towards the end of 1940; became 'Light Engineer Company' with a single parachute platoon under Second Lieutenant Lütke; a whole parachute unit from the Autumn of 1941 on).
Commander: Lieutenant (promoted Captain) Kürschner, then Lieutenant Gerlach.

II Battalion (Baden-Unterwaltersdorf).
Commander: Lieutenant Walther, then Captain (promoted Major)
Dr. P. Jacobi +, then Captain G. Pinkert.
Adjutant: Second Lieutenant Ullmann,
then Second Lieutenant Mohrmann.

5th Company (created in June 1940; then became a mountain infantry company).
Commander: Lieutenant Kotschke, then Lieutenant H. Pinkert,
then Lieutenant Dr. Kniesche, then Lieutenant Zülch +,
then Second Lieutenant Steidl.

6th Company (created in August 1940 from the 1st Company;
then became 'reconnaissance company', then *West-Kompanie)*.
Commander: Lieutenant Meissner, then Lieutenant
(promoted Captain) Bansen.

7th Company (created in April 1940 from the Brandenburg
Battalion's 1st Company; then became mountain infantry company like
the 5th).
Commander: Lieutenant Koteschke, then Second Lieutenant
(promoted Lieutenant) Oesterwitz.

8th Company (created in May 1940 from the 2nd Platoon, 4th
company of the Brandenburg Battalion; then became mountain
infantry company like the 5th and the 7th).
Commander: Lieutenant Grabert, then Captain Buchler, then
Lieutenant Grabert, then Lieutenant Knaak +, then Lieutenant
(promoted Captain) Grabert +, then Second Lieutenant Renner, then
Captain H. Pinkert, then Lieutenant Renner.

17th 'Special Company' (created in Baden April 1941; became 1st Company in December).
Commander: Lieutenant Babuke.

Light Engineer Company (coastal raider company created in Swinemünde in February 1942 from the 4th Company).
Commander: Captain Horlbeck, then Lieutenant Kriegsheim.

Signals Company (created in January 1941; detached its troops to other units of the regiment).
Commander: Captain Eltester.

V-Leute [1] **Company** (created in Brandenburg in the Spring of 1940; merged with the 1st Company of the regiment in May 1941 to form the A Company of the future *V-Leute* Battalion).

Training Company (created in April 1941).
Commander: Captain Harbich.

Interpreter Company (created in the Spring of 1940 in Brandenburg).

These last three units contributed to forming a *V-Leute* Battalion at the Regenwurmlager, near Meseritz, which took shape at the end of 1942. It was commanded by Captain Walther, then by Major Heinz.

---

1. *Vertrauensleute* : men of confidence (intelligence agents).

APPENDIX VI

ORDER OF BATTLE OF THE BRANDENBURG DIVISION zbV 800
(April 1943 to September 1944)

Staff (Berlin-Wilmersdorf).
Commander: Colonel (promoted Major-General) von Pfuhlstein,
then Lieutenant-General Kühlwein.
Operations (Ia): Major Franfurth, then Captain Wülbers, then Major Erasmus.

1st LIGHT INFANTRY REGIMENT (Brandenburg/Havel
then Freiburg/Breisgau).
Commander: Major (promoted Lieutenant-Colonel) Walther.

I Battalion.
Commander: Captain Plitt, then Captain John,
then Lieutenant Kohl, then Lieutenant Hebeler.

1st Company

2nd Company

3rd Company

4th (Legionnaire) Company
(disbanded in August 1943 in Baden)

II Battalion.
Commander: Captain G. Pinkert, then Lieutenant
(promoted Captain) Rosenow, then Lieutenant Seuberlich,
then Major G. Pinkert.

5th Company

6th Company

7th Company

III Battalion
Commander: Captain Froboese, then Lieutenant
(promoted Captain) Wandrey.

9th Company

10th Company

11th (Heavy) Company

12th Company

2nd LIGHT INFANTRY REGIMENT
(Baden-Unterwaltersdorf then Admont, in Styria).
Commander: Lieutenant-Colonel von Kobelinsky +,
then Lieutenant-Colonel (promoted Colonel) Pfeiffer,
then Major Oesterwitz.

I Battalion.
Commander: Captain Weithoener, then Captain Steidl.

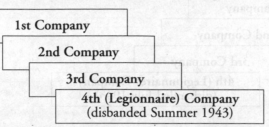

1st Company

2nd Company

3rd Company

4th (Legionnaire) Company
(disbanded Summer 1943)

II Battalion.
Commander: Captain Oesterwitz.

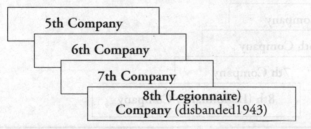

5th Company

6th Company

7th Company

8th (Legionnaire)
Company (disbanded 1943)

III Battalion.
Commander: Lieutenant (promoted Captain) Renner.

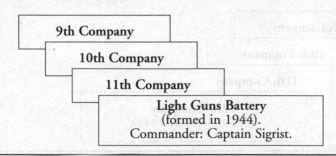

9th Company

10th Company

11th Company

Light Guns Battery
(formed in 1944).
Commander: Captain Sigrist.

3rd LIGHT INFANTRY REGIMENT (Düren).
Commander: Lieutenant-Colonel F. Jacobi.

I Battalion.
Commander: Lieutenant Kriegsheim, then Captain Wasserfall, then Captain G. Pinkert, then Captain Mertens.

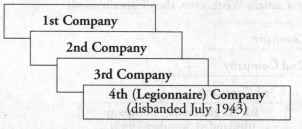

1st Company

2nd Company

3rd Company

4th (Legionnaire) Company
(disbanded July 1943)

II Battalion.
Commander: Captain Bansen, then Major H. Pinkert.

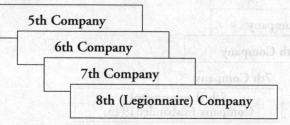

5th Company

6th Company

7th Company

8th (Legionnaire) Company

III Battalion.
Commander: Captain Grawert, then Captain Wasserfall.

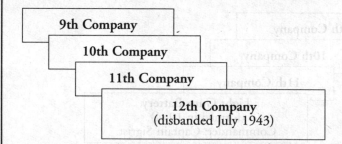

9th Company

10th Company

11th Company

12th Company
(disbanded July 1943)

4th LIGHT INFANTRY REGIMENT (Brandenburg/Havel).
Commander: Lieutenant-Colonel Heinz, then Lieutenant-Colonel von Hugo, then Major H. Pinkert, then Major Hollmann, then Major (promoted Lieutenant-Colonel) von Koenen, then Captain Kriegs-heim.

I Battalion.
Commander: Captain (promoted Major) Hollmann, then Captain Kriegsheim, then Captain Gerlach.

- 1st Company
- 2nd Company
- 3rd Company
- 4th Company

II Battalion
(disbanded 1st August 1944 and merged with I Battalion).
Commander: Captain Dr. Hartmann, then Lieutenant (promoted Captain) Lau.

- 6th Company
- 7th Company
- 8th Company
- 9th (Legionnaire) Company

III Battalion
Commander: Captain (promoted Major) von Koenen.

- 11th Company
- 12th Company
- 13th Company
- 14th Company (formerly the 15th Light Company, Brandenburg Regiment; became 16th (Light) Company in July 1943). Commander: Lieutenant Hettinger, then Captain Benesch.
- 15th (Parachute) Company
  Commander: Lieutenant Oschatz.
- 16th (Light) Company

COASTAL RAIDER BATTALION
Commander: Captain von Leipzig.

- 1st Company
- 2nd Company
- 3rd Company
- 4th (Heavy) Company

PARACHUTE BATTALION
(created in March 1944 at Stendal from 15th Company, 4th Regiment). Commander : Captain Weithoener.

- 1st Company
- 2nd Company
- 3rd Company
- 4th Company

SIGNAL BATTALION
(Berlin-Zehlendorf). Commander: Captain Eltester.

- 1st (Transmissions) Company
- 2nd (Transmissions) Company
- 3rd (Transmissions) Company
- 4th (Transmissions) Company
  (created in October 1943)
- Telephone Company
  (created in October 1943)

In practice, the companies were attached to the regiments of the division.

BRANDENBURG TRAINING REGIMENT
(created in May 1943).
Commander: Major Martin.

> **I Battalion** (Brandenburg/Havel then Veldes).
> Commander: Captain Hollmann.

> **II Battalion** (Baden, Veldes then Sankt-Veit).
> Commander: Captain von Einem-Josten.

> **III Battalion** (created in 1944 at Stein).

> **IV Battalion** (created in 1944 at Domzale).

> **Legionnaire Battalion 'Alexander'.**
> Commander: Captain Auch.

> **1st 'White Company'**

> **2nd 'Black Company'**

HOLDERS OF THE KNIGHT'S CROSS OF THE IRON CROSS WITH OAK LEAVES OF THE BRANDENBURG UNITS:

- Reserve Captain Siegfried Grabert, commanding the 8th Company, *Lehr-Regiment Brandenburg zbV 800* (6th November 1943, posthumously).

- Lieutenant-Colonel Karl-Heinz Oesterwitz, commanding the 2nd Light Infantry Regiment, Brandenburg *Panzergrenadier* Division (10th February 1945).

- Major Max Wandrey, commanding II Battalion, 1st Light Infantry Regiment of the Brandenburg *Panzergrenadier* Division (16th March 1945).

HOLDERS OF THE KNIGHT'S CROSS OF THE IRON CROSS

- Lieutenant Wilhelm Walther, commanding the 4th Company, *Bau-Lehr-Battalion Brandenburg zbV 800 (24th June 1940).*

- Reserve Lieutenant Siegfried Grabert, commanding the 8th Company, *Lehr-Regiment Brandenburg zbV 800* (10th June 1941).

- Second Lieutenant Adrian von Foelkersam, Staff of I Battalion, *Lehr-Regiment Brandenburg zbV 800* (14th September 1942).

- Reserve Second Lieutenant Ernst Prohaska, 8th Company, *Lehr-Regiment Brandenburg zbV 800* (16th September 1942, posthumously).

- Captain Hans-Wolfram Knaak, commanding the 8th Company, *Lehr-Regiment Brandenburg zbV 800* (3rd November, 1942, posthumously).

- Reserve Second Lieutenant Werner Lau, commanding the 1st Half-Company, 5th Company of the *Lehr-Regiment Brandenburg zbV 800* (9th December 1942).

- Reserve lieutenant Erhard Lange, commanding a company in a Kampfgruppe of the *Lehr-Regiment Brandenburg zbV 800* (15th January 1943).

- Lieutenant Karl-Heinz Oesterwitz, commanding the 7th Company, *Lehr-Regiment Brandenburg zbV 800* (30th April 1943).

- Captain Friedrich von Koenen, commanding III Battalion, 4th Regiment of the Brandenburg Division *zbV 800* (16th September 1943).

- Reserve Lieutenant Max Wandrey, commanding III Battalion,1st Regiment of the Brandenburg Division *zbV 800* (9th January 1944).

- Reserve Captain Konrad Steidl, acting commander of I Battalion, 2nd Regiment of the Brandenburg Division *zbV 800* (26th January 1944).

- Colonel Erich von Brückner, commanding the 1st Light Infantry Regiment, Brandenburg *Panzergrenadier* Division (11th March 1945).

- Lieutenant Erhard Afheldt, II Battalion, 2nd Light Infantry Regiment of the Brandenburg *Panzergrenadier* Division (17th March 1945).

- Lieutenant Erich Röseke, commanding the 9th Company, 1st Light Infantry Regiment of the Brandenburg *Panzergrenadier* Division (14th April 1945).

- Reserve Second Lieutenant Helmut von Leipzig, platoon commander in the Reconnaissance Battalion, Brandenburg *Panzergrenadier* Division (28th April 1945).

- Major Wilhelm Bröckerhoff, commanding the Armoured Artillery Regiment, Brandenburg *Panzergrenadier* Division (7th May 1945).

BIBLIOGRAPHY

BARTZ, Karl. *Die Tragödie der deutschen Abwehr.* Verlag K.W. Schütz KG, 1972 (reprint).

BERTHOLD, Will. *Division Brandenburg.* Heyne-Taschenbuch, 1977.

BORCHER, Will. *Krieg ohne Menschlichkeit (Jugoslawein im August 1942).* Cornett-Verlag, 1975.

BROCKDORFF, Werner. *Geheimkommandos des zweiten Weltkrieges (Geschichte und Einsätze der Brandenburger, usw.).* Verlag Welsermühl, 1967.

DUGAN, J. and STEWART, C. *Raz de marée sur les pétroles de Ploesti.* Robert Laffont, Paris.

KRIEGSHEIM, Herbert. *Getarnt, Getäuscht und doch Getreu* (Die *geheimnisvollen 'Brandenburger').* Verlag Bernard u. Graefe, 1958.

KUROWSKI, Franz. *The Brandenburgers (Global Mission).* J.J. Fedorowicz Pub. 1997.

LUCAS, James. *Kommando (German Special Forces of World War Two).* Arms and Armour Press, 1985.

SCHRAML, Franz. *Kriegsschauplatz Kroatien.* Kurt Vowinckel Verlag, 1962.

SPAETER, Helmuth. *Die Geschichte des Panzerkorps Grossdeutschland* (vol II). Selbstverlag Hilfswerk ehem. Soldaten für Kriegsopfer und Hinterbliebene e.v. des Traditionsgemeinschaft Panzerkorps Grossdeutshland, 1958.

SPAETER, Helmuth. *Die Brandenburger (Eine deutsche Kommandotruppe zbV 800).* Verlagsagentur W. Angerer, 1978.

STEFFENS, Hans Von. *Aus Rommels Spuren.* Karlsruhe, 1959.

STEFFENS, Hans von. *Salaam (Geheimkommando zum Nil, 1942).* K. Vowinckel Verlag, 1960.

TIEKE, Wilhelm. *Der Kaukasus und das Öl (Der deutsch-russische Kampf in Kaukasien, 1942-43).* Munin-Verlag, 1970.

WEINER, Dr Friedrich. *Partisanenkampf am Balkan (Die Rolle des Partisanenkampfes in der jugoslawischen Landesverteidigung).* Verlag Carl Ueberreuter, 1976.

CONTENTS

CONTENTS